Rameau's Nephew
and Other Works

Rameau's Nephew
and Other Works

Denis Diderot

In translations by
Jacques Barzun
and
Ralph H. Bowen

With an Introduction by
Ralph H. Bowen

Hackett Publishing Company, Inc.
Indianapolis/Cambridge

For further information, please address:

Hackett Publishing Company, Inc.
P. O. Box 44937
Indianapolis, IN 46244-0937

www.hackettpublishing.com

Cover design by Listenberger Design & Associates

Library of Congress Cataloging-in-Publication Data

Diderot, Denis, 1713-1784.
    [Selections. English. 2001]
    Rameau's nephew and other works / Denis Diderot ; in
translations by Jacques Barzun and Ralph H. Bowen ; with an
introduction by Ralph H. Bowen
            p.   cm.
    ISBN 0-87220-487-1 (cloth)—ISBN 0-87220-486-3 (pbk.)
    1. Diderot, Denis, 1713-1784—Translations into English. I.
Barzun, Jacques, 1907- II. Bowen, Ralph Henry, 1919- III. Title.

PQ1979 .A227 2001
848'.509—dc21   00-065036

CONTENTS

INTRODUCTION

One of the many pleasant things about reading Diderot nowadays is that no one is obliged to read him except for enjoyment or instruction. He has not yet become the hero of any fashionable literary or intellectual cult, possibly because he does not foreshadow the anxiety or the bewilderment of our troubled age. He was a cheerful believer in the possibility of human progress—although he was not sanguine enough to expect it to be automatic—and for the greater part of his life he was too busy promoting progress to have much time for gloomy meditations. Perhaps this was also the reason he never wrote a "great book." Those to whom Diderot is but a name cannot be made to feel that their exposure to Culture is incomplete. Nor is it necessary to have read Diderot for what he represents, or is alleged to represent—as Dante is said to represent "the Medieval Mind" or as Voltaire is said to represent "the Enlightenment." In the main, Diderot represents nobody but himself.

Indeed it would be best to say that Diderot should be read because almost always he *is* himself. If that were all that could be said, of course, nothing remarkable would have been demonstrated. As our author points out in *D'Alembert's Dream*, "Since I am the one who does thus and so, anyone who could act otherwise wouldn't be me." So the pleasure one takes in Diderot's uniqueness must be founded on somewhat more elaborate reasons.

One of these is that a great deal of excellent fun—and not all of it innocent merriment—would have been lost had Denis Diderot, the elder son of a master cutler in Langres, died in infancy like two of his brothers and sisters, or even if he had died at the age of forty, before writing *Rameau's Nephew, D'Alembert's Dream, A Supplement to Bougainville's "Voyage"* and *Jacques le Fataliste*. In these fictions, all but the last of which (being a full-length novel) have been included in this volume, Diderot takes his place beside Aristophanes, Rabelais, Sterne and Voltaire. Like them in spirit but unlike them in the shape of his work or the movement of his thought, he is a master at showing up the incongruities that make wise men burst out laughing.

A second reason for reading Diderot is that his best work embodies an esthetic ideal which he had learned from his model Horace, that of "mingling the pleasant with the useful" by combining business with pleasure, propaganda with entertainment, and edification with delight. One cannot read Diderot's dialogues, essays, or tales without being amused as well as taught something worth knowing. Incorrigibly a pedagogue, he was incomparable as a humorist. In either guise by itself he may now and again be objectionable, but in the combined form he is irresistible. This generality should be tested at least once by everyone who prides himself on his sense of humor or on his teachability.

The reader will find in the present volume Diderot's chief ideas, set forth, if not in Diderot's own words, at least in the nearest English equivalents that the translators have been able to hit upon. The ideas themselves are not obscure and it is not necessary to list them in an Introduction. Those persons who do not understand them in context are not likely to fare better when parts of Diderot's fabric are snipped out and mounted as samples of his "essential thought." As for his characteristic attitude, his view of life, his prevailing tone, they will be found thoroughly modern. The reader will often imagine that he is reading a twentieth-century critic rather than a spokesman of the neoclassical, rationalistic, "artificial" eighteenth century. The reason is that Diderot was thoroughly in sympathy with two great currents of modern thought—humanism and science—which have shaped the minds of all educated people living in the West today.

His attachment to these tendencies was so strong at times as to be clairvoyant, which accounts for many a passage in which his speculation leaps over an entire century of physical

and social science and joins the most recent hypotheses of
contemporary biology or psychology. Diderot's democratic
humanism, too, makes him resemble a fellow citizen of our
twentieth century rather than a late-eighteenth-century French
classicist. This can be accounted for, at least in part, by the
fact that Diderot was one of the earliest and most influential
of the "pre-romanticists" who began, around the middle of
the eighteenth century, to experiment with new, less con-
straining, modes of expression. Again, therefore, a direct chain
of descent through the various kinds of Romanticism and
Realism binds us to Diderot, and it is not strange that we can
so easily find in him the essential properties of our own "modern ego."

II

Diderot's collected works comprise twenty solid volumes in
the most nearly complete French edition,* and important new
items have been discovered from time to time in the seventy-
five years since that collection was made. Even if one sets aside
a good portion of the collected writings on the ground that
it is nothing but hack work of a superior order—and this description applies to at least three volumes of routine articles
written for the *Encyclopédie;* even if one sets aside several
volumes more of correspondence (which is *not* hack work) and
of art criticism, from which a representative selection would
be hard to make, one is still left with an inconvenient wealth
for an anthology. Any choice is bound to leave out excellent
things and thus to disappoint, no matter what the rationale of
selection may be. The present editor has applied two criteria
with a view to making the book as interesting and varied as
possible.

The first has been to include only those pieces which represent Diderot's best work as a literary artist; the second has
been to include writings that embody his most mature, most
original and most significant ideas. No doubt many personal

* That of J. Assézat and Maurice Tourneux (Paris: Garnier frères,
1875–77).

likes and dislikes have entered into the application of these standards, but a deliberate attempt has been made to take account of the views of the best qualified critics, living and dead, and it may be hoped that pure caprice at least has played no part.

There is not likely to be any dispute about the inclusion in this volume of its title piece, *Rameau's Nephew*, about which Jacques Barzun, whose English version is reproduced here, has written a critical and bibliographic note which will be found on a later page. It makes unnecessary here a recapitulation of the merits and meaning of this masterpiece.

Of the other major works composing our selection, the one that could least easily be spared is undoubtedly *D'Alembert's Dream*. It is clear that in this piece, as in *Rameau's Nephew*, Diderot took the trouble to put his text in order at the time he wrote his original draft, and he probably revised it again at the very end of his life. His correspondence makes it possible to be fairly certain that the work was first written in August and September 1769, during a rare interval of leisure and solitude occasioned by his wife's and daughter's absence in the country, while his friends were also inaccessible for one reason or another. On September 11 he wrote to his mistress, Sophie Volland (who was likewise out of town): "I have written a dialogue between myself and D'Alembert in which we talk quite gaily, and even with some clarity, in spite of the dryness and difficulty of the topic. After this dialogue there comes another one, much longer, which serves to clarify the first. The second is called 'D'Alembert's Dream'; the speakers are D'Alembert, who is dreaming; Mlle. de L'Espinasse, D'Alembert's friend; and Dr. Bordeu. If I had wanted to sacrifice richness of subject matter to nobility of tone, my characters would have been Democritus, Hippocrates and Leucippus, but then, in order to be true to life, I should have been obliged to shut myself up within the confines of ancient philosophy, and the cost would have been too great. The whole thing is the most extravagant performance possible, yet, it is full of the deepest kind of philosophy. It was, I think, a neat trick to put my ideas in the mouth of a man who is dreaming—

one must often dress wisdom up as foolishness in order to procure it an entrée. I much prefer to have people say, 'All the same, it isn't so crazy as you might think,' than 'Pay attention to these words of wisdom I am about to utter.' "

Excessive modesty was never one of Diderot's shortcomings, and this passage shows him in a typical mood of self-approval, while it describes and appraises *D'Alembert's Dream* adequately enough. It indicates moreover that Diderot was aware of what he was doing when he set out to discuss that most difficult subject—the origin and nature of conscious life—doing it in a manner that just barely avoids being frivolous. The recipe was evidently sound, for it is difficult to see how so much antiquated science could otherwise retain the vitality and fascination that Diderot's essay in dialogue still manages to hold.

Of the shorter pieces in this volume the best known is probably *A Supplement to Bougainville's "Voyage."* Written in the form of a "dialogue between A and B," probably because Diderot's discursive mind found the conversational manner especially congenial, this work ranks close to *D'Alembert's Dream* as a successful example of how to treat the most serious subjects without being solemn or tedious: it is a searching and at the same time scintillating discussion of religion, morality, government, property, marriage, imperialism, and how to bring up children.

Diderot had been thinking hard about all these matters at least since 1749, when he and Rousseau discussed the notion that the progress of the arts and sciences had perhaps *not* increased human happiness or virtue—the idea that was to make Rousseau's reputation in the following year when his essay sustaining that thesis, which had won the prize offered by the Academy of Dijon, was published and started a great controversy. Although Rousseau never used the expression "noble savage," and was even at some pains to prove that savages were not and had never been noble, his contention that civilized society tends to corrupt "the natural man" probably helped to foster a growing interest in primitive peoples after the middle of the eighteenth century. Diderot, without letting enthusiasm cloud his critical judgment, shared the curiosity of his contemporaries about men in the state of nature.

Even more to the purpose, he saw how this prevailing interest in savages could be made the starting point for a telling critique of civilized ways of thought and behavior. Much as Tacitus had praised the strength and valor of the Germanic barbarians in order to shame the effete Romans, Diderot celebrated the honest, uninhibited Tahitians—not as models for imitation, but in order to indict Europe, where artificial mores seemed to him to encourage useless asceticism at one extreme and a disgusting license at the other. While he seems to have been vehemently dissatisfied with the European institution of marriage, he also managed to have a good deal to say about the iniquities of private property and the injustice of colonial exploitation. Taken all in all, the *Supplement* is a striking forecast of, though scarcely a source for, the psychology of the French Revolution in its most radical phase. It remains a powerful statement of the Enlightenment's most advanced views on the equality and dignity of all human beings, women, children, and savages included.

Remarkably little of Diderot's fiction found its way into print during his lifetime, one reason probably being that until around 1770 he was fully occupied with the *Encyclopédie* or with the scientific writings on which he mainly relied to build his reputation. The only piece of imaginative literature (aside from a couple of plays) that he published before that date was a rather salacious fantasy, *Les Bijoux Indiscrets*, which appeared without his name in 1748 while he was still an obscure young translator in need of extra cash to maintain a growing family and an expensive mistress. Despite the very real merits of this piece, Diderot never seems to have taken any great pride in it.

Once the *Encyclopédie* was finished and his reputation as a serious writer solidly established, Diderot undoubtedly thought that it could do no harm to test the public's—and the royal censor's—response to some of the fictional writings he had been accumulating in his desk. Had the results of this experiment been more encouraging than they actually were, it is possible that he might have allowed *Rameau's Nephew* and other pieces of the same character to see the light of day while he himself was still alive. But the reception accorded in 1772–73 to *The Two Friends from Bourbonne* and *A Conversation Between a Father and His Children* was on the whole discouraging and it may have persuaded him to withhold the others.

We know very little about the circumstances under which the second of these pieces was composed, but it is possible to reconstruct in fairly satisfactory detail the principal steps in the production of *The Two Friends from Bourbonne*. The story was originally written in August 1770, while Diderot was staying at Bourbonne-les-Bains, a small spa in Champagne not far from his native city of Langres. His being there had to do with the presence of two attractive women, toward either or both of whom he may have had amorous intentions. These were Madame de Meaux, who in all likelihood did become his mistress later, and her married daughter, Madame de Prunevaux, who was taking the waters to recover her strength after the birth of her first child. To while away the long evenings in a drowsy provincial town, the two ladies carried on a voluminous correspondence with friends in Paris. One of these was Diderot's protégé Naigeon, who had once boasted that he could recognize the master's style anywhere. To play a joke on Naigeon, whom Madame de Prunevaux had taken to calling "my dear little brother," Diderot wrote the first part of the story; then he had Madame de Prunevaux copy it and send it to Naigeon as her own work. The trick was entirely successful, for Naigeon's reply consisted only of an urgent request for a sequel to the tale telling what became of Felix after Olivier's death. So Diderot wrote a continuation which was sent on in the same manner. Naigeon's remarks when he finally learned who the author was are unfortunately not recorded.

The title and theme of Diderot's story relate to a rather stilted and highly sentimental tale, *Les Deux Amis, conte iroquois*, on the theme of true friendship among the noble redskins, published in the summer of 1770 by an acquaintance, Saint-Lambert. A friend in common, Madame d'Epinay, says that she and Grimm read this story and urged Diderot to write one like it but more true to life. He seems to have accepted this assignment all the more willingly because he had long desired to see greater realism in literature and had himself written two plays that attempted to portray real situations in the lives of ordinary people. His great admiration for the English novelist Richardson, moreover, seems to have stemmed from the singular but sincere conviction that the author of *Pamela* was blazing the trail toward a more naturalistic style in the novel.

From the vantage point of a century and a half later, it is not difficult to agree with some of the reasons Diderot presumably had for thinking *The Two Friends* an important advance in the direction of greater literary naturalism. Nor are the author's concluding remarks, in which he explains to the reader what he has been trying to do, altogether lacking in charm. The story has been included in this volume partly for the insight it gives into Diderot's conception of literary craftsmanship, partly because it can still be read with pleasure as a good short story. After all, not so many of the short stories written in the eighteenth century can meet this test, and not enough of them were by Diderot.

III

No selection from Diderot's writings would be representative of his life's work or of his stature as a missionary of ideas if it did not include something from the great *Encyclopédie ou Dictionnaire raisonné des Sciences, des Arts, et des Métiers*, whose guiding genius he was and on which he labored for the best twenty-five years of his life. This vast compilation, unified and permeated as it is by a humane, optimistic and liberating view of man, stands in somewhat the same relation to the Enlightenment as the *Summa Theologica* of St. Thomas to the centuries of Mont-St. Michel and Chartres. It had the conscious aim of "changing the general mode of thinking," and it realized that aim with extraordinary success, establishing many of the philosophical points of departure for the

French Revolution and marking out a program of intellectual and political development that has had an overwhelming influence in the formation of the contemporary world.

As the principal editor and author of the *Encyclopédie*, Diderot assumed particular responsibility for its articles on the industrial arts, while the coeditor, D'Alembert, looked after mathematics and pure science. Originally projected as a French translation of the English *Cyclopaedia* of Ephraim Chambers, the *Encyclopédie* expanded as it went forward. The prospectus of 1750 promised eight folio volumes of text and two of illustrations. By the time Diderot's work was finished in 1772 the subscribers had received seventeen volumes of text and eleven of plates.

The first volume appeared in June 1751, and was eagerly received by the reading public not only of France but of all Europe. Soon there were more than four thousand purchasers, each of whom agreed to pay, in installments, a total price equal to nearly $1,000 in present-day values. These figures, extraordinary as they were at that time for a work of non-fiction, do not even begin to indicate the number of people who read the *Encyclopédie*—many of them went through it page by page—as its volumes appeared at intervals of about six months during the first years after 1751. Copies were widely loaned; pirated editions and selections of important articles, and separate printings of many individual pieces, were sold at low prices and in large numbers; and many readers in modest circumstances were able for a very small fee to consult the volumes in public reading rooms.

Despite the fact that official censors had read every page of the manuscript before it was set up in type, the first volumes drew the fire of scandalized prelates and theologians, especially that of the Jesuits, who may have feared that their *Dictionnaire de Trévoux* was in danger of being driven off the market by the new work. After a crisis in 1752—growing out of the Sorbonne's overhasty approval and subsequent ignominious disavowal of a somewhat unorthodox doctoral thesis written by the young Abbé de Prades, one of Diderot's collaborators—the first two volumes of the *Encyclopédie* were suppressed by the authorities. Continued harassment by clericals and by the Parlement of Paris made the editors' task progressively more difficult. Rousseau broke with the Encyclopedists and took issue publicly with certain ideas he had formerly shared with them. Some of the less dedicated members of the staff, including D'Alembert, withdrew from the enterprise in discouragement or disgust. Voltaire remained loyal, but did not always give the kind or amount of help that Diderot felt he had a right to expect. Finally, in 1759, in a wave of repression that began in the aftermath of the fanatic Damiens' attempt on the life of Louis XV and that was augmented during the furor stirred up by the publication of Helvetius' *De l'Esprit* (1758), the *Encyclopédie* was deprived of its license to publish.

The government ordered a refund to subscribers for the volumes they had bought in advance but had not yet received. But to the great relief of Diderot and his employers, not a single subscriber came forward to claim his money; bankruptcy was avoided by arranging that the amounts already paid in would be credited toward the forthcoming volumes of illustrations which the authorities allowed to continue. Refusing the invitations of Catherine II and Frederick the Great to finish his task in Russia or Prussia, Diderot—with the connivance of highly placed sympathizers such as Malesherbes (head of the government censorship) and Sartine (head of the Parisian police)—laboriously completed the last ten volumes of text in "secrecy," in haste, and almost singlehandedly, between 1759 and 1763.

Though they appeared in 1765 with three asterisks in place of his name and bore the name of a fictitious Swiss publisher on their title page, these volumes were, ironically enough, printed in Paris on presses that had belonged to the Jesuits before their expulsion from France in 1764. Diderot, however, felt little sense of personal triumph, for he had discovered only when it was too late that his timid publisher had treacherously cut out a number of his more telling passages and had mutilated others in the hope of appeasing the opposition. (We now know that the damage was much less extensive than Diderot

believed.) His bitterness was increased by the knowledge that
his publishers had cleared more than a million dollars in
profits, while he had earned scarcely more than an artisan's
wage for the twenty-five years of labor that had worn out his
health and his eyesight.

Still the battle had been won, for between 1770 and the
Revolution of 1789 the enemies of the *Encyclopédie* com-
manded no more than a feeble and faltering hold on French
public opinion. The dominant spirit was that of the *philosophes*, and they no longer encountered more than token
opposition. Restrictions on the expression of their views virtually ceased to operate, and the diffusion of their ideas among
the literate middle and upper classes of French society went
on unimpeded.

The selection chosen to represent here Diderot's contribution, both as author and as editor, is an essay defining the
word *"encyclopédie"* which appeared in Volume V (1755).
Here he sketches in language that often achieves real eloquence the grandiose scheme of classification according to
which the *Encyclopédie* was seeking to unify all human knowledge by placing man himself at the center of things. He dwells
with special force on his ardently held belief that the increase
and improvement of knowledge offers men their best hope of
achieving greater well-being and happiness, and he argues with
equal conviction that wider diffusion of this knowledge will
be likely to promote the interests of freedom and virtue. Although today we are doubtless not so confident as Diderot that
better education is the sure specific for all moral and social
ills, still we should probably not write his program off as a
failure until more conclusive experiments in popular education are made, or until a more promising means of restraining
the driving power of ignorance has been discovered.

The remainder of the essay supplies a quantity of fascinating details on how the modern world's first really compre-
hensive encyclopedic dictionary was put together. We learn, for
example, how difficult it was to obtain reliable information
about industrial processes, many of which were jealously
guarded guild mysteries or trade secrets. Here, too, we are

taken into the editor's confidence and shown some of the ingenious devices used to turn an encyclopedia—of all things— into a powerful engine of liberal propaganda under the very noses of a vigilant and mistrustful board of censors. Finally, we find a highly persuasive (and ever timely) plea on behalf of free expression and circulation of ideas both within and among nations.

The concluding piece in the present book is one that has no particular literary or historical importance, but does afford an intimate glimpse into Diderot's workroom as well as into his generous and appealing character. *Regrets on Parting with My Old Dressing Gown* was in origin simply a charming little note of thanks to Madame Geoffrin, a wealthy friend who had sent him a splendid new dressing gown along with some handsome pictures and some rather ornate furniture. The piece is given here mainly because it seemed likely to establish the mood of unbuttoned relaxation most suitable for bidding a reluctant *au revoir* to the prince of informal philosophers.

RALPH H. BOWEN

NOTE: The introductory note to *Rameau's Nephew,* and the translation of *Rameau's Nephew,* are the work of Jacques Barzun. All the other translations, and the introductory notes to them, are the work of Ralph H. Bowen.

RAMEAU'S NEPHEW
AND OTHER WORKS

1

PREFACE

The unique creation—part satire, part character sketch, part gossip column—by which Diderot is best known today did not exist for his contemporaries and formed no part of his living fame. For obvious reasons he did not publish it; he did not even show it or write about it to his friends. He kept the manuscript by him, revising and enlarging it for a dozen years at least, beginning probably in the 1760s, when he was rid of the heroic burden of the *Encyclopédie*.

After Diderot's death in 1784 his books went to Catherine the Great of Russia, who had bought their reversion by way of subsidy and delayed investment. Among the books was a bound volume of manuscripts, and *Rameau's Nephew* would perhaps still be hidden away in Russia if an illicit second copy had not been smuggled into Germany at the turn of the eighteenth century. It reached Schiller, then Goethe, who saw its greatness and promptly translated it. Thus Diderot's masterpiece first broke upon the world in German, its date of birth 1805. Its illustrious sponsorship secured it the attention of the happy few, but the larger public held back and the German publisher gave up the project of issuing the French original.

From then on the work appeared in French and other languages in various mangled states as other copies were hunted out and found. Until very recently the textual problem remained uppermost in scholarly minds, the work being in itself sufficiently allusive, elliptical, and abrupt without the blunders of hasty transcribers. Fortunately, a fair copy in Diderot's own hand came to light in 1891 and resolved the worst puzzles.

3

It is now in the Morgan Library and from it was made in
1950 the first annotated critical edition.*

Previous French texts and the English translations based
upon them naturally differ from one another and from the
present rendering. Yet errors, expurgations, variants, and
downright nonsense have not discouraged twentieth-century
readers, to whom the persons and situations of the dialogue
seem plain despite the minor mysteries of a retort or an allu-
sion here and there. Just as Petronius is meaningful with all
the gaps and corrupt passages, so Diderot's Second Satyricon
speaks a language we read fluently—and we know now that
the words are as the author left them after much polishing.

This certainty implies another: we can no longer doubt that
we are dealing here with a finished work of art. *Rameau's
Nephew* is no fragment or first draft. Goethe saw truly even
though his copy was imperfect: "What unity in the dialogue!
Those who think they see the fits and starts, the incoherence of
a conversation, are much mistaken: it has of a conversation
only its vivacity. Everything is held together . . . by a chain
of steel which is hidden from our eyes by a wreath." A critic
following the fashion of today might point to the "musical"
development of the work. No theme enters without preparation, none is forgotten; each is fully treated once and each is
emphatically recapitulated. The form is a kind of rondo, with
the theme of music itself as the refrain between variations.

But the music is also dramatic: all the motifs, large or small,
are associated with personages, most of them contemporaries
of the speakers. These several dozen characters fall into three
general classes and the context usually discloses the nature or
profession of the person named; it is seldom necessary to know
more than this in order to understand the point of the reference. In the first class are well-known musicians, artists and
writers, notably: Lully ("The Florentine"), Rameau (uncle
of Diderot's interlocutor), Pergolesi, Locatelli, Duni, Philidor
(also a famous chess player), Jomelli, Galuppi, Alberti, etc.;

---

* By Jean Fabre of the University of Strasbourg; published by Droz
in Geneva and Giard in Lille. My own earlier English version has been
thoroughly revised to conform with this latest text.

Greuze the painter; Voltaire, Racine, and other writers: Marivaux, Helvetius, Thyard de Bissy, Crébillon fils, Fontenelle, Quinault, D'Alembert, and so on. More about them can be found in appropriate biographical dictionaries, but it should perhaps be pointed out that Voltaire appears here exclusively as a poet and dramatist, the author of *Mohammed, Merope, Tancred* and other tragedies.

The second class comprises men such as Palissot, La Morlière, Poinsinet, Baculard d'Arnaud, Le Brun, La Porte, Robbé, David, Fréron, and others linked with them in the dialogue. They are the hangers-on of literature, booksellers or journalists, and sometimes professional spongers. An exception must be made for Duhamel, who was a writer of textbooks on practical subjects, and for Briasson, who was the distributing agent of the great *Encyclopédie* edited by Diderot and D'Alembert.

The third class consists of financiers, judges, and other officials. To it belong D'Argenson, onetime foreign minister and friend of Voltaire's; Maupeou, chancellor of France and protégé of Mme. Du Barry; Bouret, one of the farmers-general or wealthy tax collectors; Villemorien, colleague and son-in-law of the preceding; Samuel Bernard, multi-millionaire banker to Louis XIV and Louis XV; Bertin, of the treasury department.

It should be sufficiently clear that the women's names preceded by "La" (though sometimes without this particle) e.g. Clairon, Dangeville, Guimard, Deschamps, Lemierre, Arnould, and Hus, were those of actresses of the time who were usually courtesans also. The various noblemen and abbés referred to were fashionable or semifashionable figures whom Diderot uses as embodiments of current morals and manners. There is no difficulty about catching his drift.

The only remaining mystery is what utterances we may consider as expressing the author's own views. What philosophy, ethics, esthetics, is Diderot propounding? How much are we to believe in his concessions to the great Immoralist with whom he converses? The answer congenial to our century is that Diderot is ironic in both his guises. Diderot-He and Diderot-Myself are two halves of the same man, or, as it has been put

by several critics, Diderot the successful man of ideas dis-
covers within himself the shameless sensualist and failure that
was Rameau.

This is all very well as far as it goes, but there are a good
many moments when the two men flatly contradict each other
about such trifling matters as honesty, genius, marriage, business, civic duty, art, education, appetite, fame, and friendship.
To say that Diderot could perceive the force of many of his
antagonist's arguments is one thing; to say that he was equally
convinced by all of them and by his own opposing ones is another and a false generalization. It is impossible to imagine
Diderot "considering" the betrayal of a friend or reveling in
treachery. It is impossible to think of Diderot as despising
genius or making sensual gratification his permanent program.
Even if their minds largely interpenetrate, Diderot and
Rameau are two, not one.

For this we have confirmation from the best source—Rameau
himself, whom Diderot represents as saying in divers ways:
"My mode of life would not suit you, yours would not suit
me. We belong to different species." The fact that at times
the interlocutors switch positions—Diderot advising Rameau
what tricks to play, and Rameau taking the philosopher's part
—only exhibits the role of imagination in social judgments and
strengthens Diderot's underlying thesis that morality is rarely
simple, easy, absolute, and never transferable like a recipe.

At the same time, Diderot shared with his century a taste
for preaching goodness in sentimental storybook terms. The
traces here are evident though not numerous, for this lifelong
bent was held in check by the second intention of the dialogue:
to show the reality of passion. Rameau does not counter
Diderot's fine speeches with Hamlet's impatient "Words, words,
words!" but he is ever ready with facts, facts, facts, all of which
testify to the primacy of life and its emotional substance.
Rameau dwells on the Belly and is unanswerable. And this
singular parasite does not tediously remain a crude hedonist
goaded by necessity. See how he ascends from visceral truth
to the conception of modern music and the critique of stratified

society; and how convinced we are, like Diderot, that he is a great artist *manqué* and a clear-eyed revolutionist *in posse*.

Of the two in the dialogue, Rameau is the uncompromising observer, Diderot the imaginative reformer, each incomplete and also burdened with superfluous notions. Together, despite irrelevancies which make their wrangling all the more lifelike, they rout all moral platitudes, copybook maxims, and good advice given *in vacuo*. They compel us to see in the protean aspects of man's emotional being the central problem of social organization and moral choice.

We may therefore say that with the flight of Diderot's secret manuscript to L'Ermitage in 1784, the eighteenth century is over and the latest phase of the modern age, in which we still live, has begun. Romanticism, Naturalism, Symbolism, Psychoanalysis, the cult of genius, education for self-development, the ascendancy of music, the colloquializing of literature —all are to be found stated or adumbrated in this short work, in its sarcastic words and mad evocative pantomime, just as they occurred (unbelievably and quite impossibly) some spring afternoon in a Paris garden, A.D. 1761.

RAMEAU'S NEPHEW

*Vertumnis, quotquot sunt, natus iniquis.**
HORACE

Rain or shine, it is my regular habit every day about five to
go and take a walk around the Palais-Royal. I can be seen,
all by myself, dreaming on D'Argenson's bench. I discuss with
myself questions of politics, love, taste, or philosophy. I let
my mind rove wantonly, give it free rein to follow any idea,
wise or mad, that may come uppermost; I chase it as do our
young libertines along Foy's Walk, when they are on the track
of a courtesan whose mien is giddy and face smiling, whose
nose turns up. The youth drops one and picks up another,
pursuing all and clinging to none: my ideas are my trollops.

If the weather is too cold or rainy, I take shelter in the
Regency Café, where I entertain myself by watching chess
being played. Paris is the world center, and this café is the
Paris center, for the finest skill at this game. It is there that
one sees the clash of the profound Legal, the subtle Philidor,
the staunch Mayot; that one sees the most surprising strokes
and that one hears the stupidest remarks. For although one
may be a wit and a great chess player, like Legal, one may
also be a great chess player and a fool, like Foubert and Mayot.

One day I was there after dinner, looking hard, saying little,
and listening the least amount possible, when I was accosted
by one of the oddest characters in this country, where God
has not stinted us. The fellow is a compound of elevation and
abjectness, of good sense and lunacy. The ideas of decency
and depravity must be strangely scrambled in his head, for he
shows without ostentation the good qualities that nature has

---

* Born under all the changeful stars there are.

8

bestowed upon him, just as he does the bad ones without shame. Apart from this, he is endowed with a strong constitution, a special warmth of imagination, and an unusual power of lung. If you ever meet him and are not put off by his originality, you will either stuff your fingers into your ears or run away. Lord, what lungs!

He has no greater opposite than himself. Sometimes he is thin and wan like a patient in the last stages of consumption; you could count his teeth through his skin; he looks as if he had been days without food or had just come out of a Trappist monastery. The next month, he is sleek and fat as if he ate regularly at a banker's or had shut himself up in a Bernardine convent. Today his linen is filthy, his clothes torn to rags, he is virtually barefoot, and he hangs his head furtively; one is tempted to hail him and toss him a coin. Tomorrow he is powdered, curled, well dressed; he holds his head high, shows himself off—you would almost take him for a man of quality. He lives from day to day, sad or cheerful according to luck. His first care on arising in the morning is to ascertain where he will dine; after dinner he ponders supper. Night brings its own worries—whether to return on foot to the garret where he sleeps (unless the landlady has taken back the key from impatience at receiving no rent); or whether to repair to a suburban tavern and await the dawn over a crust of bread and a mug of beer. When he hasn't as much as sixpence in his pocket, as sometimes happens, he falls back on a cab-driving friend of his, or the coachman of a noble lord, who gives him a shakedown in a stable, alongside the horses. The next morning he still has bits of his mattress in his hair. If the weather is mild, he perambulates all night up and down the Cours-la-reine or the Champs-Elysées. Daybreak sees him back in town, all dressed from yesterday for today and from today perhaps for the remainder of the week.

I have no great esteem for such eccentrics. Some people take them on as regular acquaintances or even friends. But for my part it is only once a year that I stop and fall in with them, largely because their character stands out from the rest and breaks that tedious uniformity which our education, our social conventions, and our customary good manners have brought about. If such a character makes his appearance in some circle, he is like a grain of yeast that ferments and restores to each of us a part of his native individuality. He shakes and stirs us up, makes us praise or blame, smokes out the truth, discloses the worthy and unmasks the rascals. It is then that the sensible man keeps his ears open and sorts out his company.

I knew my man from quite a while back. He used to frequent a house to which his talent had given him entrée. There was an only daughter; he swore to the father and mother that he would marry her. They shrugged it off, laughed in his face, told him he was crazy. But I lived to see it happen. He asked me for a little money, which I gave him. He had somehow made his way into a few good families, where he could always dine provided he would not speak without asking permission first. He kept quiet and ate with fury. He was remarkable to see under that restraint. If he had the inclination to break the treaty and open his mouth, at the first word all the guests would shout "Why, Rameau!" Then rage would blaze in his eyes and he fell to eating with greater fury still. You wanted to know his name and now you know it. He is the nephew of the famous musician who delivered us from the plainsong of Lully that we had intoned for over a century, and who wrote so much visionary gibberish and apocalyptic truth about the theory of music—writings that neither he nor anyone else ever understood. We have from him a number of operas in which one finds harmony, snatches of song, disconnected ideas, clatter, flights, triumphal processions, spears, apotheoses, murmurings, endless victories, and dance tunes that will last for all time. Having eliminated "the Florentine" in public favor, he will be eliminated by the Italian virtuosos—as he himself foresaw with grief, rancor, and depression of spirits. For no one, not even a pretty woman who wakes up to find a pimple on her nose, feels so vexed as an author who threatens to survive his own reputation—witness Marivaux and the younger Crébillon.

He accosts me: Ha ha! So there you are, master Philosopher! And what are you up to among all these idlers? Do you waste your time, too, pushing wood? (That is the contemptuous way of describing chess and checkers.)

MYSELF. No, but when I have nothing better to do, I enjoy watching those who push well.

HE. In that case you don't enjoy yourself very often. Apart from Legal and Philidor, the others don't know what they're doing.

MYSELF. What of M. de Bissy?

HE. Oh that one is to chess what Mlle. Clairon is to acting: they know about their respective playing all that can be *learned.*

MYSELF. I see you're hard to please. You forgive nothing but sublime genius.

HE. True: in chess, checkers, poetry, eloquence, music and other nonsense of that kind, what's the use of mediocrity?

MYSELF. Not much use, I admit. But it takes a crowd to cultivate the game before one man of genius emerges. He is one out of many. But let it go. It's an age since I've seen you. I don't think about you very much when I don't see you but I'm always glad when I do. What have you been doing?

HE. What you and I and the rest do, namely, good and evil, and also nothing. And then I was hungry and I ate when I had the chance. After eating I was thirsty and I have occasionally drunk. Meanwhile my beard grew and when grown I had it shaved.

MYSELF. There you did wrong. A beard is all you lack to be a sage.

HE. Right you are. My forehead is broad and wrinkled; I have a glowing eye, a beaky nose, spacious cheeks, thick black brows, a clean-cut mouth, curved-out lips and a square jaw. Cover this ample chin with a flowing beard and I assure you it would look splendid in bronze or marble.

MYSELF. Side by side with Caesar, Marcus Aurelius, and Socrates.

HE. No. I should like it better between Diogenes and Phryne. I am as cheeky as the one and often visit the sisters of the other.

MYSELF. And you are still in good health?

HE. Usually, yes, but not so well today.

MYSELF. How is that? You have a paunch like Silenus and a face like——

HE. A face like its counterpart behind. That's because the spleen which is wasting my dear uncle seems to fatten his dear nephew.

MYSELF. Speaking of the uncle, do you ever see him?

HE. I see him pass in the street.

MYSELF. Doesn't he do anything for you?

HE. If he ever has done anything for anybody, it must be without knowing it. He is a philosopher after a fashion: he thinks of no one but himself; the rest of the universe doesn't matter a tinker's dam to him. His wife, his daughter, may die as soon as they please. Provided the parish bells that toll for them continue to sound the intervals of the twelfth and the seventeenth, all will be well. It's lucky for him and that's what I envy especially in men of genius. They are good for only one thing—apart from that, zero. They don't know what it is to be citizens, fathers, mothers, cousins, friends. Between you and me, one should try to be like them in every way, but without multiplying the breed. The world needs men, but men of genius, no; I say, no! No need of them. They are the ones who change the face of the earth. Even in small things stupidity is so common and powerful that it is not changed without fracas. What results is partly the reformer's vision, partly the old status quo—whence two gospels, a parti-colored world. The wisdom of the monk Rabelais is the true wisdom for his own peace of mind and other people's too: to do one's duty, more or less, always speak well of the father superior, and let the world wag. It must be all right since the majority is content with it. If I knew history, I could prove to you that evil has always come here below through a few men of genius; but I don't know any history because I don't know anything at all. The devil take me if I've ever learnt a single thing and if, having learnt nothing, I am worse off. One day I was at table with one of the King's Ministers who has brains enough for ten. Well, he showed us as plain as two and two make four that nothing is more useful to the nations of the earth than lies, nothing more harmful than the truth. I don't quite recall his proof but it followed very clearly that men of genius are poisonous and that if at birth a child bore the mark of this dangerous gift of nature, he should be either smothered or thrown to the dogs.

MYSELF. And yet those people who are so down on genius all pretend to have some.

HE. I'm sure they think so inside, but they don't dare admit it.

MYSELF. From modesty! So you developed from then on an undying hatred of genius?

HE. Which I'll never get over.

MYSELF. But I remember the time when you were in despair at the thought of being a common man. You'll never be happy if the pros and cons weigh with you equally. You should make up your mind and stick to it. I agree with you that men of genius are usually odd, or—as the saying goes, "great wits are sure to madness near allied"; but that doesn't change the truth that ages without genius are despised. Men will continue to honor the nations where genius thrived. Sooner or later they put up statues to them and call them benefactors of the race. With all due respect to the sublime minister you were quoting, I believe that although a lie may serve for a while, it is harmful in the long run; and, contrariwise, truth necessarily is best in the long run, even though it may do harm at the moment. From which I incline to think that the man of genius who denounces a common error or who establishes a general truth always deserves our veneration. Such a man may fall a victim to prejudice or existing law; but there are two kinds of laws—those based on equity, which are universally true, and those based on whim, which owe their force only to blindness or local necessity. These last cast odium on their violator for only a brief moment, an odium which time casts back upon the judges and the peoples who carried out the law. Which of the two, Socrates or the judge who made him drink hemlock, is today the dishonored man?

HE. A great comfort to Socrates! Was he any the less convicted? any the less put to death? Was he less of an agitator?

In violating a bad law, did he not encourage fools to despise
the good ones? Wasn't he in any case a queer and troublesome citizen? A while ago you yourself were not far from marking down the man of genius too!

MYSELF. Listen, my dear fellow. A society should not tolerate
any bad laws, and if it had only good ones it would never
find itself persecuting men of genius. I never said that genius
went with evil nor evil with genius. A fool is more often a
knave than a genius is. And even if the latter is difficult to
get on with, irritating and irritable—add wicked, if you like—
what do you infer from it?

HE. That he should be drowned.

MYSELF. Gently, dear fellow. Look and tell me—I shan't take
your uncle as an example. He is a hard man, brutal, inhuman,
miserly, a bad father, bad husband, and bad uncle. And it
is by no means sure that he is a genius who has advanced his
art to such a point that ten years from now we shall still discuss
his works. Take Racine instead—there was a genius, and his
reputation as a man was none too good. Take Voltaire——

HE. Don't press the point too far: I am a man to argue
with you.

MYSELF. Well, which would you prefer—that he should have
been a good soul, at one with his ledger, like Briasson, or with
his yardstick, like Barbier; legitimately getting his wife with
child annually—a good husband, good father, good uncle, good
neighbor, fair trader and nothing more; or that he should
have been deceitful, disloyal, ambitious, envious, and mean,
but also the creator of *Andromaque, Britannicus, Iphigénie,
Phèdre,* and *Athalie?*

HE. For himself I daresay it would have been better to be
the former.

MYSELF. That is infinitely truer than you think.

HE. There you go, you fellows! If we say anything good, it's
like lunatics or people possessed—by accident. It's only people
like you who really know what they're saying. I tell you,
Master Philosopher, I know what I say and know it as well
as you know what you say.

MYSELF. Let's find out: why better for Racine?

HE. Because all those mighty works of his did not bring him in twenty thousand francs, and if he had been a good silk merchant of rue St. Denis or St. Honoré, a good grocer or apothecary in a large way of business, he would have amassed a huge fortune, in the course of doing which there is no pleasure he would have failed to enjoy. From time to time he would have given a dollar to a poor buffoon like me and I would have made him laugh, besides procuring for him an occasional young girl to distract him a little from eternally living with his wife. We would have eaten excellent meals at his table, played high, drunk excellent wines, coffee, liqueurs; we would have had delightful picnics—you can see I knew perfectly well what I was saying—you laugh, but let me finish—it would have been better for those around him.

MYSELF. Unquestionably. Provided he hadn't used unworthily the riches acquired in legitimate trade, and had kept from his house all the gamblers, parasites, sycophants, idlers, and debauchees, as well as ordered his shopboys to beat up the officious gentlemen who would help husbands to a little distraction from habitually living with their wives.

HE. Beat up, my good sir, beat up! No one is beaten up in a well-ordered city. The profession is respectable; many people, even persons of title, are in it. And what in hell do you think money is for, if not to have good board, good company, pretty women, every kind of pleasure and every sort of amusement? I'd rather be a beggar than own a fortune without these enjoyments. But to come back to Racine. The fellow was of use only to people he didn't know, at a time when he had ceased to live.

MYSELF. Granted. But compare the good and the evil. A thousand years from now he will draw tears, will be admired by men all over the earth, will inspire compassion, human kindness, love. People will wonder who he was, from what country, and France will be envied. As against this, he brought suffering on a few persons who are dead and in whom we take no interest. We have nothing more to fear from his vices or his errors. It would no doubt have been preferable if nature had bestowed upon him the virtues of a good man as well as the talents of a great one. He is a tree which has stunted a few trees in his vicinage and blighted the plants growing at his feet; but his topmost branch reached the sky and his boughs spread afar. He has afforded shade to those past, present, and future who come to rest close to his majestic trunk. He bore fruit of exquisite savor and that will not perish. Again, it would be desirable if Voltaire had the sweetness of Duclos, the ingenuity of Abbé Trublet, the rectitude of Abbé d'Olivet;* but as that cannot be, consider the really interesting side of the problem; forget for a moment the point we occupy in time and space, and project your vision into centuries to come, into the most remote places, and nations yet unborn. Think of the welfare of our species and, supposing that we ourselves are not generous enough, let us thank nature for knowing her business better than we. If you throw cold water on Greuze's head, you will extinguish his talent together with his vanity. If you make Voltaire less restive under criticism, he will not delve into the soul of Merope and will no longer move you.

HE. But if nature is as powerful as she is wise, why not make them as good as they are great?

MYSELF. Don't you see that if you argue this way you upset the general order of things? If everything here below were excellent, nothing would be excellent.

HE. You are right. The important point is that you and I should exist, and that we should be you and I. Outside of that, let everything carry on as it may. The best order, for me, is that in which I had to exist—and a fig for the most perfect world if I am not of it. I'd rather *be*—and be even a silly logic-chopper—than not be at all.

MYSELF. There is nobody who thinks otherwise and yet who fails to attack the scheme of things, blind to the fact that in doing so he repudiates his own existence.

HE. True enough.

MYSELF. So let's accept things as they are, find out their worth and their cost, and forget whatever we do not know well enough to assess it. It perhaps is neither good nor bad, but only necessary, as so many good people think.

* These compliments are ironic.—TR.

HE. I don't follow all that you're preaching to me. Apparently it's philosophy and I tell you I will have no truck with it. All I know is that I'd be quite well pleased to be somebody else, on the chance of being a genius, a great man. I have to admit it. Something tells me I'd like it. I have never heard any genius praised without its making me secretly furious. I am full of envy. When I hear something discreditable about their private lives, I listen with pleasure: it brings me closer to them; makes me bear my mediocrity more easily. I say to myself: to be sure, you would never have been able to write *Mohammed*, but then neither would you have praised Maupeou. So I have been and I still am vexed at being mediocre. Yes, it's true, I am both mediocre and vexed. I have never heard the overture to *Les Indes Galantes*, nor the singing of *"Profonds abîmes du Ténare, Nuit, éternelle nuit,"* without thinking painfully: these are things I shall never be author of. I was obviously jealous of my uncle, and if at his death were found some grand pieces for harpsichord, I would not hesitate to remain myself and be him too.

MYSELF. If that's all that's troubling you, it isn't worth it.

HE. It's nothing, just a passing shadow.

[Then he started to sing the overture of *Les Indes Galantes* and the air *"Profonds abîmes,"* adding:]

The whatever-it-is inside me speaks and says to me: "Rameau, you'd give a great deal to have composed those two pieces; if you had done two, you would surely have done two more; and after a certain number you would be played and sung everywhere. You would walk about with head erect, your mind would bear witness to your own merit. Other people would point you out and say—'That's the man who wrote those lovely gavottes.' " [And he sang the gavottes. Then with the appearance of a man deeply moved by a rush of happiness, he added with a moist eye, while rubbing his hands together:] "You would have a comfortable house" [measuring its breadth with his arms], "a good bed" [he made as if to recline carelessly on it], "good wine" [tasting it with a smack of tongue against palate], "a good carriage and pair" [raising his foot to climb in], "pretty women" [whom he seized by the breast and gazed at voluptuously]. "A hundred loungers would come

and flatter you daily." [He thought he saw them around him—
Palissot, Poinsinet, the Frérons father and son, La Porte. He
heard them, preened himself, agreed with what they said,
smiled at them, ignored them, despised them, sent them off,
recalled them—then continued:] "Thus you would be told at
breakfast that you are a great man, you would read in *Three
Centuries of French Literature* that you are a great man, by
nightfall you would be convinced that you are a great man,
and that great man, Rameau the Nephew, would fall asleep
to the soft hum of praise buzzing in his ears. Even while asleep,
he would look sated, his chest would rise and fall with bliss,
he would snore like a great man."

[In saying this, he collapsed softly on the bench, closed his
eyes and imitated the blissful sleep he was imagining. Having
enjoyed this felicity of restfulness for a few moments, he awoke,
stretched, yawned, rubbed his eyes and looked about him for
the dull flatterers who might linger.]

MYSELF. You think, then, that a happy mortal snores in his
sleep?

HE. Think so! When I, poor wretch, am back in my garret
for the night and I have stuck myself within covers, I am
shriveled up, my chest is tight and my breath uneasy—it is a
sort of feeble plaint that can hardly be heard; whereas a financier makes the whole house resound and astonishes the entire
street. But what grieves me today is not that I sleep meanly
and snore wretchedly.

MYSELF. That's sad enough.

HE. What's happened to me is far worse.

MYSELF. What is it?

HE. You've always taken an interest in me because I'm a
good fellow whom you despise at bottom but who amuses
you——

MYSELF. I don't deny it.

HE. —so I'm going to tell you.

[Before he begins he gives a mighty sigh and puts both his
hands to his head; then he recovers his composure and says:]
"You know that I am an ignoramus, a fool, a lunatic, a lazy,
impudent, greedy good-for-nothing—what we Burgundians call
a ne'er-do-well—a blackguard, in short."

MYSELF. What a eulogy!

HE. Gospel truth from beginning to end, not a word out of place. Let's not argue about it, please; no one knows me better than I and I haven't said all I know.

MYSELF. I don't mean to annoy you: I accept everything you say.

HE. Well, I used to live with people who had taken a liking to me precisely because I had all these qualities to a rare degree.

MYSELF. Strange! Until now I had thought that one hid them from oneself, or that one forgave oneself while condemning them in others.

HE. Hide them from oneself! Who can? You may be sure that when Palissot is alone and reflects upon himself he tells himself different. In tête-à-tête with his colleague he and the other confess that they're a pair of prize scoundrels. Despise defects in others! My people were fairer than to do that and my character was a pleasure to them. I was treated like a king. They missed every moment I was away from them. I was their dear Rameau, pretty Rameau, *their* Rameau—the jester, the buffoon, the lazy dog, the saucy rogue, the great greedy boob. Not one of these epithets went without a smile, a chuck under the chin, a pat on the back, a cuff, a kick. At table it was a choice morsel tossed to me; elsewhere a liberty I could take with no consequence—for I am truly a person of no consequence. Anyone can do what he pleases with me, about me, in front of me. I never get on my high horse. Ah, the little gratuities that came my way! What a consummate ass I am to have lost all that! I have lost it all because once, once in my life, I showed common sense. I promise you, never again!

MYSELF. What was it all about?

HE. A piece of incredible folly, unimaginable, unforgivable.

MYSELF. But what kind of folly was it?

HE. Rameau, Rameau, you weren't taken on for your folly, the folly of possessing a little good taste, a little wit, a little sense. Rameau my friend, this will teach you to stay the way God made you, the way your patrons wanted you. Failing which, they seized you by the shoulder and showed you the door. They said: "Faker, beat it and don't come back. It wants to be sensible, does it? Beat it! Good sense, we have more of that than we know what to do with." You went, biting your fingernails: it's your tongue you should have bitten off first. You thought of that too late and here you are, in the gutter, penniless, and nowhere to go. You were being fed like a fatted calf, and now you're back at the slop shop; well-housed, and now you'll be lucky to have your garret back. You had a bed; now the loose straw awaits you between the coachman of M. de Soubise and Robbé, the grubstreet hack. Instead of sweet silent sleep, as you had it, one ear will be filled with the neighing and stamping of horses, the other with the far worse noise of a thousand harsh verses. Wretch, idiot, lunatic at the mercy of a million damnable fiends!

MYSELF. But is there no way to regain your passport? Did you commit so unpardonable a crime? Were I in your place, I'd go back to my patrons: you must be more indispensable than you think.

HE. Oh, I'm convinced that without me around to make them laugh, they're bored stiff.

MYSELF. That's why I'd go back. I wouldn't give them time to get used to my absence, or to take up some decent amusement. Who knows what might come of it!

HE. That's not what I'm afraid of: it couldn't happen.

MYSELF. Well then, some other genius may take your place.

HE. With difficulty.

MYSELF. Granted. Just the same, I'd go back as you are—my face fallen, my eyes wandering, unbuttoned and unkempt—in the really tragic attire in which you are. I'd throw myself at the feet of the goddess, glue my face to the ground, and without once getting up, I'd say in a weak sobbing voice: "Forgive, my lady, forgive! I am a wretch, a monster, the victim of a momentary lapse, for you know very well I am not subject to suffering from common sense. I promise it will never happen again."

[What is amusing is that while I was saying this, he was acting it out in pantomime. He was prostrate at my feet, his face on the ground, and seemed to be clutching in both his hands the tip of a slipper. He was crying and sobbing out words: "I swear it, my dear Queen, I promise, never will I do it again, never, never, never." Then, suddenly jumping up, he said in a perfectly sober, serious way:]

HE. You're right, of course. I can see it's the better way. She is kind. M. Vieillard says she is very kind, and I know somewhat that she is. But still, to go and humiliate myself before the little bitch, to cry mercy at the feet of a second-rate actress who is invariably hissed off the stage! I, Rameau, son of M. Rameau, apothecary at Dijon, a man of substance who has never crooked the knee to anyone, I, Rameau, the nephew of him who is called the great Rameau, him who can be seen pacing the Palais-Royal upright and with arms akimbo ever since M. Carmontelle depicted him bent and with his hands behind his back! I who have composed keyboard works that no one plays but which may be the only works of today posterity will like, I (in short) would go and—no, my dear sir, impossible! [And putting his right hand on his heart he added:] I feel something here which swells in pride and says to me: "Rameau, you will do no such thing. A certain dignity attaches to the nature of man that nothing must destroy. It stirs in protest at the most unexpected times, yes, unexpected, for there are days when I could be as vile as required without its costing me anything. On those days, for a penny I'd kiss the arse of the little Hus."

MYSELF. But see here, she's pretty, kind, plump, and white-skinned, and that's an act of humility that even a prouder man than you could condescend to.

HE. Let's be clear about this—there's kissing and kissing, literal and metaphorical. Consult that old Bergier who kisses the arse of the Duchess de La Marck, both literally and metaphorically—a case in which the two species disgust me equally.

MYSELF. If my suggestion does not seem expedient to you, then at least be courageous enough to be poor.

HE. It's very hard to be poor while there are so many wealthy fools to sponge on. And then contempt for oneself—that's unbearable!

MYSELF. Do you ever feel such a thing as self-contempt?

HE. Do I! How many times have I not exclaimed, "Rameau, ten thousand fine tables are set every day in Paris—a dozen to a score of covers laid there, and not one for you. Purses overflow with gold, right and left, and not a coin rolls toward you. A thousand witlings without talent or merit, a thousand creatures without charm, a thousand schemers, are well dressed and you must go naked. Are you then so stupid? Can't you lick boots like the rest? Haven't you learned to lie, swear, forswear, promise, perform, or cheat like anyone else? Can't you walk on all fours too? Can't you help my lady's affair as well as another and carry my lord's *billet-doux* equally well? Could you not, like the next fellow, encourage this young man to address that young miss and persuade Missy to hear him? Is it that you're incapable of imparting to a daughter of our bourgeoisie the fact that she is badly dressed, and that earrings, rouge, lace, or a dress *à la polonaise* will make her into a new woman? Tell her that those tiny feet were never made to tread the pavement, that there is a handsome young man who is rich and wears gold lace on his coat, owns a coach and four, and is served by six tall footmen, has seen her, finds her adorable and has in consequence lost the power of eating and sleeping and will surely die of it.—But what will Father say?—To be sure, your father; he'll be a little cross at first.— And Mamma, who says I must be an honest girl because nothing in the world is more important?—An old wives' tale which doesn't mean anything.—And my father confessor?—Stop seeing him, or if you insist on favoring him with an account of your pastimes, all it will cost you is the price of a few pounds of coffee and sugar.—But he's severe and has already refused me absolution for having sung 'Come into my nook.'—That's because you had nothing to give him, but when he sees you in a lace dress. . . .—Shall I have a lace dress?—Undoubtedly, many dresses, and diamond earrings.—Diamond!—Yes.—Like those of the marquise who buys gloves in our shop?—Just so, and a fine carriage with dapple grays, two footmen, a Negro boy, and a courier to go before. Rouge, patches, a train carried behind you . . .—For a ball?—At balls, at the play, at the Opera. (Already her heart is aflutter, so you begin to play with a slip of paper.)—What's that?—Nothing.—But what is it?—It's a note.— To whom?—To you, if you really want to know.—Can't you tell that I do? (She reads it)—A meeting, it can't be done.—It can, when you go to mass.—Mamma always goes with me. But perhaps he could come here, early. I'm up first and behind the counter. . . . He comes, he is liked; one evening the damsel disappears, and I am paid my couple of thousands. You see, poor fool, you are skilled in this art and you lack food and drink! Aren't you ashamed of yourself?" I can call to mind a crowd of knaves not fit to hold a candle to me and who were well-to-do; I was in buckram while they went in silks, leaning on gold-headed sticks, their fingers bejeweled with the cameo likeness of Plato or Aristotle. Who were they? Music masters, originally; today a kind of nobility.

It used to give me courage, uplift my soul, sharpen my mind. I felt equal to anything. But the mood did not last, apparently, because up to now I haven't managed to make my way. However that may be, those are my thoughts when I soliloquize. You can embroider them as you like, provided you agree that I do know what self-contempt is like, that torment of the soul due to neglect of the talents entrusted us by Providence. It's the cruelest form of remorse. Better a man had never been born.

[I listened to him, and while he was acting the procurer and the girl being seduced, his soul divided between opposite motives, I hardly knew whether to burst with laughter or with indignation. I was in pain: a dozen times laughter kept my anger down; a dozen times my deepening anger had to end in a shout of laughter. I was overcome by so much cunning and baseness, by notions so exact and at the same time so false, by so complete a perversion of feeling, by such turpitude and such frankness, both equally uncommon. He noticed the conflict raging within me. "What's the matter?" he asked.]

MYSELF. Nothing.

HE. You seem upset.

MYSELF. And so I am.

HE. But what do you advise me to do?

MYSELF. To talk of something else. Unhappy man, to have been born or fallen so low!

HE. I admit it. But don't let my condition weigh on you too much. My purpose in confiding in you was not to cause

you pain. I've saved a little money at my patrons'. As you know
I had everything I wanted, absolutely everything, and they
gave me an allowance for my casual expenses.

[Once more he beat his forehead with his fists, bit his lip
and turned up his eyes to the ceiling like one distracted, adding: "But the die is cast. I have some savings and time has
gone by, it's that much gained."]

MYSELF. You mean lost?

HE. No, no, gained. One gets richer by the minute: one day
less to live is the same as one banknote more. The important
thing is to keep the bowels moving freely, agreeably, copiously,
every night. *O stercus pretiosum!* That is the great end of life
in all social conditions. At the last all are equally rich: Samuel
Bernard, who by dint of stealing, swindling, and fraud leaves
twenty-seven millions in gold is no different from Rameau
who leaves nothing, Rameau who will have a shroud from
public charity to be buried in. The dead man hears no bells
toll. A hundred priests making themselves hoarse in church
are wasted on him, and so is the long procession of burning
candles. His soul is not walking in step with the leader of the
service. To rot under marble or to rot in bare earth is still
to rot. To have around your bier the Blue Boys or the Red
Boys or nobody is all one. Just look at my wrist. It was stiff
as anything; the ten fingers were like so many rods stuck in a
wooden palm; the tendons were old catgut more brittle and
stiff than that which moves a turner's wheel. But I so thoroughly pulled and broke and worked them—ah, you won't,
eh? But I say you will and they will, it works——

[Saying which, he had seized with his right hand the fingers
and wrist of his left and was bending them this way and that,
until the tips touched the forearm and the joints cracked and
I was afraid the bones would be dislocated.]

MYSELF. Be careful, you will maim yourself.

HE. Never fear, they're used to it. For the last ten years I've
shown 'em worse than that. In spite of their bloody stub-
bornness they've had to learn to find their places on the keys
and on the strings; so that now it works, it works.

[By now he has the stance of a violinist; he hums an allegro by Locatelli, his right arm moves an imaginary bow, his left hand fingers the strings. If he plays out of tune he stops and adjusts the peg, tries the string with his thumb and takes up the piece where he left off. His foot beats time and he sways and twists from top to toe as you have often seen, at the concerts of sacred music, a Ferrari, Chiabran, or other virtuoso in the like convulsions. It causes me the same distress by suggesting the same torture, for is it not a painful thing to witness the torments of someone who is busy depicting pleasure? Draw a curtain between such a man and myself if he absolutely must exhibit a victim on the rack.

[If in the midst of this agitation and these cries, there occurred a passage of slow held notes, one of those harmonious moments when the bow moves slowly across several strings at once, his face took on an ecstatic expression, his voice grew mild, he listened to himself in rapture, certain as he was that the chords were sounding in his ears and mine. Then putting his instrument under his left arm, holding it with that hand and letting the bow arm fall, he said: "Well, what do you think of it?"]

MYSELF. Marvelous!

HE. I'm in form, I think; it sounds pretty good, like the others——

[And immediately he sat down at the keyboard.]

MYSELF. I beg you to desist, for your sake and mine.

HE. No, not while I have you here; you must hear me. I don't want to be praised on no evidence. You will be more assured in your encomiums and they may bring me a pupil.

MYSELF. I know so few people: you are going to tire yourself for nothing.

[As I saw that my compassion for the man was useless (for the violin sonata had put him in a sweat), I made up my mind to let him go ahead. So there he is, seated at the keyboard with bent legs, staring at the ceiling as if he read his notes there, singing, improvising, performing a piece by Alberti or Galuppi—I don't remember which. His voice went like the

wind and his fingers flew over the keys, leaping from treble
to bass, dropping the accompaniment to stress the melody.
On his face successive emotions could be read as they passed:
tenderness, anger, bliss, sorrow. One could distinguish piano
from forte, and I am sure that a cleverer man than I could
have recognized the piece by the tempo and dynamics, by the
grimaces and the phrases that he sang out from time to time.
But what was strangest was that every so often he would
stumble and grope around, as if making a mistake and being
annoyed at his fingers' forgetfulness.

["Now you've seen for yourself," said he straightening up
and wiping the drops of sweat from his face, "that we too
can correctly use a tritone, an augmented fifth, and that the
handling of dominant progressions is familiar to us. Those
enharmonic modulations about which the dear uncle has made
so much fuss are by no means superhuman: we manage, we
manage."]

MYSELF. You've taken a great deal of trouble to show me
that you are very talented, but I was ready to take you at
your word.

HE. Very talented? Oh, no! I know my trade more or less
and that's more than enough. I ask you, does one in this
country need to know the subject one teaches?

MYSELF. No more than to know what one learns!

HE. Quite right, you know, quite right. Now, Master Philosopher, cross your heart and tell me true, wasn't there a time
when you were not so well off as you are today?

MYSELF. I'm not so very well off now.

HE. Still you wouldn't be going to the Luxembourg gardens,
in summer—you remember?

MYSELF. Let's forget it; of course I remember.

HE. In a shaggy gray coat.

MYSELF. Yes, yes.

HE. Worn through on one side, your cuffs ragged and your
black woolen stockings mended up the seam with white thread.

MYSELF. All right—whatever you say.

HE. Well, what were you doing in the Avenue of Sighs?

MYSELF. Cutting a rather poor figure.

HE. Once outside you would dash about the streets?

MYSELF. To be sure.

HE. You used to give lessons in mathematics.

MYSELF. Without knowing the first thing about it—is that what you're getting at?

HE. Just so.

MYSELF. I learned by teaching others and I turned out some good pupils.

HE. Perhaps. But music isn't like algebra or geometry. Now that you are an important person——

MYSELF. Not so important.

HE. —and have feathered your nest——

MYSELF. Very few feathers.

HE. You have tutors for your daughter.

MYSELF. Not yet. Her mother attends to her education, for one must have peace in the house.

HE. Peace in the house! That's only for the master or the servants and it's better to be the master—I've had a wife, God rest her soul. But sometimes when she piped up I'd get on my high horse and thunder at her, like God himself saying "Let there be light." And there was light. As a result, during those four years we didn't squabble more than ten times all told. How old is your child?

MYSELF. What has that to do with it?

HE. How old is your child?

MYSELF. Damn it, leave my child and her age alone and let's go back to the tutors she should have.

HE. Lord, may I never meet anyone more pigheaded than a philosopher! Would it be possible by dint of humble supplications to ascertain from His Excellency the Philosopher the approximate age of his honorable daughter?

MYSELF. Let's say about eight.

HE. Eight! Then she should have been touching the keys for four years.

MYSELF. But perhaps I am not especially concerned to include in her education a study that takes up so much time and is of so little use.

HE. What then will you teach her, if you please?

MYSELF. To think straight, if I can—a rare thing among men, and still rarer among women.

HE. Oh, let her think as wildly as she likes if she is only pretty, lively, and well-dressed.

MYSELF. Since nature has been so unkind to her as to endow her with a delicate constitution and a sensitive soul, and has exposed her to the same troubles as if she had a strong body and a heart of bronze, I'll try to teach her how to bear life with courage.

HE. Oh, let her cry, suffer, simper, and throw fits like the rest, if only she is pretty, lively, and well-dressed. And I say, no dancing?

MYSELF. No more than one needs to curtsy, know how to stand, walk, and enter a room.

HE. No singing?

MYSELF. No more than one needs to enunciate clearly.

HE. No music?

MYSELF. If I knew a good teacher and theorist I'd let him come for two hours a day for a year or two, no more.

HE. And in place of these essentials that you omit, what?

MYSELF. I put in grammar, mythology, history, geography, a little drawing, and a great deal of ethics.

HE. How easy it would be for me to prove to you the futility of all those things in the world as we know it! Did I say futility? I should perhaps say the danger. But I limit myself for the moment to one question: won't she need a master or two?

MYSELF. Of course.

HE. There we are, then. You'll expect those masters to know grammar, mythology, history, geography, and morals, and to give lessons in them. Twaddle, my dear philosopher, twaddle: if they knew these subjects well enough to teach them, they wouldn't teach them.

MYSELF. Why not?

HE. Because they would have spent their whole life learning them. A man must have gone deep into art or science to master the elements. Classic works are written only by white-haired practitioners. The darkness of the beginnings lights up only toward the middle or the end. Ask your friend D'Alembert, the dean of mathematicians, whether he would be too good to teach its rudiments. Not before thirty or forty years of application did my uncle begin to see the glimmer of musical theory.

["Oh you master crackpot!" I broke out. "How does it come about that in your silly head some very sound ideas are all muddled up with extravagant ones?"]

HE. Who the devil can tell? Chance sows them there and there they grow; which would tend to show that until one knows everything one knows nothing worth knowing, ignorant of the origin of this, the purpose of that and the place of either. Which should come first? Can one teach without method? And where does method spring from? I tell you, Philosopher mine, I have an idea physics will always be a puny science, a drop of water picked up from the great ocean on the point of a needle, a grain of dust from the Alps. Take the causes of phenomena—what about them? Really, it would be as well to know nothing as to know so little and so poorly. That's the conclusion I had reached when I took up music teaching. What are you thinking about?

MYSELF. I'm thinking that everything you've just said is more specious that solid. Let's drop it. You've been teaching, you say, composition and thoroughbass?

HE. Yes.

MYSELF. And you were entirely ignorant of both?

HE. Not really. That's why others were worse than I, namely those who thought they knew something. I at least never spoiled the minds or the hands of children. When they went from me to a good master, having learnt nothing they had nothing to unlearn, which was time and money saved.

MYSELF. What did you do actually?

HE. What they all do. I'd arrive and hurl myself into a chair. "Whew! What wretched weather! Dreadful walking!" I would gossip about this and that: "Mlle. Lemierre was to play the Vestal virgin in the new opera, but she's having her second child. Her understudy hasn't been announced. Mlle. Arnould has just broken with her little Count; they say she's dickering with Bertin.* And yet the little Count has found [the secret of] M. de Montamy's china. At the last concert of the Friends of Music there was an Italian girl who sang like an angel. As for that Préville fellow, he's a rare body: you must see him in *Mercure galant;* the scene of the riddle is killing. But la Dumesnil, poor thing, doesn't know what she's saying or doing any of the time. Come, now, Miss, your book."

While Miss takes her time finding the book, calls the chambermaid and scolds whoever mislaid it, I continue: "Clairon is really beyond making out. I hear there's an odd marriage in the wind—Miss, er, What's-her-name, that little thing so-and-so was keeping; he had two or three children by her, though before him many others had . . ."—"No, Rameau, you're talking rot, it can't be."—"I am not and it can: they say she *is* married. They also say that Voltaire is dead, which makes me glad."—"Why glad?"—"Because that means he's about to let off a wonderful squib: he usually 'dies' a couple of weeks beforehand. . . ."

Do you want to hear more? I would repeat a few risqué remarks I'd heard elsewhere; we're all gossips, you know. I acted the fool. They'd listen, laugh, exclaim "Always a charmer!" Meanwhile the young lady's book had been found under a chair where the lap dog or the cat had been at it. She would sit at the keyboard and begin the noise by herself. Then I would go nearer after having nodded my approval to the mother.

Mother: "Not bad. It would be better with a little effort, but effort is the last thing one thinks of. One prefers to babble, play with ribbons, gad about, what not. You've hardly turned your back before the book is closed—and you never scold her." Since I had to do something, I would take her hand and rearrange the fingers on the keys. I would get huffy and shout: "G, G, G, Miss, it's a G!"

Mother: "Missy, have you no ear? Even I, who know nothing and can't see the book, feel instinctively that it's a G. You make it extremely difficult for M. Rameau. I don't see how he

* Not the same as his namesake mentioned below.

stands it. You don't remember a thing he says and make no progress. . . ."

I would then mitigate the blows and nodding would say: "Forgive me, madam, forgive me. It *could* go better if the young lady would study a little, but it is not too bad."

Mother: "If I were you, I'd keep her on the same piece for a year."—"Oh, as for that, she will stick to this until all the difficulties are overcome; and it won't take as long as you may think."—"M. Rameau, you're flattering her. You are much too kind, and that's the only part of the lesson she will remember and repeat to me if she sees need." The hour would go by, the pupil would present me with my fee, as graceful of arm and manner as the dancing master had managed to make her. I put it in my pocket while the mother said: "Very good, Missy; if Javillier were here he'd compliment you. . . ." I would chat a minute more for politeness' sake and then disappear: that's what used to be called a lesson in thoroughbass.

MYSELF. And is it different today?

HE. By God, I should say it is! I arrive, my mien is grave. I hurriedly throw off my muff. I open the clavier. I try a run. I am in a perpetual hurry. If I am kept waiting one instant, I yell as if I were being robbed. An hour hence I must be elsewhere; two hours hence at the duchess's. For dinner I'm expected at the house of a marquise—a handsome one. Dinner over, there's a concert at Baron De Bagge's in the rue Neuve des Petits-Champs.

MYSELF. Whereas in fact you're not expected anywhere?

HE. Right.

MYSELF. Why resort to these vile little tricks?

HE. Why vile, if I may ask? They are part of my profession. There's nothing degrading in acting like everybody else. I did not invent these tricks. And I should be a clumsy oaf not to make use of them. I know well enough that if you apply to my case certain general principles of morals which they all talk about and never put into practice, it will turn out that white is black and black is white. But, Master Philosopher, it is with universal morality just as with universal grammar:

there are exceptions in each language that you learned people call—what is it you call them?

MYSELF. Idioms?

HE. That's what I mean. Well, each profession makes exceptions to universal morality and those I'd like to call *trade idioms*.

MYSELF. I follow you. Fontenelle speaks and writes well even though his style is full of French idioms.

HE. Likewise the sovereign, the minister, the financier, the judge, the soldier, the writer, the lawyer, the public prosecutor, the merchant, the banker, the workman, the singing teacher, the dancing master, are very respectable people even though their conduct deviates in several ways from absolute good behavior and is full of moral idioms. The older the profession the more the idioms; the worse the times become, the more the idioms multiply. A man is worth what his trade is worth; in the end they're equal; hence people make the trade go for as much as they can.

MYSELF. What appears clearest in all this tangle is that there are no honest trades and no honest men in them.

HE. Have it your own way. But as a compensation there are but few gougers outside their own shops. The world would get on pretty well if it weren't for a number of people who are called industrious, reliable, conscientious followers of duty, strict. Or what amounts to the same thing: ever in their shops practicing their trades from morn till night and doing nothing else. Result is: they're the only ones to get rich and full of reputation.

MYSELF. By sheer strength of idiom!

HE. Exactly. I see you understand. Now an idiom that is common to all trades—as there are some common to all nations and no less common than folly—is to try to get as many customers as possible. The common folly is to think that the largest tradesman is the best. Those are two exceptions to universal ethics one can do nothing about. Call it credit or "good will," it is nothing in itself but it's worth a great deal in public opinion. Don't they say: "A good name is worth a money belt?" Yet plenty of people have a good name who have no money belt, and I notice that nowadays the money insures the name. The great thing is to have both and that is precisely what I am after when I employ what you call my vile tricks. I give lessons and give them the right way—that's the absolute rule. I make people believe that I have more pupils than there are hours in the day—that's my idiom.

MYSELF. And you really give good lessons?

HE. Yes, or not bad, passable. The ground bass theory of the dear uncle has simplified everything. Formerly I swindled my pupil, yes, undoubtedly swindled. Nowadays I earn my fee at least as much as my colleagues.

MYSELF. Did you formerly swindle without qualms?

HE. Without qualms. They say, when one thief robs another the Devil laughs. My pupils' parents were fat with ill-gotten gains. They were courtiers, tax collectors, wholesalers, bankers, stockbrokers. I merely helped them—I and some others in their employ—to make restitution. In Nature all species live off one another; in society all classes do the same. We square things up with one another without benefit of the law. La Deschamps some time since, and now la Guimard, avenges the King upon his tax collector; after which the dressmaker, the jeweler, the upholsterer, the lacemaker, the confidence man, the lady's maid, the cook, and the saddler avenge the tax collector upon la Deschamps. Amid all this no one but the idiot or the loafer is taken advantage of without levying tribute on anybody else—and it serves him right. You can infer from this that the exceptions to universal ethics, or moral idioms, about which people make so much fuss under the name of mutual depredations, don't amount to anything, really. When all is said and done the only thing that matters is to see straight.

MYSELF. I admire you for that.

HE. And think of poverty! The voice of conscience and honor is pretty feeble when the guts cry out. Isn't it enough that if I ever get rich I shall be bound to make restitution? I am prepared to do this in every conceivable way—through gorging, through gambling, through guzzling, and through wenching.

MYSELF. But I'm afraid you will never get rich.

HE. I suspect it too.

MYSELF. Suppose it did work out, what then?

HE. I would act like all beggars on horseback. I'd be the most insolent ruffian ever seen. I'd remember every last thing they made me go through and pay them back with slings and arrows. I love bossing people and I will boss them. I love being praised and they will praise me. I'll have the whole troop of Villemorien's bootlickers on salary, and I'll say to them what's been said to me: "Come on, dogs, entertain me." And they will. "I want decent people pulled to pieces." And they will be—if any can be found. Then too, we'll have women, and when drunk we'll thee-and-thou one another. We will drink and make up tales and develop all sorts of whims and vices. It will be delightful. We'll prove that Voltaire has no genius; that Buffon is always up on stilts like the turgid declaimer he is; that Montesquieu was only a wit. We'll tell D'Alembert to stick to his ciphering and we'll kick behind and before all the little stoics like you who despise us from sour grapes, whose modesty is the prop of pride, and whose good conduct springs from lack of means. Ah, what music you'll hear from us!

MYSELF. Knowing what worthy use you would make of wealth, I see how deplorable it is that you are poor. You would certainly be doing honor to human nature, good to your compatriots and credit to yourself.

HE. I almost think you're making fun of me, Master Philosopher. But you don't even suspect with whom you're tangling; you don't seem to know that at this very moment I represent the most important part of Town and Court. The well-to-do of every description have either said or not said to themselves the words I've just confided to you; the fact remains that the life I would lead in their position is precisely theirs. That's where you fellows are behind the times. You think everybody aims at the same happiness. What an idea! Your conception presupposes a sentimental turn of mind which is not ours, an unusual spirit, a special taste. You call your quirks virtue, or philosophy. But virtue and philosophy are not made for everybody. The few who can, have it; the few who can, keep it. Just imagine the universe philosophical and wise, and tell me if it would not be devilishly dull. Listen! I say hurrah for wisdom and philosophy—the wisdom of Solomon: to drink good wines, gorge on choice food, tumble pretty women, sleep in downy beds—outside of that, all is vanity.

MYSELF. What! And fighting for your country?

HE. Vanity! There are no countries left. All I see from pole to pole is tyrants and slaves.

MYSELF. What of helping your friends?

HE. Vanity! No one has any friends. And even if one had, should one risk making them ungrateful? Look close and you'll see that's all you get for being helpful. Gratitude is a burden and burdens are to be shuffled off.

MYSELF. To hold a position in society and discharge its duties?

HE. Vanity! What difference whether you hold a position or not, provided you have means, since you only seek a position in order to get wealth. Discharge one's duties—what does that bring you?—jealousy, worries, persecution. Is that the way to get on? Nonsense! Pay court, pay court, know the right people, flatter their tastes and fall in with their whims, serve their vices and second their misdeeds—there's the secret.

MYSELF. Watch over the education of one's children?

HE. Vanity! That's a tutor's business.

MYSELF. But if a tutor, imbued with your principles, neglects his duty, who will pay the penalty?

HE. Not I anyhow. Possibly, some day, my daughter's husband or my son's wife.

MYSELF. But suppose that either or both plunge into vice and debauchery?

HE. Then that is part of their social position.

MYSELF. If they disgrace themselves?

HE. It's impossible to disgrace yourself, no matter what you do, if you are rich.

MYSELF. Ruin themselves, then?

HE. Too bad for them.

MYSELF. It seems to me that if you overlook the conduct of

your wife, your children and your servants, you might easily overlook your own affairs.

HE. Not so, if you will permit me: it is sometimes difficult to procure money, hence one uses a prudent foresight.

MYSELF. You will pay little attention to your wife?

HE. None, an it please you. The best behavior toward one's dearer half, I think, is to do what suits her. Do you suppose company would be tolerable if everyone minded his own business?

MYSELF. Why not? I'm never so happy in the evening as when I'm pleased with my forenoon.

HE. Me too.

MYSELF. What makes society people so choosy about their entertainment is that they are utterly idle.

HE. Don't you believe it: they are always on the go.

MYSELF. They never tire themselves and so can never feel refreshed.

HE. Don't you believe it: they are constantly weary.

MYSELF. Pleasure is always their business, never a desire.

HE. All the better: desires are ever nagging.

MYSELF. They wear everything out. Their soul gets dull, boredom masters them. Whoever should take their life at the height of their load of plenty would be doing them a good turn. For they know of pleasure only that portion which soonest loses its zest. I am far from despising sensual pleasures. I have a palate too and it is tickled by a delicate wine or dish; I have eyes and a heart and I like to look at a pretty woman, like to feel the curve of her breast under my hand, press her lips to mine, drink bliss from her eyes and die of ecstasy in her arms. Sometimes a gay party with my friends, even if it becomes a little rowdy, is not displeasing to me. But I must confess that I find it infinitely sweeter to succor the unfortunate, to disentangle a bad business, to give helpful advice, to read some pleasant book, to take a walk with a man or woman who is dear to me, to spend a few instructive hours with my children, to write a page of good prose, to carry out my duties, or to tell her whom I love something tender and true which brings her arms about my neck.

I know of certain deeds which I would give all I possess to have done. Voltaire's *Mohammed* is a sublime work, but I would rather have rehabilitated the Calas family. A man I know left home for Cartagena; he was a younger son in a country where primogeniture is the law. While abroad he learns that his elder brother, a spoiled child, has ruined his father and mother, driven them out of the castle, and left them to languish in some provincial town. What does the younger son do, who after the harsh treatment meted out by his parents had gone to seek his fortune far away? He sends them help. He winds up his affairs, comes back rich, restores his parents to their home, marries off his sisters. Ah, my dear Rameau, that man looked upon this period as the happiest in his life. He had tears in his eyes as he spoke of it and as I tell you this, I feel my heart dilate with gladness and my tongue falter with emotion.

HE. Queer people, you are!

MYSELF. And you are people to be pitied, unless you can see that one can rise above one's fate and make oneself independent of misfortune by actions such as I have described.

HE. That's a kind of happiness I would find it hard to become familiar with, it is so rarely found. Then according to you people should be decent?

MYSELF. To be happy?—Certainly.

HE. Yet I see a quantity of decent people unhappy and a quantity of people happy without being decent.

MYSELF. So it seems to you.

HE. Wasn't it because I acted sensibly and frankly for one instant that tonight I don't know where to find a meal?

MYSELF. Not at all: it's because you have not always been sensible and frank; because you did not learn soon enough that the first step is to secure the means of life apart from servitude.

HE. Apart or not, my way is surely the easiest.

MYSELF. And the least assured and the least decent.

HE. But the most consistent with my nature, which is idle, stupid, and crooked.

MYSELF. Granted.

HE. Since I can secure my well-being with the aid of vices natural to me, that I have acquired without labor and that I retain without effort, vices congenial to the habits of my countrymen, agreeable to the tastes of my protectors, and closer to their little needs than any virtues could be—for virtues would annoy them all day long like so many accusations—in view of all this, it would be strange indeed for me to bedevil myself like a damned soul and turn myself into what I am not; to acquire a character alien to mine, with laudable traits, no doubt (I won't argue), but difficult to maintain and make use of. It would do me no good, perhaps worse than no good, by implying a satire of the rich people in whose company paupers like me must find their livelihood.

Virtue is praised, but hated. People run away from it, for it is ice-cold and in this world you must keep your feet warm. Besides, I would grow bad-humored, infallibly. For note how often devout people are harsh, touchy, unsociable. The reason is that they have compelled themselves to do an unnatural thing. They're in pain, and people in pain make others suffer. That's not the life for me, nor for my patrons. I must be gay, easy, jolly, droll, entertaining. Virtue earns respect and respect is inconvenient; virtue is bound to be admired, and admiration is no fun. I deal with people who are bored and I have to make them laugh. Now what is laughable is absurdity and folly. I must consequently be absurd and a fool. Even had nature not made me such, the quickest way would be to put on the appearance. Fortunately, I don't need to be a hypocrite; there are enough of them around, not counting those who deceive themselves. The Chevalier Morlière who snaps his hatbrim on his ear, sniffs the air and looks at every passer-by over his shoulder; who drags the longest sword next to his thigh and has an insult ready for anyone unarmed; in short, who defies every man on principle, what is he really up to? He does what he can to persuade himself that he is a man of spirit, though he's a coward. Tweak his nose and he will take it mildly. If you want to make him pipe down, just raise your voice, lift your cane, or let your foot contact his buttocks. Full of surprise at finding himself a coward, he will ask you who told you of it, how you knew. Himself did not suspect it the moment before. His long and habitual aping of bravery had fooled him; so much mimicry had ended by seeming real.)

And what of that woman who mortifies her flesh, who visits prisons, who attends all meetings organized for charity, who walks with lowered lids and would not dare look a man in the eye; who is continually on guard against the temptations of the senses—does any of this keep her heart from burning, her breast from sighing, her flaming desires from obsessing her? Her imagination at night rehearses the scenes of the *Portier des Chartrains* and the postures of Aretino. What then happens to her? What does her maid think when she has to get up in her shift and fly to the aid of her mistress who is suffocating? Justine, you can go back to bed, it isn't you your mistress is calling for in her fever.

And if friend Rameau himself should ever show indifference to wealth, women, good cheer, and idleness, if he should begin to stoicize, what would he be? A hypocrite. Rameau must stay what he is—a scoundrel in luck among well-heeled scoundrels; not a holier-than-thou character nor even a virtuous man eating his dry crust alone or near some other beggar. To cut it short, I want none of your kind of happiness, none of the satisfactions of a few visionaries like yourself.

MYSELF. I can see, my dear fellow, that you don't know what I refer to and that you are apparently not made to find out.

HE. Thank God for that! It would only make me starve to death, die of boredom, and croak with remorse.

MYSELF. That being so, the one piece of advice I can give you is to hurry back into the place whence you so carelessly got kicked out.

HE. You want me to do that which you do not object to when it's literal, but which is a little repugnant to you when metaphorical?

MYSELF. That's my advice.

HE. Well—apart from the metaphor, which repels me now and may not repel me later——

MYSELF. How odd you are!

HE. Not in the least. I'm perfectly ready to be abject, but not under duress. I'm willing to lower my dignity——you're laughing!

MYSELF. Certainly. Your dignity makes me laugh.

HE. To each man his own kind. I'm willing to forget mine, but at my pleasure, not on somebody else's order. Shall it be said that at the word "Crawl!" I am to crawl? That's the worm's natural gait and it is mine too, when we are left alone, but we turn and rear, both of us, when stepped on. I was stepped on and mean to rear off. And then you have no idea what a shambles that house is. Imagine a melancholy crotchety individual, a prey to vapors, wrapped up in two or three layers of dressing gown, who likes himself but dislikes everything else; who can hardly be made to smile by one's utmost contortions of body and mind, who looks with a lackluster eye on the lively twistings of my face and the even livelier ones of my intellect. For between ourselves, compared to me the ugly Benedictine so famous at court for his grimacing is, all boasting aside, nothing but a wooden Indian. I badger myself in vain to reach the sublimest lunacy—it's no use. Will he laugh or won't he? That's what I have to keep asking myself in the midst of my exertions. You can guess what harm so much uncertainty does to talent. My hypochondriac with his head swallowed up in a nightcap down to his eyes looks like an immovable idol with a string tied to its chin and running down beneath his chair. You wait for the string to be pulled but it is never pulled; or if the jaw drops it is only to let out some chilling word, from which you learn that you have not been understood and that your apish tricks have been wasted. That word is the answer to a question you put four days ago. The word spoken, the mastoid muscle contracts and the jaw clamps.

[He then started to mimic his patron. He leaned back in a chair, his head stiff and his hat over his eyes, which were half shut. His arms hung as he moved his jaw like an automaton and said: "Yes, you are right, Miss. Be subtle there. For," he went on, "the Thing lays down the law, without appeal, morning, noon, and night—at dinner, at a café, at the gaming table, in the theater, over supper, in bed, and, God forgive me, in his mistress's arms as well. I am not by way of hearing those last sentences being handed down, but I'm fed up with the others. Gloomy, sullen, and final as fate—such is our patron.

["Opposite him is a prude who puts on important airs and to whom one manages to say that she's pretty, for she still is, despite a few lumps on her face and a tendency to fat. She is trying to outdo Mme. Bouvillon in gross tonnage. I like curves when proportionable, but too much is too much, and matter needs motion! *Item.* She is meaner, prouder and stupider than a goose. *Item.* She strives for wit. *Item.* You have to persuade her that you think she has more of it than anybody else. *Item.* She knows nothing and lays down the law too. *Item.* You have to applaud her with your hands and your feet, jump for joy, and faint with admiration: 'How beautifully put, deeply felt, shrewdly judged. How do you women do it—by sheer intuition and without study, by the light of nature—it's a miracle! Don't tell me that experience, education and reflective thought are of any help!' And similar absurdities amid buckets of joyful tears; ten times a day you bow low, the forward knee bent, the other leg straight back. Arms stretched out to the goddess, you read her wishes in her eyes, you hang upon her lips, receive her command and—off like a flash! Who would want to subject himself to play such a part unless it be a poor wretch who finds in it twice or thrice a week the means to quell the tumult of his intestines? What can one think of the others, such as Palissot, Fréron, Poinsinet, Baculard, who are not destitute and whose abjectness cannot be excused by the audible pangs of a complaining stomach?"]

MYSELF. I should never have thought you so fastidious.

HE. I am not. In the beginning I just watched the others and acted like them, better, perhaps, because I am more frankly impudent, a better actor, hungrier and stronger of lung. I must be descended direct from the famous Stentor. . . .

[To give me an exact idea of his pulmonary strength, he began to cough with violence enough to break the plate-glass windows of the café and to arrest the chess players in mid-air.]

MYSELF. But of what use is this power?

HE. Can't you guess?

MYSELF. No, I'm a little slow.

HE. Suppose an argument in progress and victory uncertain. I rise and let loose my thunder, I say: "The truth is precisely as Mademoiselle states it. What judgment! I defy any of our great minds to come anywhere near it. The very form is impeccable!" Of course, you mustn't always back her up in the same way. It would be monotonous. It wouldn't sound genuine. It would lack savor. Your only chance is to keep your wits about you, to be fertile. You must know how to prepare and establish your major keys, seize the right instant. When, for example, opinions are divided and the debate has reached the highest pitch, no one listening and all talking at once, you should be somewhat to one side, in the corner of the room farthest from the battlefield, and your explosion should be timed after a long pause so as to crash suddenly like a bombshell among the combatants. No one has mastered this art like me. Yet my really surprising skill is in the opposite vein. I have mild notes accompanied by smiles, an infinite variety of faces expressing agreement. In these, nose, mouth, brows, and eyes participate. I have a flexibility of spine, a way of twisting it, of shrugging or sagging, of stretching out my fingers, of nodding and shutting my eyes, of being thunderstruck as if I heard a divine angel's voice come down from heaven—this it is to flatter. I don't know whether you grasp the whole force of this last attitude of mine. I did not invent it, but no one has surpassed me in performance. Just look!

MYSELF. You are right. It is unique.

HE. Can you imagine any female brain of any degree of vanity capable of resisting this?

MYSELF. No, I must admit that you have carried the art of making fools and abasing yourself as far as it can go.

HE. They try what they like, any of them, they will never overtake me. Not the best of them, Palissot for example, will

hardly be anything more than a good apprentice. Still, even
if the part is fun to play at first, by making one laugh inwardly
at the stupidity of those one fools, after a while the game
loses its charm. After a number of innovations one repeats
oneself, for art and wit have their limits. Only God and some
few rare geniuses can keep forging ahead into novelty. Bouret
may be one of those. Things are reported of him that strike
me, yes me, as sublime. The trick of the lap dog, the Treatise
on Happiness, the torches on the road to Versailles, are inventions that confound and humble me. I could give up the
art from self-disgust just to think of them.

MYSELF. What do you mean by the lap-dog trick?

HE. Where have you been? Do you mean to tell me you
don't know how that amazing man went about it to alienate
from himself the affections of a little dog and attach them to
the Keeper of the Seals who had taken a fancy to the animal?

MYSELF. Really, I never heard of it.

HE. Well then. It is one of the greatest conceptions ever
formed. All Europe marveled at it; every courtier envied it.
Now you are not without guile—how would you have gone
about it? Remember that Bouret's dog loved him. Bear in mind
that the dog was frightened by the strange uniform of the
Keeper of the Seals. And don't forget the problem had to be
solved in a week. You must note all the conditions if you are
to appreciate the elegance of the solution. Well?

MYSELF. I freely admit that in that kind of business I'd be
stumped by the simplest thing.

HE. Then listen [said he, tapping me on the shoulder, for
he takes familiarities] listen and admire. He has a mask made
to look like the Keeper of the Seals. He borrows from the
Keeper's valet the voluminous gown, puts it and the mask on.
He calls his dog and pats him and gives him a sweet.

All of a sudden, the scene changes. It's no longer the Keeper,
it's Bouret who calls his dog and whips him. Less than three
days of this steady course make the dog flee Bouret the tax
collector and run to Bouret the Keeper of the Seals. But I'm
too good to you. You are a layman who doesn't deserve to be
instructed in the miracles that go on in your vicinity.

MYSELF. None the less, tell me about the Treatise on Happiness and the torches on the road to Versailles.*

HE. No, no. Ask the paving stones and they'll tell you, and take advantage rather of the fact that I know things nobody else knows.

MYSELF. You are right.

HE. Borrowed the gown *and wig* of the Keeper of the Seals. I'd forgotten the wig! The idea of having a mask made—that mask goes to my head. No wonder the man is a millionaire and enjoys the greatest respect. There are holders of the military Cross of St. Louis who go without bread—hence the folly of seeking the cross at the risk of life and limb. Why not instead go after a position absolutely free of danger and invariably rewarded. I call that aiming at true greatness. But such paragons are discouraging; they make one despise oneself and fall into the dumps. The mask! The mask! I'd give a finger of my right hand to have thought of the mask.

MYSELF. But drawn as you are toward all higher things and possessing such a ready genius, have you made no inventions of your own?

HE. If you please, I have. For example, that spinal expression of admiration I mentioned to you. I consider it mine, though the jealous might dispute it. I concede that it had been used before me, but no one had discovered how convenient it is for laughing the while at the coxcomb one is admiring. I have, in addition, more than a hundred ways to begin seducing a young girl, next to her mother, without the latter's noticing it, and indeed, making her an unwitting accomplice. I'd hardly started in my career before I gave up the conventional ways of delivering a *billet-doux*. I have ten ways of getting it snatched from me, and some I daresay are new. Above all, I know the way to spur a timid youth; I have in-

---

* During a visit of the King's to Bouret's country house, he found a volume entitled *True Happiness*. On every page was written: "The King paid a visit to Bouret." Again, when the King went once by night to Versailles, he found every twenty feet a servant of Bouret's holding a torch. Bouret made and spent forty-two million francs and died owing five more millions.—TR.

sured the success of some who had neither brains nor presence. Were this recorded no one could deny me a touch of genius.

MYSELF. An unusual kind of fame.

HE. No question about it.

MYSELF. If I were you, I would note down some of these things. It would be a pity if they were forgotten.

HE. I agree with you. But you'd be surprised how little I think of methods and rules. The man who needs a textbook can't go far. Geniuses seldom read, and they experiment a great deal; they are their own masters. Consider Caesar, Turenne, Vauban, the Marquise de Tencin, her brother the Cardinal, and his secretary, Abbé Trublet. And then Bouret? Who ever gave Bouret lessons? Nobody. Nature creates the superior man. Do you suppose the theory of the lap dog and the mask was written down somewhere?

MYSELF. Still, when you have leisure, when the anxiety of your empty stomach or the toiling of your well-filled paunch drives away sleep——

HE. I'll think about it. Better write of great feats than perform small ones. For it uplifts the soul, fires and expands the imagination, instead of contracting it with mock surprise (when speaking to the little Hus woman) at the applause given by a stupidly obstinate public to the simpering Dangeville and her dull acting. She walks on nearly bent over double, looks affectedly up into the eyes of her interlocutor and yet plays under his chin, taking all these goings-on for subtlety and her scampering about for gracefulness. And that bombastic Clairon!—scrawnier, stiffer, stuffier, stodgier than words can say! The witless audience claps till their hands are raw and never seems to notice that we are a bundle of charms (a growing bundle, to be sure, but never mind), that our skin is the finest, our eyes the handsomest, our snout the cutest— no great heart, it is true, and no sylphlike walk, but far from clumsy, in spite of what people say. And when it comes to emotional power, we can outplay every last one of them.

MYSELF. How do you mean all this—truthfully or ironically?

HE. The trouble is that this emotional power is all within. Not a glimmer of it transpires. But I give you my word she's full of it. Or if it isn't the real thing, it's very close to it. You should see, when we're in the mood, how we deal with footmen, how the maids get slapped, how we administer kicks to the Petty Outlay Department,* whenever it fails in the respect due our person. She is a cute little devil, I tell you, full of sentiment and poise. Now you know what to make of this, don't you?

MYSELF. I confess I don't know whether you are speaking in good faith or cattily. I am a plain man and I wish you would be good enough to talk plainly and leave your "art" outside.

HE. Why, that's what we hand out to the little Hus about la Dangeville and la Clairon, except that I sprinkled in a few words here and there to tip you off. I'm willing to have you think me a scoundrel but not a fool; and only a fool or a man sunk in love could seriously retail so much nonsense.

MYSELF. How then does one muster up courage to utter it?

HE. It doesn't come easy all at once, but gradually. *Ingenii largitor venter.***

MYSELF. It must be a cruel hunger that drives you on.

HE. No doubt. Yet you may be sure that though they sound like enormities to you, they are more familiar to those who hear them than to us who offer them.

MYSELF. Is there anybody in that house with the strength of mind to agree with you?

HE. What do you mean by anybody? Mine's the opinion and the common speech of society at large.

MYSELF. Those in your circle who are not great knaves must be great fools.

HE. Fools? In that place? I promise you there is only one, and that's the man who feeds us in exchange for our deceiving him.

MYSELF. But how is it possible to be so grossly deceived? Because when all is said and done, the superior merit of Dangeville and Clairon is unquestionable.

* I.e. Mlle. Hus's protector Bertin, who had charge of that department in the Treasury.

** From Persius: "The belly's the spur of genius."

HE. One gulps down the flattering lie and sips the bitter truth. And then we *seem* so convinced, so sincere!

MYSELF. Yet you must have sinned at least once against the rules of art, you must have let fall one of those wounding, bitter truths—for I believe that in spite of the vile, abject, scoundrelly part you play, you have at bottom some delicacy of soul.

HE. I? Not a bit of it. The devil take me if I know what I am like at bottom. As a general rule, my mind is as whole as a sphere and my character as fresh as a daisy. I'm never false if my interest is to speak true and never true if I see the slightest use of being false. I say whatever comes into my head—if sensible, well and good; if silly, no one minds. I take full advantage of free speech. I have never in my life thought before speaking, nor while speaking, nor after speaking. The upshot is, I offend nobody.

MYSELF. Still it did happen with those fine people you were living with, who were so good to you.

HE. What do you expect? Accidents will happen. It was one of those bad days. Life knows no perpetual bliss. I was too happy, it could not last. Our house, as you know, receives the largest and most select society. It is a school of civilization, a return to the hospitableness of antiquity. All the fallen poets, we pick up; we had Palissot after his *Zarès* failed, Bret after *Le Faux Généreux;* also the despised musicians, unread authors, hissed actors—in short a mob of shamefuls, of poor dull parasites at whose head I have the honor to be, myself the brave leader of a timorous band. It's I who exhort them to eat the first time they come, it's I who order their glasses refilled—they are so diffident. A few ragged young men who don't know where to go, though presentable enough; some others, real scoundrels who cozen the master for the sake of gleaning after him in the fields of the mistress. We seem to be jolly, but actually we are all grumpy and fiercely hungry. Wolves are not more voracious nor tigers more cruel. We devour one another like wolves when the snow has long been on the ground. Like tigers we tear apart whatever succeeds. Sometimes the Bertin, Monsauge and Villemorien mobs join forces. It's then you should hear the noise of the menagerie! You have never seen such a collection of sullen, soured, malignant, and enraged animals. You hear nothing but the names of Buffon, Duclos, Montesquieu, Rousseau, Voltaire, D'Alembert, and Diderot. God alone knows by what adjectives they are characterized. No one shall be deemed bright if he is not as stupid as ourselves. Among that crowd was born the idea of the comedy against the *philosophes:* I supplied the scene of the book peddler, patterned after *The Woman Preacher, or Theology in Skirts.* You weren't spared in it any more than the rest.

MYSELF. That's fine. Maybe it's a greater honor than I deserve. I should be humiliated to find that people who malign as many good and able men were praising me.

HE. There are a lot of us and each must do his bit. When we have sacrificed the bigger beasts, we offer up the rest.

MYSELF. Insulting knowledge and virtue for a living—that is dearly earned bread!

HE. I've already told you, we're of no consequence. We insult everybody and injure nobody. Sometimes we see the heavy-going Abbé D'Olivet, the fat Abbé LeBlanc, the hypocritical Batteux—the fat one is only mean before dinner. After coffee he slumps into an armchair, his feet on the fender, and he goes to sleep like an old parrot on his perch. If the rumpus gets too loud, he yawns, stretches, rubs his eyes and asks: "What is going on, what is it? What is it?"—"We're discussing whether Piron is wittier than Voltaire."—"Let's be clear about this: it's wit you mean, not taste? Because taste, your Piron has no idea what it is."—"No idea?"—"None." Then we're off into a discussion of taste, and the boss makes a sign with his hand that he wants to be heard, because taste is what he prides himself on having. "Taste," says he, "taste is a thing which ——" I've forgotten what he said it was, and so has he.

At other times we have friend Robbé, who regales us with his shady stories, with his accounts of religious revivalists in convulsions—actually seen by him—and with a few cantos of a poem by him on a subject he knows thoroughly. I hate his verse but I love to see him recite. He looks like a fanatic and

everybody around cries out: "There's a poet for you! . . ."
Between ourselves, his poetry is a cacophonous noise, the very
speech of the builders of Babel. Or again, we have a visit
from a certain booby who seems base and stupid but who is
as sharp as a demon and cleverer than an old monkey. His is
one of those faces seemingly made to call forth jokes and
sarcasm but designed by God to confound people who judge
by appearances. Their mirror should have told them that it
is as easy to be intelligent and look foolish as it is to be a fool
behind a bright exterior. It's such a common piece of cowardice
to offer up a good man to the ridicule of others that people
never fail to pick on this fellow. He is a trap we set for new-
comers and they almost invariably fall into it.

[Being surprised at the justness of my madman's remarks
on men and manners, I told him so.]

That [said he] is because bad company is as instructive as
debauchery: one is indemnified for the loss of innocence by
the loss of prejudice. In a society of bad men, they stand un-
disguised and one learns to see them as they are. And then
I've done some reading.

MYSELF. What have you read?

HE. I keep rereading Theophrastus, La Bruyère and Molière.

MYSELF. Excellent books.

HE. They're even better than people think, but who knows
how to read them?

MYSELF. Everybody according to his capacity.

HE. I should say almost no one. Can you tell me what they
look for in them?

MYSELF. Instruction mixed with entertainment.

HE. But what kind of instruction: that's the point!

MYSELF. The knowledge of one's duty, the love of virtue
and the hatred of vice.

HE. Now what I find there is a compendium of what to do
and what not to say. When I read *The Miser*, I say to myself:
"Be as miserly as you like, but don't talk like the miser."
When I read *Tartuffe*, I say: "Be a hypocrite if you choose,
but don't talk like one. Keep any useful vices, but don't acquire the tone and air which would make you ridiculous. Now

to avoid these one must know what they are, and the authors
mentioned have given us excellent portraits. I am myself and
I remain such, but I act and speak just as I ought to. Far from
despising the moralists, I find profit in them, particularly those
who depict morals in action. Vice offends men only from time
to time; but the symptoms of vice offend day and night. It
is surely better to be arrogant than to look it. The arrogant
character insults you only now and then; the arrogant look
insults you continually. And by the way, don't suppose that
I am the only reader of my kind. My sole merit is to have
accomplished systematically, through good judgment and right
reason, what most other people do by instinct. Hence their
reading does not make them better than I, and they remain
ridiculous despite their efforts; whereas I am such only when
I choose, and so surpass them by far. The same skill which
saves me from ridicule on certain occasions, enables me at
other times to incur it with high art. I recall whatever others
have said, whatever I have read, and I add to all this my original contribution, which is surprisingly abundant.

MYSELF. It was wise of you to impart these mysteries to me,
else I would have thought you self-contradictory.

HE. I'm nothing of the kind, for if it is necessary to avoid
ridicule once, it is fortunately just as necessary to incur it a
hundred times. There is no fitter role in high society than
that of fool. For a long time the King had an appointed fool.
At no time was there an appointed sage. I am Bertin's fool
and that of many others—yours, possibly, this minute; or maybe
you are mine. A real sage would want no fool; hence he who
has a fool is no sage; and if no sage, must be a fool. And were
he the King himself, he may be his own fool's fool. In any
event, remember that in a subject as variable as manners and
morals nothing is absolutely, essentially, universally true or
false—unless it be that one must be whatever self-interest requires, good or bad, wise or foolish, decent or ridiculous, honest or vicious. If virtue by chance led to fortune, I should have
been as virtuous—or virtuous-seeming—as the next man. I was
bidden to be ridiculous and I made myself so. As to vice,
nature alone took care of that; though when I say vicious I

am merely using your language. For if we really thrashed things out, we might find ourselves each calling virtue what the other calls vice and t'other way round.⟩

At our house we also see the authors of the Opéra-Comique, their actors and actresses and even oftener their managers, Corbie, Moette—all people of wealth and superior merit.

And I was forgetting the great literary critics, the whole gang of penny-a-liners: *l'Avant-Coureur*, *les Petites Affiches*, *l'Année littéraire*, *l'Observateur littéraire*, *le Censeur hebdomadaire*—all of them.

MYSELF. How can that be? *L'Année littéraire* and *l'Observateur* hate each other.

HE. True, but all beggars are friends at the trough. That damned *Observateur*, the devil take him and all his sheets! It's he, that stinking, miserly, money-lending little priest, who is responsible for my disgrace. He came within our ken for the first time yesterday. He arrived at the time which finds us all coming out of our lairs, the dinner hour. When the weather is bad, he's a lucky man who has the needed coin. One has been known to make fun of his neighbor for coming all muddy and wet through and through, who finds himself in the same condition when he gets home. One of the lot, I don't remember which, had a fearful quarrel with the Savoyard porter who has taken his stand at our door; they had deals together; the creditor wanted the debtor to pay up; the latter was in low water and couldn't.

Dinner is served. They put the Abbé in the seat of honor at the head of the table. I come in and see him. "How is that, Abbé, you're presiding? It's all right for today, but tomorrow you will please go down one cover; day after tomorrow, another cover, and so from cover to cover, to right or left, until, from having occupied the spot I held once before you, Fréron once after me, Dorat once after Fréron, and Palissot once after Dorat, you come to rest next to me, another poor bugger like you who *siedo sempre come un maestoso cazzo fra duoi coglioni.*"

The Abbé, who is a good fellow and takes everything in good part, began to laugh. Mademoiselle, struck by my remark and the accuracy of my simile, began to laugh. All those who sat to the left and right of the Abbé or whom he had displaced by one seat, began to laugh. The whole table laughed except Monsieur, who got huffy and began to use language which would have been of no consequence had we been alone: "Rameau, you are impertinent——" —"I know it, that's the condition of my being here."—"A scoundrel."—"Like the next man." —"A beggar."—"Should I be here if I weren't?"—"I'll have you turned out of doors." "After dinner I'll leave of my own accord."—"I charge you not to forget to do so."

We dined; I did not miss a mouthful. Having eaten and drunk my fill, for after all, it came to the same thing, and Messer Gaster is a person I've never treated to the sulks, I made up my mind to get ready to go. I had given my word in front of such a large group of people that I had to keep it. I took quite a while wandering around the rooms looking for my hat and stick where I knew they weren't, and hoping that the boss would burst out anew in a flood of fresh insults, that somebody would intervene and that we would end up making friends by dint of altercation. I turned and turned about, having of course no spleen to discharge; but the boss, the boss looked blacker than Homer's Apollo when he let his arrows rain down upon the Greek hosts. With his nightcap jammed lower down than usual over his eyes, he was pacing back and forth, his fist under his chin. Mademoiselle comes up to me. "Tell me," I ask her, "what is there out of the ordinary? How have I acted differently from other days?"—"I want him to go!" —"I *am* going—but I have given no ground for offense."—"I beg your pardon: we invite the Abbé and you . . ."—"It's he who offended himself by inviting the Abbé and me and so many other noodles like me."—"Come, come, dearest Rameau, just beg the Abbé's pardon."—"But I have no use for his pardon!" "Now, now, do it and everything will calm down." She takes me by the hand and drags me toward the Abbé's chair. I stretch out an arm and look down at him in wonder—who has ever begged the Abbé's pardon? "Abbé," say I, "all this is most absurd, isn't it?" And I burst out laughing and he does too. So my excuses were made in that quarter. But there was the other one to deal with and that was a horse of another color. I don't recall quite how I phrased my excuse: "Sir, behold this well-known fool . . ."—"I've stood him about long enough: not another word."—"He is very sorry." "It's I who am sorry."— "It shan't happen again."—"Till the next blackguard . . ."

I don't know whether he was having one of those bad days when Mademoiselle herself is afraid to go near him and has to use kid gloves, or whether he misheard what I said, or yet whether I said the wrong thing, but it fell out worse than before. Damn it all! Doesn't he know me as I am? Doesn't he know I'm like a child and that now and then I have no control over what's inside me? And by God, come to think of it, I wouldn't have a moment's respite. You'd wear out a marionette of steel if you pulled the string and jerked it all day long. I have to entertain them—granted—but I must have some fun too. In the midst of this confusion there came to me a sinister idea, an arrogant idea, an idea that filled me with insolent pride, and this was that they could not get along without me. I am the irreplaceable man.

MYSELF. Yes, I rather think they need you badly, but you need them more. You won't find again, at will, a house as congenial. But they can replace one missing fool by a hundred.

HE. A hundred fools like me, Master Philosopher! No, no: they are by no means so common. Dull fools, yes. But people are harder to please in folly than in talent or virtue. My species is scarce, very scarce. Now that they've lost me, what do they do? They're as sad as dogs. I am an inexhaustible store of silliness. Every minute I said things that reduced them to tears from laughter. I was worth to them a whole lunatic asylum.

MYSELF. In return for which you had bed and board, coat, vest, pants, shoes, and pocket money.

HE. That's the rosy side, the profit. But you don't look at the reverse, the obligations. In the first place, if there was a rumor of a new play written, regardless of weather I must ferret out the author from whatever Paris attic; I must get to read the piece, and must cleverly hint that one of the parts would be ideally suited to somebody I knew.—"And who is that, pray tell?"—"Who indeed! The three graces in one, subtlety, gentility itself."—"You mean Mlle. Dangeville? Do you happen to know her?"—"Slightly, but she's not the one I mean."—"Who, then?" I would name her in a low voice.—"That one!"—"Yes, that one," I would say blushing a little, for once in a while I can feel shame and it was something to see the poet pull a long face at her reiterated name; that is, when he didn't laugh in my face instead. In spite of all, I would have to drag my man to the house for dinner willy-nilly. He'd be afraid to commit himself, would make excuses, proffer thanks. When I did not succeed in my embassy, my reception at home was a caution: they called me a clodhopper, a bungler, a dolt; I was good for nothing and not worth the drink of water they let me have.

But it was even worse when she would get the part and I had to stand gallantly amid the hisses and jeers of the public (who are good judges, no matter what people say) and perform as a solitary claque, drawing on myself everybody's astonished eyes and sometimes depriving her of her hisses. People around me would whisper: "He's a footman in disguise—belongs to the man who sleeps with her. Will he never stop that racket!" People can't imagine what might lead a man to do what I did. They take it for stupidity, whereas it's a motive that would excuse any action.

MYSELF. Including breaking the law?

HE. After a time, however, I came to be known. They said, "That's only Rameau." All I could do to avoid the ridicule incurred by my isolated applause was to throw in a few ironic words which gave it a contrary interpretation. You must admit that it takes a strong interest to brave the assembled public as I did, and that I deserve more than a fiver for each encounter.

MYSELF. Why didn't you hire help?

HE. I did now and then, and made something on it. Before going into the torture chamber we had to burden our memory with the brilliant passages where we must take the lead. If I forgot or confused them, I would be blown up when I went back: you have no idea what an earthquake it was. And then the house had a pack of dogs for whose care I was responsible—

my own fault for offering to do it. I was likewise steward for
the cats, and lucky when Micou did not tear my hand or my
cuff. Criquette was often subject to colic—up to me to rub
her belly. Formerly Mademoiselle suffered from vapors, now
it's nerves, not to mention other slight indispositions which no
one bothers to conceal from me. Let that pass, I'm not the one
to insist on formal manners. I've read somewhere that a King
called "The Great" would lean on the back of his mistress's
chair when she was at stool. Familiarity breeds contempt, and
on those occasions I was treated more familiarly than anybody.
Well, I'm all for it and I used familiarity in return without
their objecting. They should have continued in that frame
of mind. I have sketched the boss for you. Mademoiselle is
getting heavy; you should hear the stories told about her.

MYSELF. I hope you don't help to spread them?

HE. Why not?

MYSELF. Because it is a good deal less than right to contribute to your patrons' being mocked.

HE. Isn't it far worse to take advantage of one's own philan-
thropy in order to revile one's protégé?

MYSELF. If the protégé weren't vile to begin with, nothing
would enable his patron to vilify him.

HE. And if the people in question were not ridiculous in
themselves they couldn't be mocked. Is it my fault that they
grow fouler with the years? Is it my fault if their disgusting
habits get betrayed and mocked? When people make up their
minds to keep company with the likes of me, common sense
should tell them to be ready for the blackest disloyalty. When
we're taken in tow, we are known for what we are—parasites
whose souls are treacherous and vile. Knowing us, they can't
complain. There's a tacit agreement that we'll reap benefits
and return evil for good, sooner or later. Isn't that the agreement between a man and his pet monkey or parrot? Le Brun
cries out that Palissot, his friend and guest, has made a squib
about him. Palissot had to make the squib and Le Brun is
in the wrong. Poinsinet cries out that Palissot has attributed
the squib to him. Palissot had to make the attribution and
Poinsinet is in the wrong. The little Abbé Rey cries out that

his friend Palissot has snatched his mistress, to whom the Abbé had introduced him: this only proves he should not have introduced a Palissot to his mistress, or else resigned himself to losing her. Palissot did his duty and it is the Abbé Rey who is in the wrong. The bookseller David cries out that his partner Palissot has slept or tried to sleep with his wife; the wife of the bookseller David cries out that Palissot has intimated to anyone willing to hear that he did sleep with her. Whether Palissot did or did not—a nice question, since she had to deny the fact and Palissot may have invented it—it is clear that Palissot was only acting as he must and the bookseller and his wife are in the wrong.

Helvitius may well cry out because Palissot lampoons him as a villain, though Palissot still owes him money for medical expenses as well as food and clothing; but should Helvetius have expected anything else from a man defiled by every kind of infamy, a man who for fun induces a friend by false promises to change his religion, a man who cheats his business associates, a man who is without faith, morals, or feelings, who seeks his fortune *per fas et nefas*, whose length of days is measured by the number of his crimes, and who has even represented himself on the stage as the most dangerous bully alive—a piece of impudence unequaled in the past and not likely to be matched in the future? Exactly!—Hence it is Helvetius and not Palissot who is in the wrong.

If you take a young provincial to the zoo at Versailles, and he is fool enough to push his hand through the bars of the tiger's or panther's cage and lose his arm to the wild beast, which of the two is in the wrong? The answer to all this is written down in the tacit agreement. It's too bad for the man who hasn't studied it or has forgotten it. How I wish I could defend under the terms of this universal and sacred compact the people who are accused of wickedness when one should rather accuse oneself of stupidity! Yes, my fat countess, *you* are in the wrong when you gather about you the kind of persons called in your circle "types," and when these "types" play you dirty tricks or make you their accomplice to the point of turning decent people against you. Decent people act as they

must and so do types. You have no business with types. If
Bertin had lived quietly and peacefully with his mistress, if
the integrity of their character had brought them reputable
friends, if they had gathered about them men of talent and
persons renowned for virtue, if they had kept for some choice,
enlightened company the hours taken from the pleasure of
being together and loving each other in their quiet retreat,
do you suppose they would be the theme of stories, good or
bad? What has befallen them is only what they deserved.
They've been punished for their brashness and we are the
predestined instruments of Providence, now and forevermore,
to mete out justice to the Bertins of the moment. Likewise
our counterparts among our descendants will see justice done
to the Monsauges and Bertins to come. And while we carry
out these just decrees against them you, who depict us for
what we are, carry out the same decrees against us. What
would you think of us if with our shameful conduct we laid
claim to public regard? You would think us mad. Why then
call sane those people who expect good from debased characters or creatures born vicious? Everything in the world gets
its due. There are two attorneys-general—the one at your beck
and call, who prosecutes offenders against society. The other
is Nature. It takes cognizance of all the vices that escape the
law. Give yourself over to debauchery with women and you
die of dropsy; live fast and you end consumptive. Open your
door to riffraff, consort with them, and you get betrayed,
mocked, and despised. The simplest thing is to concede the
justice of all this and say to oneself: "It is as it should be."
Turn over a new leaf and mend your ways—or else stay as you
are and abide by the terms of the contract aforesaid.

MYSELF. You are right.

HE. To come back to those "good stories," I do not make
them up; I content myself with repeating them. They say
that a few days ago, about five o'clock in the morning, a furious randan broke out; all the servants' bells ringing, and the
incoherent shouts of a man being smothered: "Help, help . . .
murder!" The cries came from the boss's apartment. Help
arrives, he is saved. It was our fat creature who had lost her

head completely—as often happens in such a circumstance—
and who kept accelerating her motion by raising herself on
her hands and collapsing to the tune of two or three hundred
pounds on the Petty Outlay Department with all the momen-
tum imparted by furious desire. Rescuing him was a job, but
what a devilishly queer notion in a tiny hammer to go and
lodge itself under a huge anvil.

MYSELF. Enough of your naughtiness, will you! Let's talk
of something else. I've had a question on the tip of my tongue
since we started chatting.

HE. Why have you held it back so long?

MYSELF. I was afraid to be inquisitive.

HE. After what I've told you, I can't imagine what secret
I could withhold from you.

MYSELF. You are in no doubt about the opinion I have
of you?

HE. No doubt at all. You think me most abject and contemptible. And so I am in my own eyes—sometimes. Not often.
I congratulate myself on my vices more often than blame
myself. But your contempt does not vary.

MYSELF. Just so. But then why show yourself to me in all
your turpitude?

HE. First, because you know a good deal of it to start with,
and I stand to gain more than I lose by confessing the rest.

MYSELF. How is that, tell me?

HE. If there's one realm in which it is essential to be sublime, it is in wickedness. You spit on ordinary scum, but you
can't deny a kind of respect to a great criminal: his courage
amazes, his ferocity overawes. People especially admire integrity of character.

MYSELF. But this admirable integrity, you haven't reached
it yet. I find you now and again weak in principle. You don't
seem to know if your wickedness comes from nature or from
study, nor whether you have pursued your studies far enough.

HE. I grant you that. But I've done my best. Haven't I with
due modesty acknowledged superiors in my kind? Haven't
I spoken of Bouret with the deepest admiration? To my mind,
Bouret is the greatest man on earth.

MYSELF. You come right after Bouret?

HE. No.

MYSELF. Then it must be Palissot?

HE. Yes, but not Palissot all by himself.

MYSELF. And who is worthy of sharing second place with him?

HE. The Renegade from Avignon.

MYSELF. I've never heard of him. He must be a remarkable man.

HE. He is that.

MYSELF. The lives of great men always interest me.

HE. I should hope so. This great man lived with a good and decent descendant of the tribe of Abraham, which as you know was guaranteed to equal the number of the stars in heaven.

MYSELF. With a Jew?

HE. With a Jew. He had earned, first, his host's compassion, then his good will, finally his entire trust. For as always happens, we are so sure of the effect of our kindness that we seldom hide our secret from those on whom we have showered benefits. How can you expect to do away with ingratitude when you expose men to the temptation of being ungrateful with impunity? This is a sound proposition which our Jew failed to ponder. He therefore confided to the renegade the truth that he could not conscientiously eat pig. You will be amazed to hear all that an inventive mind was able to make of that avowal. For a few months the renegade was full of kindness. When he deemed his Jew entirely won over, devoted, convinced by his care of possessing the best friend in all the tribes of Israel . . . Marvel at the man's circumspection: no haste, he lets the fruit ripen before shaking the branch; too much eagerness might ruin his project. Observe that greatness is usually the result of a natural equilibrium among opposite qualities.

MYSELF. Spare me your reflections and get on with your story.

HE. Impossible. There are days when I am compelled to reflect. It's a disease I have to give in to. Where was I?

MYSELF. The intimate friendship between the Jews and the renegade.

HE. Ah yes, the fruit was ripe. But you're not listening. What's on your mind?

MYSELF. I was thinking of the unevenness of your style—now elevated, now colloquial.

HE. Can the style of the vice-ridden be otherwise? . . . He comes home one night to his host with a petrified air, his voice broken, his face pale as death, and shaking in every limb. "What's wrong?"—"We are done for!" "How, done for?" —"Done for, I tell you; hopelessly done for."—"Explain yourself."—"Just a second, till I catch my breath."—"Yes, yes do." says the Jew instead of saying "You're a thorough scoundrel. I don't know what you're about to say, but you're a scoundrel and pretending to be terrified."

MYSELF. Why should he have said such a thing?

HE. Because he was lying and had overdone it. It's perfectly clear to me—and don't interrupt. "We're done for, done for, it's hopeless." Can't you sense make-believe in the repetition of "done for"? "An informer has denounced us to the Holy Inquisition, you as a Jew and me as a renegade—a loathsome renegade." Do you see how the traitor blithely goes in for the foulest expression? It takes more courage than you'd think to call oneself by one's right name. You have no idea how painful it is to achieve.

MYSELF. I have no idea, I'm sure. And this loathsome renegade?

HE. Was lying. Very adroitly lying. The Jew takes fright, pulls out his beard by the roots, rocks in anguish, sees the police at his door, himself wearing the *san benito* and his auto da fé in readiness. "My dear, dear friend, my only friend, what shall we do?"—"What to do? Why, show ourselves, affect the greatest self-assurance, behave as usual. The procedure of the court is secret but slow. We must use the time to sell and dispose of everything you own. I shall go and charter a ship, or have a third party do it—yes, that would be better—and we'll stow your money in the hold; for it's your money they're after. Then you and I will sail and find in other climes the right to worship our God, and so follow the law of Abraham and of our own conscience. The main thing in our present state of danger is to do nothing rash . . ." No sooner said than done. The ship is chartered, stored with provisions, manned, the Jew's fortune put on board. Tomorrow at dawn they sail; now they can sup and sleep more cheerfully. Tomorrow they flee from persecution. In the night, the renegade gets up, takes the Jew's purse, wallet, and jewels, makes for the ship—and he is off.

You think that's the end? You're wrong. When I was told the story I guessed what I haven't yet mentioned in order to test your intelligence. You did well to be an honest man; you would have made but half a scamp. Up to this point the renegade is not much more than that—a contemptible cur whom no one would wish to emulate. The stroke of genius in his evil-doing is that he himself was the informer who denounced his good friend the Jew to the Inquisition, which seized him that morning and made a bonfire of him a few days later. Such is the way the renegade came to peacefully enjoy the wealth of the accursed descendant of those who crucified our Lord.

MYSELF. I hardly know which I loathe more, the dastardliness of your renegade or the way in which you speak of him.

HE. Precisely what I was saying to you: the atrociousness of the deed lifts you beyond contempt and accounts for my sincerity with you. I wanted you to know how far I excelled in my art and to make you admit by main strength that I am at least original in my vileness. I want you to consider me in the great tradition of the master scoundrels. Then I can exclaim: "*Vivat Mascarillus, fourbum imperator!*"* Come, a cheer, Master Philosopher; chorus: *Vivat Mascarillus, fourbum imperator!*

Whereupon he began to sing an extraordinary kind of fugue. At one moment the melody was solemn and majestic, at other times gay and lightsome. Now he imitated the bass, now one of the upper parts. With his arms and outstretched neck he indicated the held notes, and so composed and per-

---

* From Molière's *Etourdi*: "Long live Mascarille, Emperor of Cheats."

formed in his own honor a song of triumph, from which it was clear that he understood good music far better than good morals.

[As for me I hardly knew whether I should come or go, laugh or get angry. I stayed, wanting to turn the conversation to some subject that would drive out of my soul the horror that filled it. I was beginning to find almost unbearable the presence of a man who could discuss a dreadful deed, an abominable crime, in the way a connoisseur in poetry or painting discusses the fine points of a work of art—or as a moralist or an historian points out the merit of an heroic action. I felt gloom overwhelming me. He noticed it and asked:]

What is wrong, are you unwell?

MYSELF. Somewhat. It will pass off.

HE. You look disturbed like a man pursued by dark fancies.

MYSELF. Just so.

[After a moment when neither of us spoke but during which he walked about whistling and singing, I began again in order to bring him back to a discussion of his talent. I said:]

What are you doing these days?

HE. Nothing.

MYSELF. That must be very fatiguing.

HE. I was lightheaded enough to begin with, but I went to hear the music of Duni and our other young composers and that finished me.

MYSELF. So you like this new genre?

HE. No doubt about it.

MYSELF. You manage to find beauty in these newfangled melodies?

HE. Do I manage! Ye gods! Don't doubt for a moment that I do! What declamation! What truth of expression!

MYSELF. Every imitative art finds its models in nature. What is the musician's model when he fashions a melody?

HE. Let's begin with a more general question: what is a melody?

MYSELF. I confess that is beyond me. We are all alike, really; we remember words, which we think we understand from the frequent and even correct use we make of them. But our minds contain only vague notions. When I utter the word "melody," I have no clearer idea than you and most of your colleagues when you say: "reputation, blame, honor, vice, virtue, modesty, decency, shame, ridicule."

HE. A melody is a vocal or instrumental imitation using the sounds of a scale invented by art—or inspired by nature, as you prefer; it imitates either physical noises or the accents of passion. You can see that by changing a few words in this definition it would exactly fit painting, eloquence, sculpture or poetry.

Now to come to your question. What is the musician's or the melody's model? It is declamation if the model is alive and a thinking being; it is physical noise if the model is inanimate. Consider declamation as one line and song as another, which twists snakelike about the former. The more the declamation, which is the prototype of song, is vivid and true, the more the song shaped upon it will intersect it at many points. The truer the melody, the more beautiful it will be— and that is what our younger musicians have so well understood. When one hears "I am but a poor wretch" one recognizes the complaint of a miser. Were he not singing he would be using the same inflections to address the earth in which he has buried his gold, saying "O earth, receive my treasure." And that young girl who feels her heart going pitapat, who blushes, is upset and begs my lord to let her go—could she express herself otherwise than as she does? One finds in these new works every type of character, an infinite variety of utterance. Take it from me, it's sublime. Go, go and hear the piece in which the youth feels the hand of death and sings "My heart is gone." Listen to his song, listen to the orchestra, and then tell me what difference exists between the form of this air and the ways of the dying. You will discover that the melodic line exactly coincides with the curve of spoken utterance.

I say nothing of meter, which is another condition of melody; I dwell on expressiveness. Nothing is more self-evident than the maxim I read somewhere: *Musices seminarium accentus:*

accent is the source of melody. From this you can infer how difficult and how important it is to know how to handle recitative. There is no beautiful air from which one cannot make a beautiful recitative, and no beautiful recitative from which an able composer cannot make a beautiful air. I would not guarantee that a good reciter will sing well, but I should be surprised if a good singer did not know how to recite well. You must believe all I have been saying, for it is true.

MYSELF. I should like nothing better than to believe you, if I were not prevented by a small difficulty.

HE. The difficulty is?

MYSELF. Only this, that if the new music is sublime, it follows that the music of the divine Lully, of Campra, of Destouches, of Mouret, and—be it said between us—of your dear uncle, must be a trifle dull.

HE [coming close and answering in my ear]. I shouldn't like to be overheard, for there are hereabouts plenty of people who know me—but it *is* dull. Not that I worry myself much about the dear uncle—if "dear" has to come into it. He is made of stone: he could see my tongue hanging out a foot long and he would not give me a glass of water. But try as he will—with the octave, the leading note—*Tum-tum-ta-tatum, toot-toot-toot-tra-la-toot*—even though he makes a racket like the very devil, some people are beginning to catch on; they will no longer take banging for music. The police should forbid any person, of whatever rank, to have Pergolesi's *Stabat Mater* performed. That *Stabat* should have been burned by the public hangman. Yes, these confounded *bouffons* with their *Serva Padrona* and their *Tracollo* have given us a stout kick in the butt.

Formerly a *Tancred*, an *Issé*, an *Europe galante, Les Indes, Castor, Les Talents lyriques*, would run for five or six months. The run of Lully's *Armide* was endless. Nowadays they tumble on one another's heels like jackstraws. That's why the managers, Rebel and Francœur, cry out to heaven. They say all is lost: "they are ruined; if these fair-ground musicians are allowed to keep on, our national music is done for; the so-called Royal Academy—the Opera—might as well shut up shop." And there is some truth in it. The old fogies who have been going there every Friday for thirty or forty years no longer have a good time. They are bored, they yawn without knowing why. They ask themselves and can't answer. They should ask *me*. As things are going now, Duni's prophecy will come true, and I'm willing to give up living in four or five years if after *The Painter in Love with his Model* you find as much as an alley cat in our celebrated Opera house.

The good souls! They have given up their symphonies to play the Italian ones. They thought they could accustom their ears to these new instrumental pieces without changing their taste as regards the vocal—as if symphonies were not in relation to songs (except for the greater freedom afforded by the range of instruments and the dexterity of the fingers) what songs are to declamation; as if the violin did not ape the singer, who in turn will become the ape of the violin when acrobatics will have replaced beauty. The first one who played Locatelli was the apostle of the new music. Next! Next! We shall all become accustomed to the imitation of passionate accents or of natural phenomena by means of voices and instruments— which is the whole extent of music's purpose. D'you think we'll also keep our taste for flights, dreams, glories, triumphs, and victories? Tell it to the marines. Did anyone imagine that the public could learn to weep or laugh at tragic or comic scenes when "musicated," to respond to the tones of fury, hatred, and jealousy, the true plaints of love, the irony and pleasantries of the Italian or French theater, and that in spite of all this the public would continue to admire *Ragonde* or *Platée?* Taradiddle, tol-lol-lay! That they could once learn how easily, softly, gently, the Italian tongue, with its natural harmony, flexible prosody, easy ellipses and inversions, suited the art and motion of music, the turns of song and the measured pace of sounds—and yet would overlook the fact that French is stiff, heavy, pedantic, and monotonous? Well, well, well, they persuaded themselves that after weeping with a mother bewailing the loss of her son, and shuddering at the decree of a tyrant committing murder, they would not be bored with their fairyland, their insipid mythology, their saccharine love songs, which show the poet's bad taste no less than the sterility of the music matched thereto. The good souls!

It could not and cannot be. The true, the good, and the beautiful will prevail. Their rights may at first be challenged, but in the end they are acknowledged, and people come to yield their admiration. Inferior things may be esteemed for a time but the end is a great yawn. Go ahead, gentlemen, yawn away, yawn to your heart's content, don't be afraid! The power of nature and of the trinity which I worship will never be overcome by the forces of darkness—the True which is the father, engenders the Good, which is his son, whence comes the Beautiful, which is the Holy Ghost. Change is gradual. The foreign god takes his place humbly next to the native idol, little by little asserts itself, and one fine day elbows out his fellow—before you can say Jack Robinson, there's the idol flat on its back. They say that's the way the Jesuits introduced Christianity into India and China. And the Jansenists can say what they like, the political method that aims quietly and directly at the goal, without bloodshed, martyrdom, or so much as a queue of hair cut off, is obviously the best.

MYSELF. There is some sense in almost everything you've said.

HE. Sense! I'm glad! The devil take me if I've been making any special effort. I speak as it comes. I'm like the opera musicians when my uncle came on the scene. If I'm on the point, well and good. It only shows that a man of the trade will always speak about it more sensibly than any Academy or all the Duhamels in the world.

[And now he paces up and down again humming in his throat some arias from *L'Ile des Fous, Le Peintre amoureux de son Modèle, Le Maréchal ferrant, La Plaideuse*, occasionally raising arms and eyes to the skies: "It's beautiful, my God but it is beautiful!—Why? How can a man sport a pair of ears and ask such a question?" He was getting into a passion and beginning to sing, his voice growing louder as his passion increased. Next he gesticulated, made faces and twisted his body, and I thought to myself: "There he goes—losing his wits and working himself up to a scene." True enough, he suddenly burst out very loud: "I am but a poor wretch . . . My Lord, my Lord, I beg you to let me go! . . . O Earth, receive my gold and keep my treasure safe, my soul, my life, O Earth! . . . There is my little friend; there is my little friend. . . . *Aspettare e non venire . . . A cerbina penserete . . . Sempre in contrasti con te si sta. . . .*" He jumbled together thirty different airs, French, Italian, comic, tragic—in every style. Now in a baritone voice he sank to the pit; then straining in falsetto he tore to shreds the upper notes of some air, imitating the while the stance, walk and gestures of the several characters; being in succession furious, mollified, lordly, sneering. First a damsel weeps and he reproduces her kittenish ways; next he is a priest, a king, a tyrant; he threatens, commands, rages. Now he is a slave, he obeys, calms down, is heartbroken, complains, laughs; never overstepping the proper tone, speech, or manner called for by the part.

[All the "woodpushers" in the café had left their chessboards and gathered around us. The windows of the place were occupied from outside by passers-by who had stopped on hearing the commotion. They guffawed fit to crack the ceiling. But he noticed nothing, he kept on, in the grip of mental possession, an enthusiasm so close to madness that it seemed doubtful whether he would recover. He might have to be put into a cab and be taken to a padded cell. While singing fragments of Jomelli's *Lamentations*, he reproduced with incredible precision, fidelity, and warmth the most beautiful passages of each scene. That magnificent recitative in which Jeremiah describes the desolation of Jerusalem, he drenched in tears which drew their like from every onlooker. His art was complete—delicacy of voice, expressive strength, true sorrow. He dwelt on the places where the musician had shown himself a master. If he left the vocal part, it was to take up the instrumental, which he abandoned suddenly to return to the voice, linking them so as to preserve the connection and unity of the whole, gripping our souls and keeping them suspended in the most singular state of being that I have ever experienced.

[Did I admire? Yes, I did admire. Was I moved to pity? I was moved. But a streak of derision was interwoven with these feelings and denatured them.

[Yes, you too would have burst out laughing at the way in which he aped the different instruments. With swollen cheeks and a somber throaty sound, he would give us the horns and bassoons. For the oboes he assumed a shill yet nasal voice, then speeded up the emission of sound to an incredible degree for the strings, for whose tones he found close analogues. He whistled piccolos and warbled traverse flutes, singing, shouting, waving about like a madman, being in himself dancer and ballerina, singer and prima donna, all of them together and the whole orchestra, the whole theater; then redividing himself into twenty separate roles, running, stopping, glowing at the eyes like one possessed, frothing at the mouth.

[The heat was stifling and the sweat, which, mixed with the powder in his hair, ran down the creases of his face was dripping and marking the upper part of his coat. What did he not attempt to show me? He wept, laughed, sighed, looked placid or melting or enraged. He was a woman in a spasm of grief, a wretched man sunk in despair, a temple being erected, birds growing silent at sunset, waters murmuring through cool and solitary places or else cascading from a mountaintop, a storm, a hurricane, the anguish of those about to die, mingled with the whistling of the wind and the noise of thunder. He was night and its gloom, shade and silence—for silence itself is depictable in sound. He had completely lost his senses.

[Worn out, exhausted, like a man emerging from a deep sleep or a prolonged reverie, he stood motionless, dumb, petrified. He kept looking around him like a man who has lost his way and wants to know where he is. He waited for returning strength and wits, wiping his face with an absentminded gesture. Just as a man who on waking should see a large number of people around his bed and not remember or be able to conceive what he had done, he began by asking: "What is it, gentlemen? Why do you laugh? You look surprised—what is it?" Then he added: "This, this merits the name of music. There is your true musician! And yet, gentlemen, it will not do to look down on all of Lully's arias. Let anyone try a better setting of the scene 'I await the dawn' without changing the words: it can't be done. Nor must you despise certain pieces by Campra, or my uncle's works for violin, his gavottes, his military and religious processions. 'Pale torches,' 'Light more dreadful than darkness,' 'Gods of Tartarus and oblivion' "—Here his voice swelled and sustained the notes, bringing the neighbors to their windows while we stuffed our fingers into our ears. He added: "Those are the places that call for lung power, a stout organ, a great volume of air. But before long, good-by to *L'Assomption, Le Carême* and *Les Rois*. They don't as yet know what to choose for setting to music, that is, what will suit a composer. True lyric poetry has yet to be born. But by dint of hearing Pergolesi, The Saxon, Terradeglias, Traetta and the rest, by dint of reading Metastasio, they'll catch on."]

MYSELF. Do you mean to say that Quinault, La Motte and Fontenelle didn't know their business?

HE. Not for the new style. There aren't six lines together in all their charming poems that you can put music to. They give you ingenious epigrams, sweet and delicate madrigals. But if you want to find out how empty of substance all that is for our own art—which is the most violent of all the arts, not excepting that of Demosthenes—get someone to recite these librettos to you. How frigid, monotonous and dull they will seem! Nothing in them supplies a pattern for songs: I'd just as soon be asked to set the Maxims of La Rochefoucauld or the Thoughts of Pascal. We want the animal cry of the passions to dictate the melodic line, and the expressive moments must come close together. Each phrase must be short, its meaning broken off for suspense, so that the musician can make use equally of the whole or of a part, omit a word or repeat it, add a new one he needs, turn the phrase inside out like a jellyfish without destroying the sense—all of which makes lyric poetry much harder to write in French than in languages that freely use inversion and naturally afford all these advantages. "Cruel barbarian, plunge thy dagger in my breast; here I stand ready for the fatal blow. Strike! Dare! Oh, I faint, I die. A secret fire pervades my senses. Cruel love, what do you ask of me? Leave me in blissful peace as heretofore; oh, restore

my reason!" Our passions have to be strong. The tenderness
of the musician and the poet must be extreme . . . the aria
must be the peroration of the scene. We need exclamations,
interjections, suspensions, interruptions, affirmations, and ne-
gations. We call out, invoke, clamor, groan, weep, and laugh
openly. No more witticisms, epigrams, neat thoughts—they
are too unlike nature. And don't get it into your head that
the old theatrical acting and declamation can give us a pattern to follow. Not likely! We want it more energetic, less
mannered, more genuine. Simple speeches, the ordinary utterance of passion, will be all the more necessary that our French
language is more monotonous, less accented. The animal cry
or that of man in a passion will supply the accent. . . .

[As he spoke, the crowd around us had withdrawn, whether
from no longer being able to hear or from having lost interest
in the subject; for, in general, man is like a child and prefers
being amused to being instructed. The chess players had resumed their boards and we were alone in our corner. Seated
on the bench, his head resting against the wall, his arms hanging and his eyes half shut, he said:]

HE. I don't know what's the matter with me; when I came
here I was feeling rested and in good form. Now I am exhausted, worn out, as if I had walked thirty miles. It came
upon me suddenly.

MYSELF. Should you like something to drink?

HE. With pleasure. My throat feels rough, I am a little
faint and my chest hurts. This happens to me every day and
I have no notion of the cause.

MYSELF. What'll you take?

HE. Whatever you say. I'm not hard to please. Poverty has
accustomed me to everything.

[They serve us beer and lemonade, of which he fills and
refills a large glass two or three times together. Then, like a
man restored to life, he coughs loudly, gesticulates and begins
again:]

HE. Now in your opinion, Master Philosopher, is it not a
very strange thing that a foreigner, an Italian, a man named
Duni, should be the one to teach us how to give force and

accent to our music, and to adapt our singing to the several
tempi, meters, intervals, and expressions without injuring
prosody? And yet it was nothing like drinking the ocean dry.
All you had to do was to listen to a beggar asking for alms,
to a man in a fury, a woman in a fit of jealousy, a lover in
despair, a flatterer—yes, a flatterer—sweetening his voice and
drawling out his honeyed syllables, in short, any Passion whatever, provided it is energetic enough to supply the musician
with a pattern. You would then have noticed two things: one,
that long and short syllables have no fixed values, not even a
fixed relation between them; and two, that passion rules over
prosody almost at will and can leap the largest intervals. The
man who exclaims "Oh, unhappy me!" raises his voice on the
first syllable to the highest pitch and sinks the rest down to
the lowest, making an octave or even more, and giving to each
sound the quantity appropriate to a melodic phrase without
offending the ear and yet without retaining the longs and
shorts of ordinary speech. What an advance since the days
when we used to quote as a prodigy of musical expression the
parenthetical remark in *Armide:* "Rinaldo's conqueror (if
such there be)" or the "Don't hesitate, obey!" in *Les Indes
galantes.* Nowadays such miracles make me shrug with pity. At
the rate art is going, there is no limit to its power. Meanwhile,
another drink.

[He drinks two, three glasses more without noticing, and
would have drowned like a spent swimmer had I not moved
the bottle, which he sought distractedly, not knowing what
he was about. I then said to him:]

MYSELF. How is it that with such fineness of feeling, so much
sensibility where musical beauty is concerned, you are so
blind to the beauties of morality, so insensible to the charm
of virtue?

HE. It must be that virtue requires a special sense that I
lack, a fiber that has not been granted me. My fiber is loose,
one can pluck it forever without its yielding a note. Or else
I have spent my life with good musicians and bad people,
whence my ear has become very sharp and my heart quite
deaf. And then there is heredity. My father's blood is the

same as my uncle's; my blood is like my father's. The paternal molecule was hard and obtuse, and like a primordial germ it has affected all the rest.

MYSELF. Do you love your son?

HE. Do I love the little savage? I am crazy about him!

MYSELF. And will you do nothing to thwart in him the effect of his accursed paternal molecule?

HE. I'll try it, but (I think) in vain. If he is fated to become a good man, trying won't do any harm. But if the molecule decides that he shall be a ne'er-do-well like his father, the pains I might take to make him an honest man would be very dangerous. Education would work continually at cross-purposes with the natural bent of the molecule, and he would be pulled by two contrary forces that would make him go askew down the path of life—like so many others I see who are equally clumsy in good and evil deeds. They are the ones we call "types," of all descriptions the worst, because it indicates mediocrity and the lowest degree of contempt. A great scoundrel is a great scoundrel; he isn't a "type." Before the molecule could recapture him and reproduce the state of perfect abjection which I have reached, it would take endless time. He would waste his best years. So at the moment I hold my hand, I simply observe him and let him come along. He is already greedy, cozening, rascally, lazy, and a liar: I am afraid he is a pedigreed beast.

MYSELF. And you will make him a musician so that the likeness can be complete?

HE. A musician! A musician! Sometimes I look at him and grind my teeth and say to myself "If you ever learn a note, I really think I'll twist your neck."

MYSELF. But why, if you don't mind telling me?

HE. It leads nowhere.

MYSELF. It leads everywhere.

HE. Yes, if you excel. But who can guarantee that his child will excel? It's ten thousand to one that he will be a wretched note-scraper like me. Do you know that it would be easier to find a child able to govern a kingdom and be a great king than a great violinist?

MYSELF. I think on the contrary that any likely talent, even if mediocre, can lead a man to fortune, provided the country has no morals and lives on luxury and debauch. I myself once heard the following conversation take place between a sort of patron and his would-be protégé. The latter had been recommended to the former as a useful and serviceable man:

"My dear sir, what can you do?"

"I am a fairly good mathematician."

"Good enough. But after you have taught mathematics for ten or twelve years by running the streets of Paris, you will have only 300 or 400 francs a year."

"I have also studied law."

"If Puffendorf and Grotius came back to life they would starve in the gutter."

"I am well versed in geography and history."

"If there were any parents who really cared about their children's education, your fortune would be made. But such parents do not exist."

"I am a tolerable musician."

"Why didn't you say so at once? Just to show you what that gift is worth to you, let me say this: I have a daughter; come every evening at seven-thirty and give her a lesson until nine. I shall pay you 250 francs a year and give you all your meals at our house. The rest of the day is yours to dispose of for your profit."

HE. And what happened?

MYSELF. If the man had been clever he would have grown rich—which is all you seem to care about.

HE. No doubt. Gold, gold is everything; and everything, without gold, is nothing. Therefore, instead of having my son's head stuffed with grand maxims which he would have to forget under pain of being a pauper, this is what I do whenever I have a gold piece—not often, to be sure: I plant myself in front of him, draw the piece from my pocket, show it to him with admiring looks, raise my eyes to heaven, kiss the gold in front of him, and to show him still more forcibly the importance of the sacred coin, I stammer out the names and point out with the finger all the things one can buy with it—

a beautiful gown, a beautiful hat, a good cake; next I put the
coin in my pocket, parade before him proudly, pull up my
coat tails and strike my waistcoat where the money lies. Thus
do I make him understand that it is from that coin I draw
the self-assurance he beholds.

MYSELF. Nothing could be better. But what if some day,
being deeply persuaded of the value of money, he should . . .

HE. I follow you! One must shut one's eyes to that. There
is no principle of conduct wholly without drawbacks. At the
worst, one goes through a bad half hour, then all is over.

MYSELF. Yet in spite of your wise and courageous views,
I continue to think it would be a good thing to make him
a musician. I know of no better way to approach the rich,
to serve their vices, and to turn one's own to advantage.

HE. True. But I have projects for even quicker and surer
success. Ah, if I only had a daughter! But no man can do
as he likes, he must take what he gets and do the best he can
with it. For which purpose one must not, like most fathers,
stupidly give children who are destined to live in Paris the
education of ancient Sparta. One might as well plot their ruin.
If the native training is bad, the fault lies with the manners
and customs of my country, and not with me. No matter who
is responsible, I want my child happy, or what amounts to the
same thing, honored, rich, powerful. I know the easiest ways
to accomplish this, and I mean to teach them to my son early
in life. If you wise men blame me, the majority (and success
itself) will absolve me. He will have gold—it's I who tell you
so, I guarantee it—and if he has a great deal, he will lack
nothing, not even your admiration and respect.

MYSELF. You might be wrong about those.

HE. If so, he can do without, like many other people.

[There was in all he said much that one thinks to oneself,
and acts on, but that one never says. This was in fact the
chief difference between my man and the rest of us. He admitted his vices, which are also ours: he was no hypocrite.
Neither more nor less detestable than other men, he was
franker than they, more logical, and thus often profound in
his depravity. I was appalled to think of what his child would
become under such a tutor. It was clear that if he was brought

up on a system so exactly framed on our actual behavior, he would go far—unless he was prematurely cut off on the way.]

HE. Never you fear! The important thing that a good father must do is not so much to give his child vices that will bring him wealth and foolish traits that will make him a favorite of the great—everybody does as much: not systematically like me, but by casual precept and example. No, what is more difficult is to teach him the golden art by which he can avert disgrace, shame, and the penalties of the law. These last are dissonances in the harmony of society, which one must know how to use, prepare, and resolve. Nothing is duller than a progression of common chords. One wants some contrast, which breaks up the clear white light and makes it iridescent.

MYSELF. Very good. Your comparison brings me back from morals to music. I digressed in spite of myself, for to speak frankly, I prefer you as musician rather than as moralist.

HE. And yet I am only second-rate in music, whereas I am a superior moralist.

MYSELF. I doubt this; but even if it were so, I am an honest man and your principles do not suit me.

HE. So much the worse for you. Oh, if I only had your talent!

MYSELF. Leave my talent alone; let's go back to yours.

HE. If I could express myself as you do! But my vocabulary is a damned mongrel—half literary and well bred, half gutter-snipe.

MYSELF. Don't think I speak well. I can only tell the truth and, as you know, that doesn't always go down.

HE. It's not for telling the truth that I envy you your gifts. Just the opposite—it's to tell lies. If I only knew how to throw together a book, how to turn a dedication, intoxicate some fool with praises and make my way among women!

MYSELF. As for all that, you know much more about it than I do; I am not even fit to be your pupil.

HE. Oh, what abilities you are letting go to waste, not even suspecting what they're worth!

MYSELF. I reap whatever I sow, no more, no less.

HE. If that were true, you wouldn't be wearing these coarse clothes—linen coat, woollen stockings, thick-soled shoes and superannuated wig.

MYSELF. Granted. One must be terribly clumsy if one isn't rich after sticking at nothing to acquire wealth. But there are people like me, you see, who don't consider wealth the most important thing in the world—queer people.

HE. Very queer. No one is born that way. It's an acquired idea; it's unnatural.

MYSELF. For man?

HE. For man. Everything that lives, man included, seeks its well-being at the expense of whoever withholds it. I'm sure that if I let my little savage grow up without saying a word to him, he would of his own accord want to be richly dressed, magnificently fed, liked by men and loved by women, and concentrate on himself all the goods of life.

MYSELF. If your little savage were left to himself and to his native blindness, he would in time join the infant's reasoning to the grown man's passions—he would strange his father and sleep with his mother.

HE. Which only proves the need of a good education. There's no argument. But what is a good education if it is not one that leads to all the enjoyments without trouble or danger?

MYSELF. I am almost with you there, but let's not go into it.

HE. Why not?

MYSELF. Because I think we are only superficially in agreement, and if we look into the question of troubles and dangers, we shall no longer be at one.

HE. And what's the harm of that?

MYSELF. Let it go, I say. What I know on the subject I shan't be able to teach you. You will have an easier time teaching me what you know about music, of which I am ignorant. Dear Rameau, let us talk music; and tell me how it is that with your remarkable power for understanding, remembering and rendering the most beautiful works of the great masters, with your contagious enthusiasm for them and for conveying them, you have never done anything that amounts to anything.

[Instead of answering me, he started nodding his head, lifted a finger heavenward, and added: "My star! my star! When Nature fashioned Leo, Vinci, Pergolesi, Duni, she smiled on them. She put on a grave imposing mien when she made my dear uncle Rameau, who for a dozen years was called 'the great Rameau,' though soon nobody will have heard of him. But when she slapped together his nephew, she made a face, then another face, and still another." As he said these words he was making all sorts of faces depicting contempt, disdain, irony; he seemed to be kneading a ball of dough within his fingers and smiling at the ridiculous shapes he was imparting to it.

[This done, he made a gesture as if throwing the outlandish idol far from him and said: "That is how nature made me and threw me down among other idols, some with fat wrinkled bellies, others with short necks and popping, apoplectic eyes, and still others with wry necks. Some were stringy, bright of glance and beaky-nosed—all burst out laughing on seeing me, and I putting my fists on my hips burst out laughing on seeing them, for lunatics and fools entertain one another; they seek one another out and are mutually drawn. If on arriving here below I hadn't found the saying ready-made which tells you that 'a dolt's money is the patrimony of the man with wits' I would have invented it. I felt that nature had put my estate in the keeping of those idols and I devised a thousand ways to recover it."]

MYSELF. I know those ways. You told me about them and I have duly admired them. But, given your large choice of means, why didn't you try fashioning a work of art?

HE. That is the remark a man of the world made to Abbé Le Blanc. The Abbé had said: "Mme. de Pompadour took me in hand and brought me as far as the doors of the Academy. There she withdraws her hand, I fall down and break both my legs." The man of the world replied: "Well, Abbé, you must pick yourself up and break in the doors with your head." To which the Abbé retorted: "I tried that and do you know what came of it?—a large bump right here."

[This little tale told, my man started pacing again, his head lowered, looking pensive and worried. He sighed, wept, seemed in despair, raised his eyes and hands to heaven, struck his forehead with his fist with a violence fit to break his knuckles or his skull, then added: "It seems to me nevertheless that I have something there, but I knock in vain, I worry it but nothing comes out." Whereupon he started again to shake his pate and to redouble his blows on his skull, saying: "Either there's nobody at home or they refuse to answer."

[The next minute he put on a look of pride, raised his head, put his right hand over his heart, took a pace forward and said: "But I feel, yes, I do feel. . . ."

[He was aping a man who grows angry, indignant, who softens, commands, and implores. He improvised speeches full of anger, compassion, hatred, and love, sketching every passionate character with astonishing accuracy and subtlety. Then he went on: "Isn't that about right? It's coming, I should say. It only shows the value of having a midwife who knows how to prod and bring on the labor pains so as to bring out the child. When I take my pen by myself, intending to write, I bite my nails and belabor my brow but—no soap, the god is absent. Though I had convinced myself that I had genius, at the end of the first line I am informed that I'm a fool, a fool, a fool. But how in the name of sense can one feel, think, rise to heights, and speak with vigor while frequenting people such as those I must frequent to live—in the midst of gossip and the meaningless words that one says and hears: 'It was lovely out today. Have you heard Mlle. Marmosette? She plays like an angel. Monsieur So-and-So has the handsomest pair of dapple grays you ever saw. As for Madame X, she is really beginning to fade. Why does she think that at forty-five she can still do her hair that way? The young one is plastered with diamonds which certainly don't cost her much.—You mean which cost her a great deal?—On the contrary.—Where have you seen her? At Goldoni's *Harlequin's Child Lost and Found*. They did the grieving scene as never before. The Punchinello has voice but no art, no soul. Madame Z has given birth to twins—that way each father will have his own. . . .' Do you suppose that things like these, repeated over and over every day, kindle the mind and lead to great ideas?"]

MYSELF. No, of course not. It would be better to shut oneself up in a garret, eat a dry crust, drink plain water and try to find oneself.

HE. That may be, but I haven't the courage. Why sacrifice one's well-being to a chancy success? And what about my name?—to be called Rameau is extremely embarrassing. Talent isn't like noble blood which is transmitted and grows in luster by being handed down from grandfather to great grandson without the ancestor's forcing any abilities on the descendant. The old line branches out into a huge spread of fools, but no matter. That's not true of talent. In order to get as much fame as one's father one has to be much more able than he. One must have inherited his fiber. I've lacked fiber—though my wrist is limber, the bow scrapes, and the pot boils. It isn't fame but it's food.

MYSELF. If I were in your place, I wouldn't take it all for granted, I'd try.

HE. You think I haven't tried? I was hardly fifteen when I first said to myself: "What's the matter, Rameau, you're dreaming. What are you dreaming about? You'd like to have accomplished something for the whole universe to marvel at. Then all you have to do is to spit on your palms and wiggle your fingers. One, two, three, and the thing is done." Later in life, I repeated the words of my youth; today I do it still and I stand near the statue of Memnon.

MYSELF. What does that mean, the statue of Memnon?

HE. I should think it's clear enough. Around the statue of Memnon there were an infinity of others, all equally struck by the rays of the sun. But Memnon's was the only one to give forth a sound. Who's a poet?—Voltaire. Who else? Voltaire. Name a third one: Voltaire. A fourth? Voltaire. As for musicians, there is Rinaldo of Capua, Hasse, Pergolesi, Alberti, Tartini, Locatelli, Terradeglias; there's my uncle and there is the little fellow Duni, who looks like nothing at all but who can feel, by God, who is full of melody and expression. The others around this handful of Memnons are so many donkeys' ears, one pair to a stick. And we're so poor, so beggarly, it's to cry a-mercy. Ah, Master Philosopher, poverty is a dreadful thing. I can see her squatting, openmouthed to catch a few drops of the icy water that flows out of the sieve of the Danaïds. I don't know whether she sharpens the wits of a philosopher,

but she surely chills the brain of a poet. You can't sing under
that sieve—and yet he's a lucky man who can hide under it.
I had a place there and wasn't capable of holding it. It had
happened to me once before. I've traveled in Bohemia, Germany, Switzerland, Holland, Flanders, to the ends of the earth.

MYSELF. Under the sieve?

HE. Under it. He was a rich and free-handed Jew who loved
my music and my wit. I played music as Providence permitted.
I played the fool. I had all I wanted. My Jew was a man who
knew his law and lived by it punctiliously—sometimes with
friends and invariably with strangers. It led him into a bad
pass which I must tell you about because it is amusing.

There was in Utrecht a charming courtesan. My man fell
for the Christian girl and despatched a messenger to her with
a sizable letter of credit. The singular creature refused his offer.
He was in despair. The messenger says: "Why be so upset?
You want to sleep with a pretty woman? Nothing is easier,
even with a prettier one than the one you're after. I mean my
wife, whom you can have for the same price." The bargain is
struck. The messenger keeps the letter of credit and my Jew
sleeps with the fellow's wife. The letter of credit reaches
maturity; the Jew lets it be protested and brings a countersuit.
"Never," he thinks, "will the fellow admit in court how he obtained possession of the letter, and I shan't have to pay." At
the trial he tackles the messenger. "This letter of credit, how
did you come by it?"—"I had it from you."—"Was it for a
loan?"—"No." "Was it for goods received?"—"No."—"Was it
for services rendered?"—"No. You're off the point. The letter
is mine, you signed it, and you'll pay it."—"I did not sign it."—
"You're calling me a forger?"—"Either you or someone whose
agent you are."—"Well, I'm a coward, but you're a swindler.
Take it from me, don't force my hand. I'll tell the whole story.
I'll lose my honor but you'll go down with me." The Jew
made light of the threat and at the next hearing the messenger
told everything. They were both castigated. The Jew was condemned to pay and the sum applied to the relief of the poor.
It was then I left him and came back to this country.

What could I do? I had to do something or starve. All sorts of projects buzzed in my head. One day I was all for joining a traveling troupe, being equally fit or unfit for the footlights and the orchestra. The next I thought of having a set of pictures painted and put up in a public place, where I would have shouted: "That's his birthplace; there he is leaving his father the apothecary; now he enters the capital looking for his uncle's house; you see him on his knees before his uncle, who shows him the door. He joins the household of a Jew, etc., etc. The day after I would get up resolved to take up with a band of street singers, and that might not have been the worst of my ideas. We could have gone to serenade my uncle under his own windows and made him turn up his toes with vexation. But I decided on something else. . . .

[There he stopped, taking in succession the pose of a man holding a violin and turning the pegs to tune it up, and the pose of a poor wretch who is worn out with fatigue, who faints and falters in the legs, who is ready to give up the ghost if one does not throw him a piece of bread. He showed his extreme need by pointing a finger at his half-open mouth. Then he said: "You understand. They would toss me the loaf and we were three or four starvelings to wrangle for a share of it. Go and have grand conceptions, create beauty, on such a diet!"]

MYSELF. It is indeed hard.

HE. From tumble to tumble I had fallen you know where. I lived there like a rat in a cheese. I left, and now we'll have to squeeze the guts again, go back to the gesture of the finger and the gaping mouth. Nothing is stable in this world. Today at the top of the heap, tomorrow at the bottom. Accursed circumstance guides us and does it very badly.

[Then drinking what was left in one of the bottles and addressing his neighbor, he said: "Sir, a pinch of snuff, for kindness' sake. You have a mighty handsome snuffbox. You are not a musician? No? So much the better for you, for they're all poor buggers, a pitiable lot. Fate has decreed that I should be one, while in Montmartre there may be in a windmill, a

miller or a miller's helper who has never heard anything but
the click of the ratchet but who would have found the most
enchanting melodies. To the mill, Rameau! To the mill, that's
the place for you!"]

MYSELF. Whatever a man tries, Nature destined him for that.

HE. Then she makes some very odd blunders. I can't for
myself see from those heights where everything comes to the
same thing—the man who prunes a tree with his shears and
the slug that eats off the leaves being just two insects each
doing his duty. You go and perch on the epicycle of Mercury,
and like Réaumur, who classifies the flies into seamstresses, sur-
veyors, and reapers, you classify mankind into carpenters,
builders, roofers, dancers, and singers: that's your affair, I
shan't meddle with it. I am in *this* world and here I stay.
But if it is natural to be hungry—I always come back to hunger,
for it's with me an ever-present sensation—I find that it is
no part of good order to be sometimes without food. What a
hell of an economy! Some men replete with everything while
others, whose stomachs are no less importunate, whose hunger
is just as recurrent, have nothing to bite on. The worst of it
is the constrained posture in which need holds you. The
needy man doesn't walk like the rest, he skips, twists, cringes,
crawls. He spends his life choosing and performing positions.

MYSELF. What kind of "positions"?

HE. Go ask Noverre the choreographer. The world numbers
more positions than his art can reproduce.

MYSELF. So you too, if I may use your expression—or rather
that of Montaigne—are perched on the epicycle of Mercury
and considering the different pantomimes of humankind.

HE. No, I tell you, no. I am far too clumsy to rise so high.
I yield to the cranes their foggy realms. I crawl on the earth,
look about me, and take my positions. Or else I entertain myself watching others take theirs. I am good at pantomime, as
you shall see.

[Thereupon he begins to smile, to ape a man admiring, a
man imploring, a man complying. His right foot forward, the
left behind, his back arched, head erect, his glance riveted as
if on another's, openmouthed, his arms are stretched out

toward some object. He waits for a command, receives it, flies like an arrow, returns. The order has been carried out; he is giving a report. Attentive, nothing escapes him. He picks up what is dropped, places pillow or stool under feet, holds a salver, brings a chair, opens a door, shuts a window, draws curtains, gazes at master and mistress. He is motionless, arms hanging, legs parallel; he listens and tries to read faces. Then he says: "There you have my pantomime; it's about the same as the flatterer's, the courtier's, the footman's, and the beggar's."]

[This man's vagaries, like the tales of Abbé Galiani and the extravaganzas of Rabelais, have often plunged me in deep reverie. Those are three storehouses from which I have drawn some absurd masks that I have then projected on the faces of the gravest figures. I seem to see Pantaloon in a prelate, a satyr in a presiding judge, a porker in a friar, an ostrich in a king's minister, and a goose in his under secretary.]

MYSELF. According to you [I went on], there are innumerable beggars in this world, for I hardly know anyone who doesn't use at least a few of your dance steps.

HE. You are right. In the whole country only one man walks—the King. Everybody else takes a position.

MYSELF. The King? Even about him there might be something more to say. Don't you suppose that from time to time he finds near him a little foot, a little nose, a little curl that makes him perform a bit of pantomime? Whoever stands in need of another is needy and takes a position. The King takes a position before his mistress and before God: he dances his pantomime steps. The minister trips it too, as courtier, flatterer, footman and beggar before his king. The crowd of self-seekers dance all your positions in a hundred ways, each viler than the next, in front of the minister. The noble Abbé, in furred cape and cloak, dances attendance once a week at least before the official who appoints to benefices. Really, what you call the beggar's pantomime is what makes the world go round. Every man has his Bertin and his little Hus.

HE. It's very consoling to me.

[While I spoke he mimicked in killing fashion the positions of the figures I enumerated. For the little Abbé, for example, he held his hat under his arm and his breviary in the left hand. With the right he lifted the train of his cloak, stepping forward with his head a little to one side, eyes lowered, and giving the very image of the hypocrite. I thought I was seeing the author of *The Refutation* petitioning the Bishop of Orleans. When he came to the courtiers and self-seekers, he crawled like a worm—the image of Bouret before the Auditor-General.]

MYSELF. Your performance is unsurpassable [said I]. But there is one human being who is exempted from the pantomime. That is the philosopher who has nothing and asks for nothing.

HE. And where does the creature hide? If he has nothing, he must be suffering; if he asks for nothing, he will get nothing—and so will always suffer.

MYSELF. No. Diogenes made fun of his wants.

HE. But a man needs clothes.

MYSELF. He went naked.

HE. Wasn't it ever cold in Athens?

MYSELF. Not so often as here.

HE. But people had to eat.

MYSELF. No doubt.

HE. At whose expense?

MYSELF. At Nature's. Whom does the savage beg from? The earth, the animals and fishes, the trees and plants and roots and streams.

HE. An inferior menu.

MYSELF. But abundant.

HE. And badly served.

MYSELF. Yet it's the one whose leavings appear on all our tables.

HE. You have to admit that our cooks, pastrymen, confectioners, and caterers add a little of their own. If your Diogenes stuck to his austere diet, his organs must have been exceedingly docile.

MYSELF. You are wrong. The Cynic's costume was that of our monks and equally virtuous. The Cynics were the Carmelites and Cordeliers of Athens.

HE. I've caught you then! Diogenes must have danced a pantomime, if not in front of Pericles, at least in front of Lais and Phryne?

MYSELF. Wrong again. The others paid dear the same courtesan who gave herself to him for pleasure.

HE. What if the courtesan was busy and the Cynic in haste?

MYSELF. He went back to his tub and did without.

HE. Do you advise me to do the same?

MYSELF. I'll stake my life it is better than to crawl, eat dirt and prostitute yourself.

HE. But I want a good bed, good food, warm clothes in winter, cool in summer, plenty of rest, money, and other things that I would rather owe to kindness than earn by toil.

MYSELF. That is because you are a lazy, greedy lout, a coward and a rotting soul.

HE. I believe I told you so myself.

MYSELF. The good things of life have their worth, no doubt, but you overlook the price of what you give up for them. You dance, you have danced, and you will keep on dancing the vilest pantomime.

HE. True enough. But it's cost me little and it won't cost me anything more. For which reason I should be quite wrong to take up another position, which would cause me trouble and which I could not hold. But from what you tell me I see that my poor dear little wife was a kind of philosopher. She had the courage of a lion. Sometimes we had no bread and no money and had already sold all our clothes. I would throw myself across the foot of the bed and rack my wits to find someone who would lend us a fiver that I'd never repay. She, gay as a lark, would sing and accompany herself at the clavier. She had the throat of a nightingale; I'm sorry you never heard her. When I took part in some musical evening I took her with me and on the way I would say: "Come, my lady, get yourself admired, display your talents and your charms, overwhelm, captivate." She would sing, overwhelm, captivate. Alas! I lost her, the poor thing. Besides her talents, she had a tiny mouth the width of a finger, a row of pearls for teeth, and then eyes, feet, a skin, cheeks, breasts, legs like a doe, thighs and buttocks for a sculptor. Sooner or later she would have had a chief tax collector at least. Her walk, her rump, ye gods, what a rump!"

[At once he imitated his wife's walk, taking little steps, perking his nose up in the air, flirting with a fan, swinging his hips. It was the caricature of our little coquettes, laughable and true. Then resuming his speech, he said: "I used to take her everywhere—to the Tuileries, the Palais-Royal, the Boulevards. She could not possibly have stayed with me. When she went across the street in the morning, hatless and in her smock, you would have stopped just to look at her and you could have held her waist with both thumbs and forefingers without squeezing her. Those who followed her and watched her trot along on her little feet or who gauged that rich rump outlined in her thin petticoats would hasten their pace. She let them come up then turned on them two big dark and glowing eyes that stopped them in their tracks. For the right side of the medal fully matched the reverse. But alas! I lost her and all my hopes of fortune went with her. I had taken her for no other reason, I had told her my plans. She was too intelligent not to see that they were assured of success and too sound of judgment not to agree with their aim."

[At which he began to sob and choke as he said: "No, no, I never shall get over it. Ever since, I've taken minor orders and wear a skullcap."]

MYSELF. From grief?

HE. If you like. But really in order to carry my soup plate upon my head. . . . But let's see what time it is, because I am going to the Opera.

MYSELF. What's on the program?

HE. Dauvergne's *Les Troqueurs*. The music has some fine things in it. Too bad he wasn't the first to write them. Among the dead there are always a few to annoy the living. Can't be helped. *Quisque suos patimur manes.** But it's half past five; I hear the bell ringing vespers for me and Abbé Canaye. Farewell, Master Philosopher, isn't it true that I am ever the same?

MYSELF. Alas! Yes, unfortunately.

HE. Here's hoping this ill fortune lasts me another forty years. He laughs best who laughs last.

* From Virgil but twisted to a new meaning: "Each of us has antecedents to live down."

2

PREFACE

The manuscript of *D'Alembert's Dream* has an even more bizarre history than that of *Rameau's Nephew*, and came even nearer to falling into total oblivion. About a month after writing it, Diderot showed it to his friend Melchior Grimm, who edited a handwritten newsletter, the *Correspondance Littéraire* for circulation (at a fancy price) among a number of sovereigns and princely families of Germany and points east. Grimm liked the dialogues and wanted to use them in his forthcoming numbers; Diderot's draft was therefore given to one of Grimm's copyists, a certain Hénault, who fortunately seems to have made an extra copy without the author's knowledge—otherwise the work would have been lost forever. While the manuscript was being copied, Diderot spent a week at Grandval, the château of his friend D'Holbach just outside Paris, and probably while browsing in the Baron's library happened to read in the *Gazette de France* of September 4, 1769, an account of the twins of Rabastens. This seemed such a striking illustration of one of his main points that he asked for the temporary return of his manuscript to insert a short passage about them.

A little later he began showing his manuscript to a few carefully chosen friends, and one of these, Suard, seems to have let the cat out of the bag by telling Julie de L'Espinasse about it. Julie was only slightly acquainted with Diderot and thought he was taking undue liberties in putting improper words in her mouth, so she made her friend and would-be lover D'Alembert go to Diderot and demand that he destroy the offending manuscript. In D'Alembert's presence Diderot threw his original and the only copy he knew about into the fire.

For nearly ten years Diderot believed that *D'Alembert's Dream* had ceased to exist. In 1774, on his return from Russia, where he had gone at the pressing invitation of his benefactress, Catherine the Great, he evidently got to thinking about his vanished dialogues and made a heroic effort to reconstitute them. But he had by then used up his best creative powers, and the attempt was (as he himself recognized) a miserable failure.

Two years later, in 1776, Julie de L'Espinasse died, embittered by the death of one lover, the Marquis de Mora, and by the marriage and growing indifference of another, the Comte de Guibert. Diderot now realized that except for D'Alembert there was no obstacle to publishing his dialogues— if only a copy could be found. D'Alembert meanwhile, being Julie's executor, had just had the shock of discovering the Marquis de Mora's love letters among her papers. Not long afterward, as a fair copy of *D'Alembert's Dream* providentially came to light—in all likelihood the extra copy made in 1769 by Grimm's copyist, Diderot promptly destroyed the new version on which he had been working with such discouraging results, and turned his attention to putting the finishing touches on what he had once described as "the only one of my works, besides a certain treatise on mathematics, in which I see no possibility of improvement."

In August 1782, and the three months following, most of the subscriber's to the *Correspondance Littéraire* received, in confidence, the revised text of *D'Alembert's Dream*. Diderot's daughter was careful to retain her father's copy, corrected in his own handwriting, when she sent manuscripts of all his writings—thirty-two volumes in all—to Russia in 1785. Remarkably enough, none of the subscribers to Grimm's newsletter allowed the text to leak out, though several publishers were eager to obtain it after its existence had been made known around the turn of the century.

Not until 1830 did the piece appear in print, and the public would not have obtained it even then if it had not been for a certain Dugour, born in France but naturalized in Russia under the name Gourov, who became Rector of the University of St. Petersburg and used his exalted position to steal hastily-made copies of several unpublished works of Diderot from the Hermitage collection. These, including *D'Alembert's Dream*, were published in Paris by the bookseller Paulin under a title that protected Dugour, alias Gourov, by pretending that the manuscript was one given by Diderot to Grimm.

All subsequent editions down to the annotated critical text published by Paul Vernière in 1951* have been based on this none-too-faithful copy of a copy. Vernière's edition is based on a copy in Diderot's own handwriting—the one preserved by his daughter, Angélique de Vandeul, and kept secret by the Vandeul family all through the nineteenth century. This copy had been made available only recently by Diderot's descendant, Baron Jacques Le Vavasseur, who allowed Herbert Dieckmann of Harvard to photograph the Vandeul papers in 1949. The English translation offered here was made from this authentic text, and will therefore be found to differ from previous versions based on the carelessly made Hermitage manuscript and its even less reliable offspring.

* The publishers are: Librairie Droz (Geneva) and Librairie Giard (Lille).

D'ALEMBERT'S DREAM

A Conversation Between
Diderot and D'Alembert

D'ALEMBERT. I'm willing to agree with you that it's very hard to believe in the reality of a Being that is said to exist somewhere, yet occupies no single point in space; a Being that has no extension, yet occupies space; that exists in its entirety in every separate part of the universe; that is essentially different from matter, yet is one with it; that moves matter and follows the movements of matter, yet does not move; that acts upon matter, but at the same time suffers all its vicissitudes. I do not have the least idea what such a Being can be like, for its nature seems utterly contradictory. Still, there are also difficulties for the man who rejects such a Being. For if you put some principle of sensitivity or consciousness in its place, if you say that consciousness* is a universal and essential attribute of matter, then you will have to admit that stones can think.

* Diderot's term is *"sensibilité,"* a word that can convey many meanings depending on the context. Its most elementary, literal meaning is doubtless "sensitivity," or "the ability to receive sense impressions." The exact scope of the term was, however, much disputed during the eighteenth century, and some English physiologists insisted that it should be used interchangeably with "irritability." Diderot sometimes uses the word in this way, and when he does the term "irritability" is given here as the English equivalent. For the most part, however, he gives *"sensibilité"* and its derivatives a much more extended meaning that seems to be best expressed in English as "consciousness." As the text of the *Dialogue* will make clear, there is still another important meaning attached to the word *"sensibilité"* in eighteenth-century usage—as applied to human temperaments the adjective "sensible" signifies the opposite of "phlegmatic," and the parent noun is perhaps best rendered by the English "sensibility."

DIDEROT. And why not?

D'ALEMBERT. That's pretty hard to swallow.

DIDEROT. Yes, for someone who cuts and shapes them, or who grinds them into powder without hearing them cry out.

D'ALEMBERT. Then I wish you'd tell me what difference you think there is between a man and a statue, between marble and flesh.

DIDEROT. Not very much. You can make marble out of flesh, or flesh out of marble.

D'ALEMBERT. But the two things are still not identical.

DIDEROT. No, just as kinetic energy is not potential energy.

D'ALEMBERT. I don't follow you.

DIDEROT. Then I'll explain. When you carry something from one place to another, that isn't motion—it is only the effect produced by motion. Motion is inherent in the thing itself, whether you carry it or whether it remains at rest.

D'ALEMBERT. Well, that's a novel way of looking at it.

DIDEROT. It's true just the same. Take away an obstacle that has been preventing the local motion of an immobile object and that object will move from one place to another. Remove, or suddenly rarefy, the air that surrounds the trunk of this enormous oak tree, and all of a sudden the water it contains will start to expand, splintering the wood into a hundred thousand pieces. The same could be said of your own body.

D'ALEMBERT. Of course. But what connection is there between motion and consciousness? Are you perhaps trying to make a distinction between actual and latent consciousness? Are you suggesting an analogy with kinetic and potential energy—between kinetic energy, which shows itself in the form of local motion, and potential energy, which takes the form of pressure? Is there an active consciousness characterized by certain actions that we can observe in animals and perhaps also in plants, and a latent consciousness which we detect only when it changes its state and becomes active?

DIDEROT. Exactly! You've said it better than I could have.

D'ALEMBERT. So a statue has only latent consciousness, while man, animals, and perhaps even plants, are endowed with active consciousness.

DIDEROT. There is certainly that particular difference between a block of marble and the fibers of living flesh, but, as you may well imagine, that isn't the only difference.

D'ALEMBERT. I should say not. Whatever resemblance there may be between the external shape of a man and that of a statue, there is surely no similarity in their internal organization. There could hardly be a sculptor skillful enough to make even so much as a real skin with his chisel. But there is a very simple method of causing potential energy to pass into the kinetic state. This phenomenon takes place before our eyes a hundred times every day. Yet I don't see very well how one can make a physical object change from a state of latent consciousness to a state of active consciousness.

DIDEROT. That can only be because you don't want to see it. It is actually rather common.

D'ALEMBERT. Well, if it is such a common phenomenon, tell me, if you please, how it takes place.

DIDEROT. I'm about to explain it to you, since you're apparently not ashamed to admit that you can't guess what it is. It is something that happens every time you eat a meal.

D'ALEMBERT. Every time I eat?

DIDEROT. Yes. What do you do when you eat? You remove the obstacles that were preventing the emergence of active consciousness in the food. You assimilate the food and make it part of yourself. You make flesh out of it. You make it become animal and you make it conscious. Furthermore, what you do with your food, I can do whenever I please with marble.

D'ALEMBERT. And just how will you manage that?

DIDEROT. How? Simply by making it edible.

D'ALEMBERT. Making marble edible doesn't strike me as a very easy thing to do.

DIDEROT. I see that it's up to me to explain the method to you. I will take that statue you see there, put it in a mortar, and after a few good blows with my pestle . . .

D'ALEMBERT. Not so fast, please. This statue is one of Falconnet's masterpieces. Of course, if it were by Huez or one of the others . . .

DIDEROT. Falconnet wouldn't mind; the statue has been paid for, and Falconnet gives little enough thought to his present-day reputation, let alone his future glory.

D'ALEMBERT. Go ahead, then. Grind it up.

DIDEROT. As soon as the block of marble has been reduced to an impalpable powder I will mix that dust with some humus or dirt containing vegetable matter. I will knead the powder into the humus, sprinkle water on the mixture, and then I will let it rot for a year, two years, a hundred years. Time means nothing to me. When the whole mass has changed into a more or less homogeneous substance—into humus—do you know what I will do?

D'ALEMBERT. I am sure you are not going to eat the humus.

DIDEROT. No, but there is a process by which I can unite the humus with myself, by which I can appropriate it—a *latus*, as the chemists would call it.

D'ALEMBERT. And I suppose the plant is this *latus*.

DIDEROT. You've hit the nail on the head. I'll plant seeds in the humus—peas, beans, cabbages and other garden vegetables. The plants will get their food from the earth and I will get mine from the plants.

D'ALEMBERT. Your notion may or may not be true, but I like the idea of this transition from marble to humus, from humus to vegetables, and from vegetables to animals—in the end to flesh.

DIDEROT. Well, that's how I make flesh, or, as my daughter says, a soul—that is, matter that possesses active consciousness —and if I have not completely solved the problem you set me, at least I am not far from a solution. You ought to be willing to admit that there is much more difference between a piece of marble and a conscious being than there is between a conscious being and one that thinks.

D'ALEMBERT. I admit it. But all the same, a creature that has feelings is not quite the same as one that can think.

DIDEROT. Before pushing ahead along that line, I would like to tell you the life story of one of the greatest mathematicians of Europe. Do you know what that marvelous being was in the beginning? Nothing.

D'ALEMBERT. How do you mean, nothing? You can't make something out of nothing.

DIDEROT. You are using the word too literally. I mean only that before his mother, the beautiful and naughty canoness Tencin,* had reached the age of puberty, and before the soldier La Touche had reached adolescence, the molecules that were to make up the first rudimentary beginnings of my mathematician were dispersed throughout the delicate young bodies of his future parents, were being filtered with the lymph through their organs, were circulating in their blood streams, until the moment when the molecules were finally collected in certain reservoirs in preparation for their final meeting— I mean the sex glands of his mother and father. Now we can observe the germination of this rare seed. See how it is carried, as most authorities believe, through the Fallopian tubes into the womb; see how it attaches itself by a long stem to the womb; see how it grows and develops by stages into a fœtus. At last the moment arrives when it is to leave its dark prison. Behold the newborn child, abandoned on the steps of the church of St.-Jean-le-Rond from which he will take his baptismal name; now he is placed in the orphanage and afterwards taken out of it again; now he is put to nurse at the breast of the good glazier's wife, Madame Rousseau. On her milk he grows strong both in body and in mind and becomes a man of letters, a physicist and a mathematician. And how did this all come about? As the result of eating and of other purely mechanical operations. I will give you the general recipe in a few words—eat, digest, distill in a closed vessel, and you have the whole art of making a man. If anyone wants to describe

* D'Alembert was the illegitimate son of Mlle. de Tencin and her lover, La Touche. His parents left their unwanted child on the steps of the little chapel close by the cathedral of Notre-Dame which, because of its circular form, was called the church of St.-Jean-le-Rond; when the baby was transferred to the Foundling Hospital he was christened "St.-Jean-le-Rond" for want of any other name. Though his father eventually assumed the responsibility of supporting him and paid for his education, D'Alembert (as he chose to call himself) never made any demands on his natural parents and never tried to assert his right to use the family name.

to the Academy the steps in the production of a man or animal, he will need to make use of nothing but physical agencies, for these can produce the successive effects required—an inert object, a conscious being, a thinking creature, a being who can solve the problem of the precession of the equinoxes—a sublime and marvelous being, but one that is still going to grow old, fall sick, die and finally return to humus.

D'ALEMBERT. Then you don't believe that the sex glands of Adam and Eve contained the seeds of the whole human race?

DIDEROT. No.

D'ALEMBERT. Bravo! I'm glad to hear you say that.

DIDEROT. The whole idea flies in the face of both experience and logic. It goes against experience because we have never been able to find sex cells in eggs or in the majority of animals before they have reached a certain age. It is illogical because logic teaches us that in nature there is a limit to the divisibility of matter—though there may be no such limit in pure theory—for reason refuses to conceive of a fully formed elephant contained in an atom, and in one atom [of this elephant] another complete elephant, and so on *ad infinitum*.

D'ALEMBERT. But if you rule out the theory of pre-existing germ cells, how can you account for the original production of animal life?

DIDEROT. If you are worrying about the question of which came first, the chicken or the egg, your difficulty is simply that you are assuming that all animals were originally just what they are now. What nonsense! We have no idea what they have been like in the past, any more than we know what they will be like in the future. Some earthworm squirming about in a dung heap is perhaps on his way to becoming a large animal, while some huge beast, who now amazes us by his size, is perhaps on his way to becoming a worm. In other words, he may be only a momentary and unique product of this earth.

D'ALEMBERT. Would you mind repeating that remark?

DIDEROT. I was only saying that . . . But we are losing the thread of our original discussion. . . .

D'ALEMBERT. What of it? We can decide later whether we want to go back and pick up the thread again.

DIDEROT. Do I have your permission to look forward a few thousand years into the future?

D'ALEMBERT. Why not? Nature takes little account of the passage of time.

DIDEROT. Will you let me snuff out our sun?

D'ALEMBERT. Go ahead, by all means. It won't be the first time a sun was extinguished.

DIDEROT. All right, the sun is extinct. What will happen next? The plants will all die, and so will the animals; the earth will be left silent and lifeless. Now light up the sun again. Instantly you have restored the necessary cause of an infinite number of new manifestations of life. I am not bold enough to assert that, after the lapse of centuries, our plants and animals of today would or would not reappear.

D'ALEMBERT. Why should they not reappear, once the same scattered elements had come together again?

DIDEROT. Why not? Because in nature everything is bound up with everything else, and whenever you introduce a new phenomenon, or try to recreate an instant that has gone by, you end up by conceiving a whole new world.

D'ALEMBERT. No one who thinks profoundly about the matter can deny what you say. But let's get back to the human race, since the universal order requires that men should exist. Remember that you left me in suspense just at the moment when a being endowed with sensations was about to be transformed into a thinking being.

DIDEROT. I haven't forgotten.

D'ALEMBERT. Frankly, I should be much obliged to you if you would get me out of that limbo. I am in somewhat of a hurry to have the thinking process begin.

DIDEROT. Even if I should not solve the riddle once and for all, what harm would be done? There would still remain a whole chain of incontestable facts.

D'ALEMBERT. No harm at all. Except that we would still be stopped short in the middle of our inquiry.

DIDEROT. And in order to get in motion again, would it be allowable to invent some agency whose attributes are mutually contradictory, some word that has no meaning, that is unintelligible?

D'ALEMBERT. Of course not.

DIDEROT. Can you tell me what the existence of a being endowed with sensation means to that being itself?

D'ALEMBERT. It must mean the awareness of having been itself, from the first instant of consciousness down to the present moment.

DIDEROT. And in what is this awareness grounded?

D'ALEMBERT. In the memory of its own actions.

DIDEROT. What if that memory were lacking?

D'ALEMBERT. If there were no memory, there would be no awareness of self, because if a creature were aware of its existence only during the instant of that awareness, it would have no history of its life. Its life would be only an interrupted series of sensations without anything to bind them together.

DIDEROT. Very good. Now tell me what memory is, and explain where it comes from.

D'ALEMBERT. It comes from a certain organization of matter—an organization that grows or disintegrates, and sometimes disappears altogether.

DIDEROT. Then if a being that has sensations, and that possesses the organization necessary for memory, binds together the impressions it receives and constructs by this process a history—the history of its own life—and so acquires an awareness of itself, then it affirms and denies; it thinks and draws conclusions.

D'ALEMBERT. Apparently. So I am left with only one difficulty.

DIDEROT. You're mistaken. There are actually many more.

D'ALEMBERT. But there is one principal difficulty. It is that we are able to think of only one thing at a time, and in order to grasp just one simple proposition—not to speak of those stupendous chains of·reasoning that are made up of thousands of separate ideas—it seems that at least two things are required: the object which remains as it were under the mind's eye, while the mind concerns itself with those qualities of the object which it will either affirm or deny.

DIDEROT. I believe so, and for that reason I have sometimes been led to compare the fibers that make up our sense organs with sensitive, vibrating strings. The string vibrates and makes a sound for a long time after it has been plucked. It is a vibration of this sort, it is this kind of necessary resonance, that keeps an object present to our minds while our understandings deal with whichever of its qualities we please to study. Besides, these vibrating strings have still another property—they can make other strings hum—so that in this way one idea can call forth another, the second can call forth a third, and so on. Hence no one can set a limit to the ideas that will occur to a philosopher, for his ideas arise out of their own necessary connections while he meditates in darkness and in silence. The instrument has an astonishing range, for a newly awakened idea can sometimes provoke a sympathetic response in a harmonic that is almost inconceivably remote. If this phenomenon can be observed in musical strings that are separate and inert, why should we not expect to find it wherever living points are connected with each other—why not in sensitive fibers that are continuous?

D'ALEMBERT. If what you are saying isn't true, it is at least most ingenious. But I am tempted to believe that you may be slipping unawares into the very difficulty that you are trying to avoid.

DIDEROT. Which one?

D'ALEMBERT. You are trying to eliminate the distinction between mind and matter.

DIDEROT. I realize that.

D'ALEMBERT. But if you don't watch out, you will end up saying that the philosopher's mind is an entity distinct from the stringed instrument, a sort of musician that listens to the vibrating strings and draws conclusions about their harmony or dissonance.

DIDEROT. I may have let myself in for that objection. But you might not even have raised it if you had sufficiently considered the difference between the two instruments—the phi-

losopher and the clavichord. The philosopher-instrument has
sensations, so he is simultaneously the performer and the instrument. Because he is conscious, he has a momentary awareness of the sound he produces; because he is an animal, he
remembers the sound. This organic faculty, by linking together the sounds inside his mind, both produces and preserves the melody. Imagine a clavichord endowed with sensation and memory, and then tell me whether it will not learn
and be able to repeat by itself the tunes you play on its keyboard. We humans are instruments gifted with sensation and
memory. Our senses are merely keys that are struck by the
natural world around us, keys that often strike themselves—
and this, according to my way of thinking, is all that would
take place in a clavichord organized as you and I are organized.
There is an impression that has its cause either inside or outside the instrument; from this impression a sensation is born,
a sensation that persists, for it is impossible to suppose that a
sensation can both arise and be extinguished in a single indivisible instant of time. Then a second impression follows
the first, arising similarly out of an external or internal cause;
then there occurs a second sensation. And these sensations
all have tones—either natural or conventional sounds—that
serve to identify them.

D'ALEMBERT. I follow your line of thought. So, then, if this
animated and sensitive clavichord were also endowed with
the ability to eat and to reproduce itself, it would be alive
and could beget—either by itself or with the help of its female
—little clavichords that would be alive and resonant.

DIDEROT. Don't you doubt it for a moment! What else do
you think a bluefinch is, or a nightingale, or a musician, or
any human being? What other difference do you think there
is between a canary and the little wooden whistle used to
teach canaries to sing? Imagine that you have an egg in your
hand. With it all the schools of theology can be overthrown,
as well as all the temples of religion on earth. What exactly
is an egg? Nothing but an insensitive mass—that is, before
the germ is put into it. Introduce a germ, and then what is it?
Still an insensitive mass, for the germ itself is nothing but

a thick, lifeless fluid. How does this substance pass over into another form of organization, into sensitivity—into life? By means of heat. What generates the heat? Motion. What stages does this development follow? Instead of answering my question, sit down and let us watch carefully what happens from one moment to the next. At first there is a litle dot that bobs about, then there is a thread that takes on color and grows larger, then there is flesh starting to form, then there is a beak, there are wing-tips, eyes and feet beginning to appear, a yellowish substance that divides to make the intestines—at last there is a living thing. This creature moves, it stirs about, it makes a noise—I can hear it peeping inside the shell. Its body begins to be covered with fuzz. It can see. The weight of its head, which wobbles back and forth, constantly forces its beak against the interior wall of its prison. At last the wall is broken, and the chick comes out. It walks, it flutters its wings, it feels irritations, it runs away, it comes back again, it makes a complaining sound, it feels pain, it shows affection, it has desires, it gets pleasure from this or that. It shows all the emotions that you show and does everything that you can do. Can you maintain with Descartes that this is nothing but an imitative machine? If so, even the smallest children will make fun of you, and philosophers will tell you that if this is a machine, you're another.

On the other hand, if you admit that there is no difference between you and the animals except in degree of organization, you will show reason and common sense as well as good faith. But then we shall have to conclude that you were wrong in your earlier opinion, and that an inert substance arranged in a certain way and impregnated with another inert substance, when subjected to heat and motion, can give rise to sensation, life, memory, conscience, passion and thought. You have left only a choice between two other positions—you must either imagine that within the lifeless substance of the egg there is some hidden element that waited until the egg had developed before it revealed its presence, or you must argue that this undetectable element made its way in through the shell at some particular moment of the egg's development.

But what could such an element be? Did it occupy space, or did it not? How did it get in, or out, without moving? Where was it? What was it doing, either in that place or somewhere else? Was it created at precisely the moment when it was needed? Did it exist earlier? Was it looking for a home? Was it, or wasn't it, of the same substance as the home it sought? If of the same substance, then it must have been matter; otherwise how can you account for its inertia before the egg began to develop, or its energy in the fully formed chick? Just listen to yourself talk and you will feel sorry for yourself. You will recognize that the price you have to pay for not accepting a simple hypothesis that explains everything—I mean irritability, a universal attribute of matter or the result of the organization of matter—will be a renunciation of common sense and a headlong plunge into an abyss of mysteries, contradictions and absurdities.

D'ALEMBERT. A hypothesis! You may be pleased to call it that. But what if this irritability of yours should prove to be essentially incompatible with matter?

DIDEROT. And who told you that irritability is *essentially* incompatible with matter—you, who know nothing whatsoever about the essence of anything under the sun—including both matter and irritability? Do you understand any better the nature of motion, or the mode of its existence in bodies, or the manner of its transmission from one body to another?

D'ALEMBERT. Although I can't clearly conceive the nature of irritability nor the nature of matter, I can see that irritability is one single, indivisible property, so it is incompatible with a divisible object or substance.

DIDEROT. Theologico-metaphysical fiddle-faddle!Listen! Don't you see that all the properties and all the tangible forms of matter are essentially indivisible? There's no question of more or less impenetrability. You can have half of a round body, but there's no such thing as half of roundness. There can be more or less motion, but you either have motion or you don't. It is as silly to talk of a half or a third or a quarter of a head, or of an ear or of a finger, as it is to speak of a half or a third or a quarter of a thought. Since in the whole universe there is not a single molecule that is just like another, and in every molecule not a single atom that is just like another atom, why won't you admit that the atom itself possesses an indivisible form and quality? Why don't you admit that division is incompatible with the essence of all forms whatsoever because it destroys them? Be a good physicist and acknowledge the reality of a result when you have seen it occur, even if you can't explain the connection between cause and effect. Be a good logician and do not throw overboard a cause that is real and that explains everything just for the sake of retaining another cause that is incomprehensible and that has even less logical connection with the observed effect, a cause that gives rise to innumerable difficulties without removing a single one of them.

D'ALEMBERT. Well, what if I give up this second cause?

DIDEROT. Then there will be only one single substance in the universe, in man and in the animals. The little whistle is made of wood; man is made of flesh. The canary is made of flesh, the musician is made of flesh that is differently organized, but both have a single origin, were formed in the same way, have the same functions, and serve the same end.

D'ALEMBERT. But how do your two clavichords manage to establish a conventional system of sounds?

DIDEROT. If we think of animals as sensitive instruments, then one of them is perfectly comparable with another that has been put together on the same plan—all will have the same strings and their keys will respond in the same way to joy and sorrow, hunger and thirst, anger, admiration and fright. Whether you play the instrument at the North Pole or at the Equator, it will necessarily make the same sounds. This is why it happens that the common interjections—oh!, ah!, eh!—are just about the same in all languages living or dead. To explain the origin of conventional sounds you need only the principles of need and proximity. The sensitive instrument, or animal, discovered that when he made a certain noise there followed a certain result outside himself; he noticed that other sensitive instruments like himself—other animals with sensations—came closer, went away, asked something of him or offered him something, hurt him or fondled him. All these results were connected in his memory and in the memories of others with the occurrence of the sounds in question. Please note that all human intercourse consists merely of making noises and doing things. If you want a clinching demonstration of my theory, just reflect that it is open to the same insurmountable objection that Berkeley raised against the real existence of physical bodies. This merely shows that there is sometimes an instant of delirium when a sensitive clavichord imagines that it is the only clavichord that exists and that it alone produces all the harmonies of the universe.

D'ALEMBERT. There would be a great deal to say on that topic.

DIDEROT. Very true.

D'ALEMBERT. For instance, according to your theory, it isn't very easy to understand how we make syllogisms and draw logical conclusions about this or that.

DIDEROT. But it's perfectly obvious that we don't draw any conclusions at all—they are always drawn by nature itself. We do nothing but describe the connections among phenomena, connections that are either necessary or contingent. These phenomena are known through experience. In mathematics and physics the connections are necessary; in morality and politics they are contingent or probable, as they are in the other branches of speculative knowledge.

D'ALEMBERT. But are the connections between the phenomena themselves any more necessary in the first group than in the rest?

DIDEROT. No. But in morality and politics the causes are subject to so many particular influences which we fail to note that we cannot be sure of the result that will follow. We cannot be as certain that a man of violent disposition will be provoked by an insult as we are that if two bodies collide, the larger will move the smaller.

D'ALEMBERT. What analogy do you see there?

DIDEROT. In the most complex situations the analogy is simply a one-two-three sequence that works itself out within the sensitive machine. If a given phenomenon observed in the natural world is followed by a second natural phenomenon, what fourth phenomenon will be the consequence of a third one that is either found in nature or conceived in imitation of nature? If the average warrior wields a lance ten feet long, how long is Ajax's lance? If I can throw a stone weighing four pounds, Diomedes should be able to move a whole cliff. The strides of the gods and the distance their horses can leap will be in the same ratio that the gods are supposed to bear to men. We have to do with a fourth harmonic string that is proportional to the other three and from which the animal always hears a sympathetic vibration set up inside itself, though this vibration does not always occur in the outside world. All this makes little difference to the poet, but it is true just the same. For the philosopher the problem is different—he must immediately start asking questions of nature because nature often confronts us with phenomena that differ from the ones we had expected to find. Then we realize that we have been led astray by a false analogy.

D'ALEMBERT. Well, my friend, I shall have to bid you good night and be off to bed.

DIDEROT. You can make jokes about all this if you like, but you are going to start dreaming about this conversation of ours as soon as your head touches your pillow, and if your dreams are incoherent, so much the worse for you, because in that case you'll end up by embracing some hypothesis far more ridiculous than anything I've suggested.

D'ALEMBERT. Don't get your hopes up. I shall lie down a skeptic and get up in the morning still a skeptic.

DIDEROT. Skeptic indeed! How can anyone be a skeptic?

D'ALEMBERT. Do you mean that when it comes to a question of whether skeptics exist, you are one yourself? Or are you going to maintain that I am not a skeptic? Who knows better than I do?

DIDEROT. Just listen to me for a moment.

D'ALEMBERT. Make it short or I shall fall asleep.

DIDEROT. It won't take me long. Do you think that there is a single debatable question on which a man can support both sides with an exactly equal measure of reason?

D'ALEMBERT. Why, no. That would be like Buridan's ass.*

DIDEROT. In that case there can be no such thing as a skeptic, because—if we leave aside mathematics, where there is never the slightest uncertainty—you can find arguments for and against every proposition. But since the scales are never equal, it is impossible that they should not tip toward the side where we think the greater probability lies.

D'ALEMBERT. Still, in the morning I find the greater probability on my right, and in the afternoon I find it on my left.

DIDEROT. You really mean that you are dogmatically *pro* in the morning and dogmatically *con* in the afternoon.

D'ALEMBERT. And in the evening, when I recall how rapidly my judgments were made and unmade, I disbelieve both my morning's opinion and the one I had in the afternoon.

DIDEROT. No, what you mean is that you no longer recall your reasons for giving the edge to one opinion or the other; hence the reasons for an earlier decision now appear to have been too frivolous to justify a definite conclusion. So you decide to stop tormenting yourself with such doubtful questions and to leave their exploration to other people, making up your mind not to argue about them anymore.

D'ALEMBERT. Perhaps.

DIDEROT. But if someone should take you aside and question you in a friendly way, asking you to say in all honesty which of the two possible viewpoints seemed to you to involve the fewest difficulties—would you in good faith be embarrassed to give a reply? Would you play the part of Buridan's ass?

D'ALEMBERT. No, I think not.

DIDEROT. All right, my friend, and if you think carefully about it, you will agree that in the end our truest opinions are not the ones we have never changed, but those to which we have most often returned.

D'ALEMBERT. You may very well be right.

DIDEROT. I think I am. So good night, my friend, and remember: Dust thou art and to dust thou shalt return.

D'ALEMBERT. That's a gloomy thought.

* Who starved to death because he could not choose between two identical piles of hay.

DIDEROT. An inescapable one, though. I don't ask for immortality—but just give man twice the length of his present life, and you can never tell what might happen!

D'ALEMBERT. What the devil do you want to happen? Besides, what difference would it make to me? Whatever is going to happen, I say, let it happen if it can. I'm going to bed. Good night.

D'Alembert's Dream

SPEAKERS: D'ALEMBERT,
MADEMOISELLE DE L'ESPINASSE,* DOCTOR BORDEU

BORDEU. Well, well, what's the trouble here? Is he sick?

MLLE. DE L'ESPINASSE. I'm afraid so. He had a very restless night.

BORDEU. Is he awake yet?

MLLE. DE L'ESPINASSE. No, not yet.

BORDEU (bending over D'Alembert's bed to feel his forehead and pulse). It won't amount to anything.

MLLE. DE L'ESPINASSE. Do you really think so?

BORDEU. No doubt about it. His pulse is good—just a little bit on the weak side. . . . His skin is moist . . . respiration is normal.

MLLE. DE L'ESPINASSE. Isn't there anything we ought to do for him?

BORDEU. No.

MLLE. DE L'ESPINASSE. That's good. He hates taking medicine.

BORDEU. And I dislike giving it. What did he eat at suppertime?

---

* Julie de L'Espinasse conducted a *salon* of which D'Alembert was the chief ornament. He was passionately devoted to her and shared her lodgings for many years. Their relations apparently remained platonic, however, because Julie was in love with Guibert, the military theorist, among others.

MLLE. DE L'ESPINASSE. He didn't seem to want anything to eat. I don't know where he spent the evening, but he came home looking worried.

BORDEU. Well, this is just a little touch of fever that shouldn't have any serious consequences.

MLLE. DE L'ESPINASSE. When he came in, he put on his dressing gown and his nightcap and flung himself into his armchair where he soon dropped off to sleep.

BORDEU. Sleep is a good thing no matter where, but he would have done better to go to bed.

MLLE. DE L'ESPINASSE. He got angry with Antoine for telling him the same thing. I had to nag him for half an hour to make him go to bed.

BORDEU. That's just the way it always is with me, even when I'm feeling perfectly well.

MLLE. DE L'ESPINASSE. When he finally went to bed, instead of resting quietly as he usually does—he generally sleeps like a baby—he began to toss and turn, thrashing about with his arms, throwing the covers off and talking in his sleep.

BORDEU. Well, what did he talk about? Mathematics?

MLLE. DE L'ESPINASSE. No, it all sounded like the talk of a crazy person—a lot of nonsense about vibrating strings and sensitive fibers. It seemed so strange that—not wanting to leave him alone in the dark, and not really knowing just what to do—I brought a little table here to the foot of his bed and started to write down all that I could catch of his muttering.

BORDEU. That was a clever thought—and just like you too. Do you mind if I read it?

MLLE. DE L'ESPINASSE. I have **no** objection. But I'd stake my life that you won't be able to **make** head or tail of any of it.

BORDEU. Perhaps not.

MLLE. DE L'ESPINASSE. All right, Doctor. Are you ready?

BORDEU. Yes, begin.

MLLE. DE L'ESPINASSE. Well, listen then: "A living point . . . No, that's wrong. Nothing at first, then a living point . . . Another living point joins itself on to the first one, then another. From a series of such additions there results a living being, for I myself am just such a being—how can I doubt that?" As he said this, he touched various parts of himself. "But how did such a unified being come into existence?" Then I said to him: "Come, come, my dear—what can it matter to you? Go to sleep!" Then he stopped speaking. After a moment of silence he began again as though he were arguing with someone. "Look here, my philosophic friend, I can see very well that there is an aggregation, a fabric of tiny sensitive beings, but where is the animal? . . . What about the whole? A system or self that is aware of forming a unity? I can't see it. No, I can't see it . . ." Doctor, can you make any sense out of all that?

BORDEU. It makes perfect sense.

MLLE. DE L'ESPINASSE. Then I envy you your good fortune. . . . "Perhaps my difficulty is that I am starting from a false premise."

BORDEU. Is that you speaking or him?

MLLE. DE L'ESPINASSE. That's what he said in his dream.

BORDEU. All right, continue.

MLLE. DE L'ESPINASSE. I'll go on. . . . Then he seemed to be talking to himself and he said: "D'Alembert, my friend, watch your step—you are assuming that there is only contiguity, but, actually, there is continuity. . . . Yes, he is really cunning enough to tell me that. . . . And how does this continuity arise? I suppose that will give him no trouble. Just the way a drop of mercury melts into another drop of mercury, one living, sensitive molecule can melt into another one. . . . At first, there were two drops, but after they touched there was only one. . . . Before assimilation, there were two molecules; afterward there was only one. . . . Sensitivity, then, exists throughout the whole mass. . . . Well, actually, why not? . . . In a given length of animal fiber I need distinguish only as many separate points as I please, but the fiber is continuous just the same—one fiber—yes, only one. . . . Continuity arises from the contact of two molecules of the same substance, of exactly the same substance. . . . And this is all that happens in the most perfect case of union, cohesion, combination or identity that can be imagined. . . . Yes, Philosopher, if only the molecules are simple, elementary substances—but what if they are compound or composite? . . . Combination will take place

just the same, and hence there will be continuity and identity.
. . . And then the usual actions and reactions. . . .

"Yet it is certain that contact between two living molecules
is quite different from the contiguity of two inert particles.
. . . Well, never mind, never mind; perhaps I could quibble
with you about that, but what's the use? I'm not one of those
people that always have to have the last word in an argument. . . . But let's get back to the question. I remember
now. . . . A thin wire of very pure gold, that was the comparison he used—a homogeneous network in the meshes of
which other molecules can be fitted in, forming perhaps a second homogeneous network, a fabric of sensitive matter assimi-
lated to the other one by the contact between them—so you
have active sensitivity here, inert matter there, and the sensitivity communicates itself just as motion does. Not to
mention, as he very acutely remarked, that there must be a
difference between the contact of one sensitive molecule with
another and the contact between two molecules that are not
sensitive—but what can be the nature of this difference? . . .
The usual actions and reactions . . . And these actions and
reactions must be of a very special kind. . . . Then everything
conspires to produce the kind of unity that exists only in a
living animal. . . . Upon my word, if that isn't the truth of
the matter, it can't be far from it. . . ." You are laughing,
Doctor; do you mean to say that you can find a grain of sense
in all that?

BORDEU. Oh yes, a great deal.

MLLE. DE L'ESPINASSE. Then he isn't out of his mind?

BORDEU. Not at all.

MLLE. DE L'ESPINASSE. After this preamble he began to shout:
"Mademoiselle de L'Espinasse! Mademoiselle de L'Espinasse"
—"What is it?"—"Have you ever seen a swarm of bees escaping
from their hive? . . . Well, the world, or rather the general
supply of matter in the universe, is nothing but a great swarm
of bees. . . . Have you ever seen how they fly off and form a
long cluster of tiny winged creatures that hang from the branch
of a tree, each one clinging to the others with his feet? Well,
that cluster is a single being, an individual, some sort of animal.—But one of these clusters must be just like any other

cluster.—Yes, if there were only one homogeneous substance.—
But have you ever seen them?—Oh yes, I've seen them.—You
have actually seen them?—Of course, I tell you.—Well, if one
of the bees takes a notion to pinch in some way or other the
bee to which it is attached, what do you think will happen?
Just tell me that.—I have no idea.—Well, say what you think
anyway. You may not know, but the Philosopher—he's sure to
know. The next time you see him—and you're bound to see
him sooner or later because he promised that you would—
he will tell you that when one bee pinches the next one, setting
off a chain of sensations that will run from one little creature
to the next one, and so on throughout the cluster, the whole
cluster will stir, quiver, change its shape and location, the
cluster will make a noise composed of many tiny cries, so that
anyone who had never seen such a cluster formed would most
likely mistake it for an animal with five or six hundred heads
and ten or twelve hundred wings. . . ." Well, what do you
say to that, Doctor?

BORDEU. I declare, you know, this dream is a splendid performance—you did very well to write it all down.

MLLE. DE L'ESPINASSE. I'm beginning to wonder if you aren't
dreaming yourself.

BORDEU. Far from it. So little, in fact, that I could almost
undertake to tell you how the rest of it goes.

MLLE DE L'ESPINASSE. I'll bet you couldn't.

BORDEU. You want to bet?

MLLE. DE L'ESPINASSE. Yes.

BORDEU. And if I guess right?

MLLE. DE L'ESPINASSE. If you guess right, I'll promise you
that . . . I'll promise to think that you're the craziest man in
the world.

BORDEU. Look at your notes and listen to me: "The man
who took that bunch of bees for an animal would be making
a mistake." But, Mademoiselle, I assume he went on as though
he were speaking to you: "Do you want to know what his considered opinion would be? Do you want to see how the bunch
of bees could be transformed into a single, unique animal?
Then soften the material in the feet by which they cling to
one another, make them continuous instead of contiguous.

Between this new condition of the bunch and its former condition there is surely a striking difference. And what can be
the nature of this difference unless it lies in the fact that the
bunch now forms a whole, a single animal, one and the same,
whereas formerly it was only a collection of animals? . . . All
our organs——"

MLLE. DE L'ESPINASSE. Did you say, "all our organs"?

BORDEU. Yes. For anyone who has practiced medicine and
made a few observations——

MLLE. DE L'ESPINASSE. Why, that's just the language he used!
Now tell me what comes after that.

BORDEU. After that? ". . . are only distinct animals held together by the law of continuity in a general bond of sympathy,
unity, or identity."

MLLE. DE L'ESPINASSE. It's astounding—that's just what he
said, almost word for word. Now I can proclaim to the whole
world that there is not the slightest difference between a wide-
awake physician and a dreaming philosopher.

BORDEU. People have had their suspicions before now. But
is that all he said?

MLLE. DE L'ESPINASSE. Not by any means—you have no idea!
After that babbling of yours, or of his, if you prefer, he spoke
to me and said: "Mademoiselle?"—"Yes, my dear."—"Come
closer . . . closer . . . still closer . . . I want you to do something for me."—"What is it?"—"Hold this bunch of bees—
there, are you sure you've got it? Good. Let's make an experiment."—"How?"—"Take your scissors—are they good and
sharp?"—"They cut beautifully."—"Then reach gently over
with them—very gently—and cut these bees apart for me. Only
take care not to snip through their bodies. Cut just at the
point where they have grown together by their feet. Don't
be afraid. You may hurt them a little, but it won't kill them.
. . . Excellent! You have a touch as light as a fairy's. . . . Now
do you see how they fly away, each in a different direction?
They fly away one by one, two by two, three by three. What
a lot there are! Well, now, if you have really understood what
I've been up to——Did you understand it all?"—"Oh yes, very
well indeed."—"Well, now we will suppose . . . we will suppose——" Really, Doctor, I took in so little of what I was

writing down, and he spoke in such a faint voice—this next part of my notes is so scribbled that I'm afraid I can't read it.

BORDEU. I'll fill it in if you wish.

MLLE. DE L'ESPINASSE. If you can.

BORDEU. Nothing could be simpler. "Suppose that these bees are very small, so small that their vital parts would always be missed by the thick blade of your scissors: then you could keep on dividing and subdividing as long as you pleased without killing a single bee. In that case the whole bunch, made up of imperceptibly small bees, would be a genuine polyp which you could destroy only by crushing it. The difference between a bunch of continuous bees and a bunch of bees that are merely contiguous is precisely the same as the difference between ordinary animals like ourselves, or like fish or worms, and the little snakelike creatures of the polyp family. We need make only a few slight modifications in this same theory——" (Here Mlle. de L'Espinasse gets up suddenly and goes to pull the bell cord to summon a servant.) Be quiet and walk softly, Mademoiselle, or you will wake him up, and he needs rest.

MLLE. DE L'ESPINASSE. I forgot all about that, I was so astonished at what you said. (To the servant, who comes into the room.) Which one of you went to fetch the doctor?

SERVANT. I did, Mademoiselle.

MLLE. DE L'ESPINASSE. How long ago was that?

SERVANT. I got back less than an hour ago.

MLLE. DE L'ESPINASSE. Did you take anything with you to give to him?

SERVANT. No, nothing at all.

MLLE. DE L'ESPINASSE. No papers?

SERVANT. Not a single one.

MLLE. DE L'ESPINASSE. Well, then, that's that. You may go. . . . I can't get over it. You see, Doctor, I was suspicious that one of them had shown you my scribbling.

BORDEU. I assure you that no one did any such thing.

MLLE. DE L'ESPINASSE. Well, Doctor, now that I have taken the measure of your abilities I can see that you would be a great help to me in polite society. In any event, his dream didn't stop at that point.

BORDEU. So much the better.

MLLE. DE L'ESPINASSE. You don't see anything alarming in it so far?

BORDEU. Not in the least.

MLLE. DE L'ESPINASSE. Well, then he went on: "Come, now, Philosopher, your idea is that there are polyps of all sorts, even human·polyps. . . . Only we do not find any such thing in nature."

BORDEU. He didn't know about those two girls who were attached to each other by the head, shoulders, back, buttocks and thighs, who lived stuck together that way up to the age of twenty-two, and who both died within a few minutes of each other. What did he say after that?

MLLE. DE L'ESPINASSE. Just some senseless talk of the sort you might hear in any insane asylum. He said: "Either that has already happened, or it will happen. And besides, who knows how things may be on some of the other planets?"

BORDEU. Perhaps there is no need to look so far afield.

MLLE. DE L'ESPINASSE. "Perhaps on Jupiter or Saturn there are human polyps! The males split up to make a new batch of males, and similarly with the females—what a joke that would be. . . ." Here he let out such bursts of laughter that I was frightened. "To think of men splitting up into an infinite number of little men the size of atoms, small enough to fold up in a sheet of paper like insects' eggs. They would spin their cocoons, which would take a certain time to pass through the chrysalis stage, then break out of the cocoon and escape as butterflies. Why, you could make a whole human society or at least populate a whole province with the pieces of one individual. I find this idea wholly fascinating to con-template. . . ." The outbursts of laughter began again. "If somewhere a man could change himself into a million little men of microscopic size, then the people there ought to be less reluctant to die. The loss of a man would be so easy to make good that it would probably be accepted with little regret."

BORDEU. That may seem like an extravagant notion, but it is what actually takes place with all the existing species of lower animals, and it will doubtless be true of future species too. Even if man does not change into an infinite number of men, at least he changes into an infinite number of tiny animals whose future changes in shape or structure it is impossible to foresee. Who knows whether our species is not simply a hatchery for another generation of beings who will supplant our species after the lapse of countless centuries, during which successive modifications will occur?

MLLE. DE L'ESPINASSE. What is that you're muttering about, Doctor?

BORDEU. Nothing at all. I was only having a dream of my own. Go on reading, Mademoiselle.

MLLE. DE L'ESPINASSE. "Taking everything into consideration, though, I prefer our own method of replenishing the population," he added. "Philosopher, you who invariably know what's going on, here or elsewhere, tell me this—when the different parts of a man are split up, won't each of them yield men of as many different kinds? The brain, the heart, the lungs, the feet, the hands, the testicles . . . Just think how that would simplify morality! . . . You would have a man who was born a . . . A woman who came from . . ." Doctor, will you excuse me if I pass over some of this? . . . "You would have a warm room lined with little vials. and on each of these vials there would be a label: warriors, magistrates, philosophers, poets—this vial for courtiers, that one for whores, that one for kings."

BORDEU. Crazy as it sounds, it's an amusing idea. All this is only a man talking in a dream, yet it puts me in mind of some actual phenomena that are rather interesting.

MLLE. DE L'ESPINASSE. At this point he began to mumble something I couldn't quite make out—all about seeds, shreds of meat ground up in water, different races of animals that he saw being born or dying out. With his right hand he seemed to be imitating the tube of a microscope while with his left hand he tried to show, I think, the aperture of a vessel. He looked through the tube into the vessel and said: "Our Voltaire may make as many jokes about it as he likes, but Needham*

---

* John Turberville Needham, English microscopist and physiologist who collaborated with Buffon. In his *Microscopic Observations* (1751) he put forward the theory of spontaneous generation to account for the existence of tiny eel-like creatures he had observed in flour that had been allowed to spoil in a jar that was closed to everything—unfortunately—but air.

is right about his little eels; I have to believe the evidence of
my own eyes and I can actually see them. My, what a swarm!
Look how they dart back and forth! See them squirm!" Then
he began comparing the vessel, in which he saw so many
instantaneous births, with the whole universe, pretending to
see in a single drop of water the history of the entire world.
This idea struck him as a great one, he thought it altogether
in the spirit of sound scientific procedure, which learns about
large bodies by studying small ones, and he said: "In Needham's drop of water everything is over and done with in an
instant. In the world at large the same phenomena occupy a
little more time; but what is our human lifetime in comparison with the infinite duration of the universe? Less, surely,
than this drop, which I take on the point of a needle, is in
comparison with the boundless space that surrounds us. You
have an infinite succession of little animals inside the fermenting atom, and the same infinite succession of tiny animals inside the other atom that is called the Earth. Who knows
how many races of animals have preceded us? Who knows how
many will follow the races that now exist? Everything changes,
everything passes away—only the Whole endures. The world
is perpetually beginning and ending; every moment is its
beginning and its end; there has never been any other kind
of world, and there never will be any other.

"In this immense ocean of matter there is not one molecule
that is just like another, not one that is exactly like itself
from one instant to the next. *Rerum novus nascitur ordo*—
A new order of things is born*—this is the unchanging device
of all that is. . . ." Then, with a sigh, he added: "Ah, how vain
is all human thought! How poor are all our glories, all our
labors! How wretched we are! How petty our ideas! There
is nothing substantial except eating, drinking, living, making
love and sleeping. . . . Mademoiselle de L'Espinasse, where
are you?"—"Here I am." Then his face became flushed. I
thought I should feel his pulse, but I couldn't find where he
had put his hand. He seemed to be having some sort of con-
vulsion. His mouth fell open; his breathing was labored;
finally he gave a deep sigh, then a weaker and still deeper

* Virgil, *Bucolics*, IV, 5.

one; then he turned his head on his pillow and fell sound
asleep. I was watching him very attentively and I felt a peculiar
kind of excitement that I could not account for; my heart began to pound violently, though not from fear. After a few moments more I noticed a gentle smile playing on his lips, and he
said very softly: "If there is a planet where men multiply the
way fish do, where a man's spawn is merely deposited on that
of a woman . . . At least my own frustration would be easier to
bear in that case. . . . It's a shame to waste anything that could
serve some useful purpose. Mademoiselle, if only this stuff
could be gathered up and sent in a closed flask the first thing
tomorrow morning to Needham . . ." Doctor, how can you say
that he isn't out of his mind?

BORDEU. In your presence, what can I say?

MLLE. DE L'ESPINASSE. In my presence or not, it all comes
to the same thing. You don't know what you're talking about.
Well, after that I had hopes that the rest of the night would
be peaceful.

BORDEU. That would ordinarily be the case after what you
have described.

MLLE. DE L'ESPINASSE. But not in this case. About two o'clock
in the morning, he began to worry again about his drop of
water, which he called a mi-cro . . .

BORDEU. A microcosm.

MLLE. DE L'ESPINASSE. That's the word. He was struck with
admiration for the acuteness of the ancient philosophers.
Either he said, or his Philosopher said—I don't really know
which one it was—"When Epicurus maintained that the earth
contained the seeds of all living things, and that all animals
were the products of fermentation, what if he had proposed
to show on a small scale the same picture that he draws to
represent the beginning of the world on a large scale—what
kind of answer could one make? . . . But you have that very
same picture in front of your eyes, and yet it teaches you
nothing. . . . Who knows—perhaps the fermentation is complete and its products have all been used up. Who can tell
what place we humans occupy in the chain of animal species?
Who knows whether those deformed bipeds who are only four

feet tall, and who are called men by those who visit the polar regions—who knows whether these creatures might not soon cease to be called men if they were only slightly more misshapen? Perhaps they are just the remnant of a race that is passing away. Who can say that the same thing is not true of any other species of animals? Who can be sure that the universe is not tending to degenerate into an inert and motionless deposit of sediment? Who can tell how long such a state of inertia might last? Who knows what new species might once again arise from such a vast heap of sensitive, living particles? Why not just one kind of animal? How did the elephant originate? Perhaps this huge beast, as he appears to us now, was once only a single atom—we know that both elephants and atoms exist, and we need appeal only to motion and to the other various properties of matter. . . . But was the elephant, with all his vast bulk, a product of sudden fermentation? Well, why not? The ratio between this great quadruped and the womb he was formed in is less than the ratio a worm bears to the grain of flour that produced it. Still, a worm is only a worm. . . . That only means, though, that the marvelous complexity of his organization is hidden from us by his extreme smallness. . . . The real miracle is life itself—sensitivity—and this miracle can be accounted for. . . . Once I have seen inert matter change into something sensitive I should no longer marvel at anything. . . . Can I not compare the small number of elements fermenting in the hollow of my hand with the immense reservoir of elements that are to be found everywhere—inside the bowels of the earth, all over its surface, in the depths of the sea, and even in the currents of the air! . . . However, since the same causes go on operating, why shouldn't the same effects follow? Why should we no longer see [Lucretius's] bull pushing his horns up through the crust of the earth, straining, with his feet pressed against the underlying rocks, as he struggles to free his heavy body from the soil? . . . Let's suppose that all the existing species of animals should die out; let us wait several million centuries while the great inert sediment goes on working. Perhaps to renew the various species it requires a period ten times as long as that of their actual duration. Consider carefully, and do not make hasty judgments about what nature can or cannot do. You have proof of two fundamental processes—the passage of matter from the inert to the sensitive state, and spontaneous generation—that should be enough for you. Draw the right conclusions from them, and in the midst of a natural order where there is neither absolute bigness nor absolute smallness, neither absolute permanence nor absolute change, beware of falling into the fallacy of the ephemeral . . ." Doctor, what does he mean by the fallacy of the ephemeral?

BORDEU. He means the mistake made by a transitory being who believes in the immutability of things.

MLLE. DE L'ESPINASSE. Like Fontenelle's rose who said that so far as any rose could remember, no gardener had ever died?

BORDEU. Precisely. The illustration is both striking and profound.

MLLE. DE L'ESPINASSE. Why don't your present-day philosophers express themselves as gracefully as Fontenelle did? Then we could understand them.

BORDEU. Frankly, I'm not sure that his frivolous manner is well suited to serious subjects.

MLLE. DE L'ESPINASSE. Well, just what do you mean by a serious subject?

BORDEU. Why, for example, the various forms of sensitivity, the formation of a conscious being, the unity of such a being, the origins of animal life, its duration, and all the different problems connected with these matters.

MLLE. DE L'ESPINASSE. As for myself, I'd call that a nonsensical hodgepodge, something that may be all right to dream about when you are asleep; but I can't see why a wide-awake person should bother his head about it, assuming that he has any common sense.

BORDEU. And why do you take that point of view, if I may ask?

MLLE. DE L'ESPINASSE. It's just that some of those questions are so obvious that it is useless to go into their explanations, while the rest are so obscure that no one can ever make head or tail out of them, and none of them has the slightest practical utility.

BORDEU. Is it your opinion, Mademoiselle, that it makes no difference whether one affirms or denies the existence of a Supreme Intelligence?

MLLE. DE L'ESPINASSE. It makes a great deal of difference.

BORDEU. Do you believe that one can decide for or against the Supreme Intelligence without knowing what basis there is for one's ideas about the eternity of matter and about its properties, about the distinction between mind and matter, about the nature of man and about the way animals come into existence?

MLLE. DE L'ESPINASSE. Well, no.

BORDEU. Then these questions are not so fruitless as you just said they were.

MLLE. DE L'ESPINASSE. I see your point. But what good will it do me to acknowledge their importance if I have no way of getting to the bottom of them?

BORDEU. How can you get to the bottom of them if you never even examine them? But will you allow me to ask you which ones seem so obvious to you that there is no need to examine them?

MLLE. DE L'ESPINASSE. Well, take for instance the question of my unity—my identity. Mercy on us! It seems to me that there is no need for so many words to arrive at the conclusion that I am myself, that I have always been myself, and that I shall never be anyone else.

BORDEU. No, of course not. The fact is obvious enough, but it isn't at all clear how the fact can be accounted for, especially if we adopt the hypothesis of those who hold that the real world is all of one substance and who account for the production of men and animals by supposing that sensitive molecules have simply been juxtaposed to one another. Each sensitive molecule had its own identity before the contact occurred. So how did it lose that identity, and how did the consciousness of the whole come into existence as the result of all these losses of identity?

MLLE. DE L'ESPINASSE. I should think that contact alone would be sufficient. There is an experiment that I have performed a hundred times . . . But, wait just a moment—I must look and see what is going on behind those bed curtains. . . .

Good, he's asleep. . . . When I put my hand on my thigh, I am very much aware at first that my hand is separate and distinct from my thigh, but after a little time has passed, and the temperature of the two parts has become equal, I can no longer tell which is which. I can't tell where one begins and the other leaves off, and it is the same as if the two parts were one.

BORDEU. Yes, unless someone comes along and pricks one or the other of them; then you know soon enough which is which. Therefore there must be something in you that knows very well whether your hand or your thigh has been pricked, and this something cannot be your foot—it cannot even be the hand that has been pricked. The hand felt the pain, but it is something else that knows what happens without feeling the pain.

MLLE. DE L'ESPINASSE. Why, I should think it's my head.

BORDEU. Your whole head?

MLLE. DE L'ESPINASSE. No, but look here, Doctor—I'll have to give you an example if I am to make myself clear. Women and poets seem to reason mostly by examples. So imagine a spider . . .

D'ALEMBERT. Who's that? Is that you, Mademoiselle de L'Espinasse?

MLLE. DE L'ESPINASSE. It's all right, go to sleep. (Mlle. de L'Espinasse and the Doctor remain silent for a time; then Mlle. de L'Espinasse says in a low voice:) I think he's gone back to sleep.

BORDEU. I think not. I hear him making some kind of noise.

MLLE. DE L'ESPINASSE. You're right. Do you suppose he is starting to dream again?

BORDEU. Shhh! Let's listen.

D'ALEMBERT. Why am I as I am? Obviously, because I had to be such. Here on this earth, to be sure. But what if I had been somewhere else? At the North Pole? Or at the Equator? Or on Saturn? . . . If a distance of several thousand leagues could alter my species, what would happen if I had been born several thousand terrestrial diameters from here? . . . And if the whole universe is in a state of flux, as the spectacle of nature everywhere plainly shows, what might not be the results, here or elsewhere, of the passage of millions of centuries with their attendant changes? Who knows what it would be like to be a conscious, thinking being on Saturn? . . . But do thought and consciousness exist on Saturn? . . . Why not? . . . Would a conscious, thinking being on Saturn possess more senses than I do? . . . Ah well, if he does, how unhappy that poor Saturnian must be! . . . Without senses we should have no wants.

BORDEU. He is right. Our organs produce our wants, and the other way around too—wants produce organs.

MLLE. DE L'ESPINASSE. Doctor, are you out of your mind too?

BORDEU. What's unreasonable about that? I have seen a pair of stumps grow slowly into a pair of arms.

MLLE. DE L'ESPINASSE. I don't believe it!

BORDEU. Well, what I said isn't strictly true. But to be precise, what I have seen is two shoulder blades gradually get longer, taking the place of two arms that were missing. They move like a pair of tweezers and finally become two stumps.

MLLE. DE L'ESPINASSE. But that's absurd!

BORDEU. It is a fact just the same. What if you had a long series of armless generations? Imagine that these same efforts go on. Eventually you might see the two parts of the pincer stretch out, grow longer and longer, cross over each other, reach around to the rear and back to the front again, sprout fingers at their extremities, and so reconstitute the missing arms and hands. The original shape of a creature changes and develops in response to necessity and habitual use. People nowadays walk so little and work so little, and they think so much, that I wouldn't be surprised if man should wind up by becoming all head.

MLLE. DE L'ESPINASSE. All head? Nothing but head! That's not good for very much. As for me, I look forward to the time when our unrestrained amorousness . . . what silly ideas you put into my mind!

BORDEU. Shhh!

D'ALEMBERT. So, then, I am what I am because it was necessary that I should be what I am. Change the entire universe, and it necessarily follows that I will be different; but the universe is always changing. . . . Man is merely a common phenomenon, while a monster is only a rare phenomenon, but both are equally natural, equally necessary, equally subject to the general order of the universe. . . . And what is there in that to cause astonishment? . . . All beings participate in the existence of all other beings; consequently every species . . . all nature is perpetually in flux. . . . Every animal is more or less human; every mineral is more or less vegetable; every plant is more or less animal. There is nothing precise in nature. . . . Father Castel's colored ribbon* . . . Yes, Father Castel, nature resembles nothing so much as your colored ribbon. Every particular thing is only more or less something—more or less earth, more or less water, more or less air, more or less fire; more or less a member of one class or another. . . . Hence we can't speak of the essence of a particular being. . . . No, beyond a doubt, because there is no single property which the being in question does not share with some other being . . . and because it is only the greater or less proportion of such a property that makes us attribute it to one being to the exclusion of another. . . . And you still speak of individuals, you poor philosophers! Stop worrying about your supposed individuals and answer me this question: Is there in all nature one single atom that is absolutely like another atom? . . . No. . . . Then will you not agree that in nature everything is bound up with everything else, and that it is impossible that there should be any gap in the chain of beings? What, then, do you mean when you talk about individuals? There isn't any such thing; no, there isn't any such thing. . . . There is only a single great individual—the whole universe. Within this whole, as in a machine or in any animal, there is a part which you may label such and such; but when you give the name of individual to this part of the whole you are making use of a false concept—just as much as if you were to give the name of individual to a bird's wing or to a feather on its wing. . . . Again, poor philosophers, you speak

---

* An attempt to produce "visual music" by means of ribbons of various colors, the unwinding of each color being regulated by pressing a key.

of essences! You had better give up your essences. Examine instead the general mass, or if your imaginations are too petty to take that idea in, examine only your own ultimate origins and your ultimate dissolutions. . . . Oh, Archytes!—you who were able to measure the globe—what are you now? A pinch of dust! . . . What is a living creature? . . . The sum of a certain number of tendencies. . . . Can it be that I myself am anything more than a tendency? . . . No, I am tending toward a limit. . . . And what about a species? . . . A species is only a tendency toward a common end that is peculiar to it. . . . And life itself? . . . Life is a series of actions and reactions. . . . As long as I am alive, I act and react as a mass; when I am dead I shall act and react in the form of disparate molecules. . . . Does this mean that I shall never die? . . . Well, of course, in that sense I shall never die, neither I nor anything else for that matter. . . . Being born, living, dying—these are only changes of form. . . . And what difference is there between one form and another? Each form experiences the happiness and unhappiness that belong to it. So it is with the elephant and the flea and all the intermediate beings. . . . So also with all those between the flea and the living, sensitive molecule, the origin of all the others—there is not an entity in all the natural world that does not know suffering and enjoyment.

MLLE. DE L'ESPINASSE. He seems to have stopped speaking.

BORDEU. Yes. And what he said was a rather fine soliloquy. It was full of philosophical insights, too. Although for the moment these ideas have to be purely speculative, I am confident that the more our knowledge of man increases, the more they will be verified.

MLLE. DE L'ESPINASSE. What had we been talking about?

BORDEU. Bless my stars, I don't remember any more—I got to thinking about so many things while I was listening to him!

MLLE. DE L'ESPINASSE. Wait, I've got it. . . . I was starting to explain about my spider.

BORDEU. Oh yes, of course.

MLLE. DE L'ESPINASSE. Doctor, please pull your chair closer to me. Now, imagine that you see a spider sitting in the center of her web. If you disturb a single thread, you will see how the alert little creature comes running. Well, then, what if the threads which this insect spins out from her body—and can swallow up again whenever she pleases—what if those threads were a sensitive part of her body?

BORDEU. I follow your thought. You mean to suggest that inside your own body, in some region of your brain—perhaps in the part known as the meninges—there may be one or more points to which are conveyed all the sensations that are produced anywhere along the threads.

MLLE. DE L'ESPINASSE. Yes, that's my idea exactly.

BORDEU. Your idea is as sound as anything can be. And don't you see that approximately the same thing takes place in the cluster of bees that we were talking about?

MLLE. DE L'ESPINASSE. Oh, I'm so glad my idea is sound! I must have been speaking prose without knowing it.*

BORDEU. You were speaking very good prose, as I hope to be able to show you. Those who know man only in the form that he presents to us at birth do not have the least idea of what man is. His head, his feet, his hands, all his limbs, all his bowels, all his organs of sense, his nose, eyes, ears, heart, lungs, intestines, muscles, bones, nerves, membranes—all these, strictly speaking, are nothing but gross extensions of a network which takes form, grows, extends, and throws out a multitude of imperceptibly fine threads.

MLLE. DE L'ESPINASSE. That's what I mean by my web, and my spider is the point from which all those threads start.

BORDEU. Perfect!

MLLE. DE L'ESPINASSE. But where in the human body do you find the threads, and where does the spider sit?

BORDEU. The threads run everywhere. There is scarcely a point on the surface of your body that is not connected to the end of one of those threads. And the spider has her nest in that part of your brain that I just mentioned—the meninges —and if you were so much as to tap lightly on that part

---

* Monsieur Jourdain, the protagonist of Molière's *Le Bourgeois Gentil-homme*, marveled that he had, without knowing it, been speaking prose all his life.

of the brain, you would induce unconsciousness in the whole organism.

MLLE. DE L'ESPINASSE. Well, if the smallest particle should set up a vibration in one of the filaments of the spider's web, she would immediately take alarm, she would run hither and yon. She sits in the center and learns everything that goes on in every single part of the wide dwelling that she has woven. Why is it that I don't know instantly all that happens in my own room—I mean the whole world—inasmuch as I am a mass of sensitive particles, and inasmuch as I am in contact with all the other particles and they with me?

BORDEU. The reason is that impulses get weaker in proportion to the distance from their point of origin.

MLLE. DE L'ESPINASSE. But if you tap ever so lightly on the end of a long rod, I will be able to hear the tap, provided I press my ear against the other end. The same result would occur if one end of the rod were touching Sirius and the other end touching the earth. If everything is continuous or contiguous with everything else, just as in the rod, if it really existed, why would I not hear everything that goes on in the vast spaces that surround me, especially if I put my ear close?

BORDEU. How do you know that you don't perhaps hear more or less of what goes on? But the distances are so great, the impulses are so weak and they jostle one another so much along the way—and besides, you are in the midst of so many assorted loud noises that dull your hearing. Finally, there are only contiguous bodies between you and Saturn, whereas what we require is continuity.

MLLE. DE L'ESPINASSE. What a pity!

BORDEU. Yes. Otherwise you would be God. Thanks to your identity with all the beings of the natural world you would know absolutely everything that takes place, and thanks to your memory you would know everything that has happened in the past.

MLLE. DE L'ESPINASSE. What about the future?

BORDEU. So far as the future is concerned, you would be able to make some highly probable guesses, but you would make some mistakes. It's exactly the same as though you were to try to guess what is going on inside your own body or at the tips of your toes or fingers.

MLLE. DE L'ESPINASSE. How do you know that the entire world does not have a brain, or that there is not in some corner of the universe a big or a little spider whose threads reach everywhere?

BORDEU. I don't know at all. Still less do I know that there never was one or that there will not be one sometime in the future.

MLLE. DE L'ESPINASSE. But how could a God of that sort——

BORDEU. Which is the only kind that makes sense——

MLLE. DE L'ESPINASSE. —have existed only at some time in the past? How could it first exist and then not exist?

BORDEU. Exactly. But since it would be a material God—part of the universe and subject to its processes—it might grow old and even die eventually.

MLLE. DE L'ESPINASSE. I have just had an even more fantastic idea.

BORDEU. You needn't bother to tell me—I know what you are thinking.

MLLE. DE L'ESPINASSE. All right, tell me what it is.

BORDEU. You see the possibility that intelligence may be implanted in bits of especially energetic matter, and you are wondering why that should not lead to the most prodigious effects imaginable. You aren't the first person to have that notion.

MLLE. DE L'ESPINASSE. I must say that I don't think any the more highly of you because you were able to guess my idea—it only proves that you have a splendid talent for nonsense!

BORDEU. I don't deny it. But is there anything in such an idea to upset anybody? You would have an epidemic of good and evil geniuses; nature's most constant laws would be turned upside down by the action of natural forces; the physical scientists would have a much harder time of it—but there still wouldn't be anything miraculous.

MLLE. DE L'ESPINASSE. Certainly it would be very rash to assert dogmatically what might happen—or to deny it either.

BORDEU. Fiddlesticks! Anyone who told you he had seen anything of the sort would be taken for the prince of liars. But let's not talk any more about these hypothetical beings, including your spider with an infinite web. Let's get back to the other network—you yourself—and the processes by which it came into existence.

MLLE. DE L'ESPINASSE. I have no objection.

D'ALEMBERT. Mademoiselle, is there someone else here with you? Who is that you're talking to?

MLLE. DE L'ESPINASSE. It's only the doctor.

D'ALEMBERT. How do you do, Doctor? What are you doing here at this hour in the morning?

BORDEU. You'll find out, but just now you'd best go back to sleep.

D'ALEMBERT. I won't deny that I need some sleep. I declare, I can't recall when I have had a more restless night. But will you still be here when I wake up?

BORDEU. Yes, I promise. . . . Now, Mademoiselle, I'll bet that when you try to think what you were like at the age of twelve, you have a mental picture of a half-size woman; for the age of eight you have the image of a quarter-size woman; you imagine that in the foetal stage you were a very tiny woman, and that in your mother's ovum you were a still tinier woman. That is, you think of yourself as having been always a woman identical in form with what you are at this moment; thus you tend to think that all the difference between what you were in the beginning and what you are now is owing only to successive increases in size.

MLLE. DE L'ESPINASSE. That's actually the way I do think of it.

BORDEU. Yet that notion is as false as anything can be. In the beginning, you were an imperceptibly small dot made up of still smaller molecules. These were dispersed throughout the blood and the lymph of your father and mother. The dot became a fine thread, then a bundle of threads. Up to this moment there wasn't the least hint of your present delightful shape—your eyes (handsome as they are now) were no more like eyes than the tip of a sea anemone's claw is like the sea anemone. But then each of the strands in the bundle of threads started to change—solely as the result of nutrition and in conformity with the special structure of each—into a particular organ: except, that is, for those organs that are produced by a complete change of form on the part of certain threads in the bundle. The bundle now comes to form a system capable of nothing but sensation; if it persisted in this form it would be capable of receiving all impressions that are nothing but pure sensations—cold, warmth, softness, hardness and the like. Perhaps memory would also be generated out of these sensations, coming, as they do, one after the other, and varying in kind and intensity; perhaps they would even produce self-consciousness and a very limited sort of reason. At any rate, this pure sensitivity, this simple sense of touch, undergoes diversification as the other sense organs develop from other threads—one forms an ear and gives rise to a sense of touch that detects noise or musical sounds, another becomes the palate and gives rise to a second sense of touch that detects flavors; a third develops into a nose and gives rise to a kind of touch that distinguishes odors; a fourth grows into an eye and provides a sense of touch that is sensitive to colors.

MLLE. DE L'ESPINASSE. If I understand your explanation, anyone would have to be a fool to deny the possibility of a sixth sense, or of a true hermaphrodite. How do we know that nature is unable to construct a bundle containing a special thread which could give rise to some sense organ of which we have no knowledge?

BORDEU. Or a bundle containing the threads to produce both sexes? I think you are quite right—it's a pleasure to discuss things with you because you not only grasp what is said to you; you go on to draw further conclusions that are astonishingly acute.

MLLE. DE L'ESPINASSE. You're just trying to encourage me, Doctor.

BORDEU. No, really, I'm only saying what I think.

MLLE. DE L'ESPINASSE. All right, I see what some of the threads in the bundle are for, but what happens to the others?

BORDEU. Do you expect me to believe that anyone but yourself would have thought of that question?

MLLE. DE L'ESPINASSE. Why not?

BORDEU. Well, at any rate you are not conceited. As for the rest of the threads, they ultimately come to form as many kinds of sensitivity as there are parts of the body or differentiated organs.

MLLE. DE L'ESPINASSE. What do you call those other organs? I've never heard of them.

BORDEU. They have no names.

MLLE. DE L'ESPINASSE. Why not?

BORDEU. Because there is not nearly so much difference between the sensations we detect through them as there is between the sensations that come through the medium of the sense organs proper.

MLLE. DE L'ESPINASSE. In all seriousness, do you really believe that we receive special kinds of sensation through our feet, hands, thighs, bellies, stomachs, chests, lungs and hearts?

BORDEU. Yes, I think so. If I dared, I would ask you whether, among those sensations that we don't discuss in polite society . . .

MLLE. DE L'ESPINASSE. I see your point. But I disagree. That sensation is the only one of its kind, more's the pity. Furthermore, how can you account for the multiplicity of these other sensations—more distressing than otherwise—with which you are pleased to endow us?

BORDEU. Account for them? It's simply a matter of being aware of most of them. If this great variety of senses of touch did not exist, we would know that we felt pleasure or pain, but we would not know where the feeling was located. Unless, of course, the source were visible. But then it would no longer be a matter of feeling; it would be a matter of experience and observation.

MLLE. DE L'ESPINASSE. You mean that if I should say that I had a pain in my finger, and someone should ask me how I could be sure that it was my finger that hurt, I would have to answer—not that I felt it—but that I felt pain and saw that my finger was injured?

BORDEU. Precisely. Come here and let me give you a kiss.

MLLE. DE L'ESPINASSE. With pleasure.

D'ALEMBERT. Doctor, I heard you kissing Mademoiselle. You show good judgment.

BORDEU. Now, to get back to the spider web—I have been giving the problem a good deal of thought, and it strikes me that the creature at the center needs to know more than just the location and direction of an impact on the web in order to make its instantaneous decisions.

MLLE. DE L'ESPINASSE. How should I know?

BORDEU. I'm glad you don't jump to a conclusion. Most people are apt to mistake acquired habits of long standing for natural qualities.

MLLE. DE L'ESPINASSE. And vice versa.

BORDEU. However that may be, you can see that it would be putting the cart before the horse, in speaking of the earliest stages of an animal's development, to limit one's attention and consideration solely to the mature creature. Instead, we must go back to its rudimentary beginnings. That's why it was essential to strip away all the complexity of your present physical constitution in order to get back momentarily to the time when you were nothing but a soft, fibrous, shapeless, wormlike substance, more comparable to the bulb or root of a plant than to an animal.

MLLE. DE L'ESPINASSE. If it should get to be the fashion to walk stark naked in the streets, I would be neither the first nor the last to conform. Therefore you are at liberty to do anything you like with me so long as I learn something. Now you say that each thread in the bundle develops into a special organ—what proof do you have that it works that way?

BORDEU. You have only to perform in thought an operation that nature often performs. Mutilate one of the threads in the bundle, the thread, for example, that is destined to form the eyes. What do you think would happen?

MLLE. DE L'ESPINASSE. Perhaps the animal would have no eyes.

BORDEU. Or perhaps it would have only a single eye in the middle of its forehead.

MLLE. DE L'ESPINASSE. A Cyclops, in other words.

BORDEU. A Cyclops.

MLLE. DE L'ESPINASSE. So perhaps Cyclops wasn't a legendary creature after all.

BORDEU. Very likely not. In fact, I can show you one any time you like.

MLLE. DE L'ESPINASSE. Does anyone know the cause of this abnormality?

BORDEU. Yes, the man who has dissected the monstrosity and found in it only a single optic thread. Now perform again in your mind one of nature's occasional experiments. Eliminate a second thread from the bundle—the one that's supposed to form the nose—and the animal will have no nose. Eliminate the thread for the ear and the animal will have no ears, or will have only one, and the anatomist who dissects it will find neither olfactory nor auditory threads, or will find only one instead of two. Keep on eliminating threads, and the animal will be deprived of its head, feet and hands; it won't live long, but it will have lived.

MLLE. DE L'ESPINASSE. Are there any cases where that has happened?

BORDEU. Yes indeed. And that's not all. If you double some of the threads in the bundle, the animal will have two heads, four eyes, four ears, three testicles, three feet, four arms, or six fingers on each hand. If you jumble the arrangement of threads in the bundle, the various organs will be out of place: the head will appear in the middle of the chest, the lungs will be on the left and the heart on the right. If you fuse two threads together, two organs will be merged: the arms will adhere to the body; the thighs, legs and feet will be all lumped into a single piece, and you will have every imaginable kind of monstrosity.

MLLE. DE L'ESPINASSE. Still, it seems to me that so complex a machine as an animal, a machine that develops from a single particle, from a turbulent fluid or perhaps from the chance mixture of two fluids—no one is any too clear about what he is doing on such an occasion, after all—a machine that builds itself little by little through a multitude of successive stages; a machine whose regularity or irregularity is determined by a packet of fine, loose, flexible threads and by a kind of embroidery frame where the smallest thread cannot be crushed, broken, displaced or removed without the most disastrous consequences for the whole organism—I should think these threads would be even more likely to get knotted or snarled in the place where the machine is constructed than would the skeins of silk in my embroidery basket.

BORDEU. The fact is that they are more frequently damaged than we generally assume. We don't perform enough dissections, so our ideas about foetal development are still very far from exact.

MLLE. DE L'ESPINASSE. But aren't there some striking cases of original deformity, aside from hunchbacks and clubfeet—misshapen babies whose malformation might be attributed to some hereditary defect?

BORDEU. Innumerable cases. Just recently, at the Charity Hospital in Paris, there died at the age of twenty-five a carpenter, a native of Troyes, by the name of Jean-Baptiste Mace, who was a victim of complications resulting from a chest fluxion. His internal organs, both in the chest and in the abdomen, were transposed—the heart was on the right instead of in its normal position on the left; the liver too was on the right; the stomach, the appendix, and the pancreas were near the right hypochondrium; the major artery bore to the liver on the left side the same relation as it would have if the liver had been on the right; in the long intestinal canal there is the identical transposition; the bowels are placed back to back against the lumbar vertebrae and form a horseshoe. And, after all that, they still want us to believe in final causes!

MLLE. DE L'ESPINASSE. Very strange!

BORDEU. Now if Jean-Baptiste Mace had been married and had had any children . . .

MLLE. DE L'ESPINASSE. Exactly, Doctor. Those children . . .

BORDEU. They would have had normal bodies, but some day the grandchild of one of those children—a century later, perhaps, for these deformities leap over several generations—would turn up with the same odd anatomy as his ancestor.

MLLE. DE L'ESPINASSE. But why do these leaps occur?

BORDEU. Who knows? It takes two to make a baby, as you are well aware. Perhaps one partner repairs the defects of the other, so that the defective network only reappears when the descendant of the freakish strain is predominant and so is able to determine the pattern of the network. In any event, the original and primary differences between animal species must be sought in the bundle of threads. And variations within the bundles of a single species account for all the individual freaks produced by that species.

(After a long interval of silence, Mlle. de L'Espinasse awakes from her reverie and arouses the doctor from his musings by making the following remark:) The silliest notion has just crossed my mind.

BORDEU. What is your notion?

MLLE. DE L'ESPINASSE. Perhaps men are nothing but a freakish variety of women, or women only a freakish variety of men.

BORDEU. That notion would probably have occurred to you a good deal sooner if you had known that a woman possesses all the anatomical parts that a man has. The only discoverable difference is this—one has a pouch that hangs outside and the other has a pouch that is reversed so as to go inside the body. A female foetus is virtually indistinguishable from a male foetus, and the part that gives rise to mistakes becomes less important in the female in proportion as the internal pouch develops. Nor does this part ever change so much that it entirely loses its original shape, for it retains this same shape in miniature, and is capable of behaving similarly. It, too, is the center of voluptuous sensations; it, too, has its glans and its foreskin; and you can see at its tip a dot that looks like the orifice of a urinary canal that has been blocked. In the man, there is a space between the anus and the scrotum that is called the perineum, and a seam extending from the base of the scrotum to the tip of the penis which seems to be the stitched-together opening of an original vulva. Furthermore, a woman whose clitoris is exceptionally large generally also has a beard, while eunuchs, who have none, exhibit well-padded thighs, hips that tend to assume the shape of a vase, and round kneecaps—in other words, after losing the characteristic organization of one sex they seem to revert to the characteristic organization of the other. Certain Arabs, who have been castrated by continual riding on horseback, have been known to lose their beards, start speaking in a treble voice, take to wearing women's clothes and to sitting with them in the wagons, crouch down to make water, and in general assume all the habits and mannerisms of women. . . . But all that is rather far afield from our discussion. Let's get back to our bundle of living, animated threads.

D'ALEMBERT. I think you are talking smut to Mademoiselle de L'Espinasse.

BORDEU. When you talk science you have to use technical words.

D'ALEMBERT. Of course, you're absolutely right. In that context they lose all the associations that would make them objectionable. Please go on, Doctor. You were just telling Mademoiselle that the womb is nothing but a scrotum that has been turned inside out and tucked inside the body. In the process, the testicles were spilled out of the pouch in which they had been contained and were tossed, one to the right and the other to the left, to the sides of the abdominal cavity. You were explaining, too, that the clitoris is a male member in miniature, and that in the female this male member gets smaller and smaller in proportion as the womb, or reversed scrotum, gets larger. Also——

MLLE. DE L'ESPINASSE. Yes, yes; but be quiet and keep your nose out of our business.

BORDEU. So you see, Mademoiselle, that in discussing the question of our sensations in general—which are all merely diversifications of the sense of touch—we must leave aside the various subsequent modifications of the network and bring all our attention to bear upon the network itself.

MLLE. DE L'ESPINASSE. All right. Now, I see that each thread of the sensitive network can be hurt or tickled at any point along its entire length. Pleasure or pain arises at this point or that, in one place or another, along one of the long "legs" of my spider—I keep getting back to my spider. Well, the spider is the central meeting place of all the "legs," and these only transmit the pleasure or pain to such and such a place, but without themselves feeling either pleasure or pain.

BORDEU. And that is the unvarying, uniform relation between all such impressions and the common center which constitutes the unity of the animal.

MLLE. DE L'ESPINASSE. And it is the memory of all these successive impressions that makes for every animal the history of its life and of itself.

BORDEU. And it is the memory and the comparisons following inevitably from all these impressions that produce thought and reasoning.

MLLE. DE L'ESPINASSE. But where are these comparisons made?

BORDEU. Why, at the center of the web.

MLLE. DE L'ESPINASSE. What about the rest of the network?

BORDEU. The center is all that matters, and at the center there is no specific or particular kind of sensitivity—the center does not see nor hear; nor does it feel pain. It is generated and then nourished; it grows out of a soft, inert, insensitive material, on which it rests just as if it were on a cushion— there it sits, listens, makes judgments and promulgates its decisions.

MLLE. DE L'ESPINASSE. But you say that it feels no pain?

BORDEU. None whatsoever. Though it is true that the slightest pressure on the right spot will make the judge suspend his sitting. Then the animal falls into a moribund condition. Remove the pressure and it resumes its vital functions; the animal is reborn.

MLLE. DE L'ESPINASSE. And how do you know all that? Has anyone ever been able to kill and then revive a man at will?

BORDEU. Yes.

MLLE. DE L'ESPINASSE. How, for goodness' sake?

BORDEU. It's a very interesting operation; I'll tell you all about it. Dr. La Peyronie, the surgeon, whom you may know, was called to attend a sick man who had received a violent blow on the head. The patient felt a pulsation inside his skull at that point. The surgeon was certain that an abscess had formed on the brain, and that there was not a moment to lose. He shaved the man's head and made an opening in the skull. The point of his instrument fell exactly on the center of the abscess, which was full of pus. The surgeon drained off the pus and was washing out the abscess with a syringe. Each time he squeezed out some liquid into the hollow of the abscess the patient would close his eyes, his limbs became rigid and still, all signs of life ceased. Then, as soon as the doctor took up the liquid again and thus relieved the center of the burden of the weight and pressure of the injected fluid, the patient would open his eyes, move his limbs, speak, feel sensations— in short, would come to life again.

MLLE. DE L'ESPINASSE. That's very odd. Did the patient get well?

BORDEU. Yes, he recovered, and when he was back on his feet again, he was able to think, to deliberate, to reason. He had as much wit, as much common sense and as much shrewdness as before—even though a very sizable part of his brain had been removed.

MLLE. DE L'ESPINASSE. I can see that this judge we are dealing with is a really remarkable fellow.

BORDEU. Yet he sometimes plays tricks on himself. He can be misled by bias arising from force of habit—for example, people sometimes feel pain in some part of their body that has been amputated. You can fool the judge whenever you please— just cross one finger over another and touch their two tips with a marble. The judge will decide that there are two marbles.

MLLE. DE L'ESPINASSE. That only means that he is like all the other judges in the world—he needs a great deal of experience; otherwise he will touch a piece of ice and cry that he has been burned.

BORDEU. There's still another aspect to the matter. The center of the web can enlarge the individual to an almost infinite size, or it can compress him practically to a pinpoint.

MLLE. DE L'ESPINASSE. I'm afraid I don't follow.

BORDEU. What is it that really limits the volume of space that your body seems to fill, that is, the sphere that really contains all your sensations?

MLLE. DE L'ESPINASSE. It seems to be limited by what I can see or touch.

BORDEU. That's all very well in the daytime, but at night how does it seem when you lie half awake in the dark, especially if you let your thoughts dwell on some abstract problem—how does it seem even in the daytime when your mind is taken up with some absorbing idea?

MLLE. DE L'ESPINASSE. There's no limit at all. I seem to be reduced to a single point in space; my body almost seems insubstantial, and I am aware only of my thoughts. I am unconscious of location, movement, solidity, distance and space. The universe is annihilated as far as I am concerned, and I am nothing in relation to it.

BORDEU. Well, then, under those conditions your being is concentrated as much as it possibly can be. On the other hand, there are perhaps no limits to its expansion, at least in theory. Once you have passed the threshold of sensory perception, whether by drawing into yourself—by condensing your being into itself—or by the opposite process of expansion, we have no longer any certainty about what will happen.

MLLE. DE L'ESPINASSE. I agree, Doctor. Often it seems to me, when I start to dream——

BORDEU. Just as with those who are suffering from dropsy——

MLLE. DE L'ESPINASSE. —that I am swelling and swelling——

BORDEU. —when they think their feet are big enough to touch the canopy over the bed.

MLLE. DE L'ESPINASSE. —that my arms and legs are stretching out toward infinity, and that the rest of my body is growing at the same rate. I feel that by comparison the giant Enceladus in the fable was only a pigmy, that Ovid's Amphitritus was just a dwarf, even though he could put his arms around the earth. I seem to tower up into the heavens, and I could easily embrace the earth.

BORDEU. Very well put. As for myself, I once knew a woman who had much the same experience, but in reverse.

MLLE. DE L'ESPINASSE. How was that? Do you mean that she thought she was getting smaller and smaller, shrinking by degrees into herself?

BORDEU. Exactly. She thought she was no bigger than a needle. She could see, hear, speak reasonably and make judgments, only she had a terrible fear of getting mislaid. She would shudder if the tiniest objects were brought near to her, and would not dare to budge from her place.

MLLE. DE L'ESPINASSE. I'd call that a very odd sort of dream—and very uncomfortable. Most disagreeable.

BORDEU. It had nothing to do with dreaming. It was just a symptom of the menopause.

MLLE. DE L'ESPINASSE. And did this delusion that she was an imperceptibly tiny woman persist very long?

BORDEU. Only an hour or two. Then she felt herself grow gradually back to her normal size.

MLLE. DE L'ESPINASSE. What in the world could have caused such extraordinary sensations?

BORDEU. In their natural, quiet state the threads that make up the bundle are under a certain tension; they have an elasticity, an habitual force that defines for us the real or imaginary size of our bodies. I say "real" or "imaginary" because the tension, or elasticity, or force is variable. Hence our bodies do not always seem the same size.

MLLE. DE L'ESPINASSE. Which goes to show that in the physical world as well as in the moral world we are inclined to think we are bigger than we actually are!

BORDEU. Cold makes us smaller, heat makes us larger, and a given individual may believe all his life that he is bigger or smaller than he actually is. If it should happen that the bulk of the bundle should be thrown into a state of excitation, if the fibers should swell up so that their incredibly numerous extremities pushed rapidly out beyond their usual limits—then the head, feet, arms and legs, and all the separate points on the surface of the body would seem to be flung out to a vast distance and the individual would feel like a giant. You will have the opposite phenomenon if the ends of the fibers are overcome by torpor, inertia or apathy.

MLLE. DE L'ESPINASSE. I can imagine that there would be no way to measure that sort of expansion. And isn't it conceivable that this torpor, apathy, or inertia that affects the ends of the fibers—this heavy feeling—might become permanently fixed after it had reached a certain degree of intensity, that it might be arrested . . .

BORDEU. That's exactly what happened to La Condamine when he lost his hearing. In that case the person would feel as though he were walking on a layer of balloons.

MLLE. DE L'ESPINASSE. In other words, he exists partly outside the limits reached by his sensory perceptions. I suppose that if all his senses should be affected by that kind of apathy, he would be a sort of miniature man who would go on living inside a dead man.

BORDEU. From which you might draw the conclusion that every animal is only a single point at its origin, and never finds out whether he is really anything more. But to get back to our subject——

MLLE. DE L'ESPINASSE. Which one?

BORDEU. Which one? Why, to the man who had his skull trepanned by La Peyronie. . . . I thought that was what you were asking me about—you wanted an example of a man who had been known to live and die by turns. . . . But there is an even better example.

MLLE. DE L'ESPINASSE. What sort of case was that?

BORDEU. It was a case of Castor and Pollux in real life—two babies, one of whom began to live as soon as the other was dead, and who died again as soon as the other began to live.

MLLE. DE L'ESPINASSE. That's a likely story! And how long did this go on?

BORDEU. The pair lived for two whole days, an existence that they shared equally by turns, so that each was alive for a day and dead for a day altogether.

MLLE. DE L'ESPINASSE. I'm afraid, Doctor, you are taking advantage of my gullibility. Watch out! If I catch you just once trying to fool me, I'll never believe another word you say.

BORDEU. Tell me, do you often read the *Gazette de France?*

MLLE. DE L'ESPINASSE. No, never. Despite the fact that it is written by two very intelligent gentlemen.

BORDEU. See if you can borrow the number for September 4th last, and you will find that at Rabastens, in the diocese of Albi, two baby girls were born who were joined together back to back, united by the last lumbar vertebra, by the buttocks and in the lower gastric region. The only way to hold one of

them upright was to turn the other upside down. When they
were put in a prone position they could look each other in
the face, for their thighs were bent upward between their two
bodies and their lower legs stuck still further up in the air
between them. Halfway around the circle where their bodies
joined in the lower gastric region you could distinguish their
sex. In a hollow in between the right buttock of one and the
corresponding left buttock of her sister there was a little anus
out of which excrement came.

MLLE. DE L'ESPINASSE. What an odd sort of creature!

BORDEU. They drank milk when it was given them from a
spoon, and they lived twelve hours each, as I told you, one
falling into unconsciousness as soon as the other revived, one
dead as long as the other was alive. The first interval, during
which one was in a coma and the other awake, lasted four
hours. After that the periods of alternating life and death grew
shorter, and finally they both died at the same instant. It was
also observed that their navels followed the same rhythm of
expansion and contraction, becoming smaller when the baby
was unconscious and larger when she came back to life.

MLLE. DE L'ESPINASSE. Well, what is your explanation for
this alternation between death and life?

BORDEU. It may be valid or it may not. But inasmuch as
everyone looks at things from the point of view of his own
theories, and inasmuch as I don't want to be an exception to
the rule, I should say that in the case of these twins we have
the same phenomenon as in the case of the man who was
trepanned by La Peyronie, only duplicated because of the
fact that two individuals were joined together. The fibrous
networks of the two babies were so completely intermingled
that they acted and reacted upon one another. When the center
of one's network became dominant, it absorbed all the sensations from the network of the other, so that the other one
lost consciousness at that moment; the contrary effect occurred when the second baby's network got control of the
whole system. In the case of La Peyronie's patient the pressure
was exerted from above downward by the weight of a liquid,
while in the twins of Rabastens the pressure was exerted from

the bottom upward in the form of tension on some of the fibers of the network. This theory is supported by the alternating movement of the navel, which seemed to bulge out when one of the babies revived and to retract when it lost consciousness.

MLLE. DE L'ESPINASSE. At any rate, it sounds like a case of two souls joined together.

BORDEU. A single animal with two sets of sensory organs and two centers of consciousness.

MLLE. DE L'ESPINASSE. Yet it only had the use of one of them at any given moment. Still, who can tell what might have happened if the animal had survived?

BORDEU. Do you mean, what sort of pattern of experience would have been gained from all their successive periods of consciousness—the source of all the strongest habits that one can imagine—what sort of reciprocal relations might have been developed between the two brains?

MLLE. DE L'ESPINASSE. I mean their double set of senses, their double memory, their double capacity for paying attention. Half the creature observes, reads or meditates, while the other half rests; then the other half starts to perform the identical functions when its partner is tired. It would be a double creature leading a double life.

BORDEU. It seems entirely possible, and since nature, if given enough time, must bring about everything that is possible, some such being is bound to occur.

MLLE. DE L'ESPINASSE. How poorly endowed we ordinary human beings would seem in comparison with a creature like that!

BORDEU. Not necessarily. There are already quite enough uncertainties, contradictions and stupidities now that we have only one mind to a person—I can't imagine what might become of us if we each had two. . . . But it is half-past ten, and I have a patient to visit out on the edge of town.

MLLE. DE L'ESPINASSE. Do you suppose it would be a great loss to him if you didn't go see him tonight?

BORDEU. Perhaps it would be a gain. If nature can't do the job without me, there's not much chance that she and I can do it together, and there's no chance at all that I can do it without her help.

MLLE. DE L'ESPINASSE. Well, then, why not stay here?

D'ALEMBERT. Doctor, just one more question, and you're free to go visit your patient. In view of all the alterations I have undergone in the course of my existence—considering that I perhaps do not possess now a single one of the molecules that were in my body when I was born—tell me this: How does it happen that I have continued to be the same person both in my own eyes and from the viewpoint of other people?

BORDEU. You told us that while you were dreaming.

D'ALEMBERT. Have I been talking in my sleep?

MLLE. DE L'ESPINASSE. All night long. And what you were saying sounded so much like raving that I sent for the doctor early this morning.

D'ALEMBERT. How about your own remarks about the spider's legs that begin to vibrate all of their own accord, keeping the spider on the alert and causing the creature at the center of the web to speak? By the way, what does the creature say?

BORDEU. That he was able, thanks to his memory, to remain the same person both for himself and for others, and I would add that the slow rate of change in his molecular make-up also had something to do with it. If you had been whisked in an instant from infancy to old age, you would find yourself adrift in the world with the mind of a newborn baby. You would no longer be able to look back and say that you had been yourself either in your own eyes or in those of others, and, as far as you were concerned, the others would not have been themselves either. All sorts of relationships would have been annihilated; the whole history of your life would have been rendered meaningless so far as I'm concerned, and vice versa.

How could you know that this same fellow had not so long ago walked with a spring in his step, shifted heavy objects around with the greatest of ease, possessed the mental vigor for the most profound cogitation and the physical strength required for the most arduous as well as the most delicate exertions? You would be utterly unable to understand your own books, you would be unable to recognize yourself, you would be unable to recognize anyone else, and no one else would be able to recognize you. The appearance of the whole world would be entirely different so far as you were concerned.

Remember that there was less difference between what you were as a baby and what you were as a young man than there was between your youth and your sudden decrepitude. Remember, too, that while there was a continuous series of sensations between your babyhood and adolescence, the first three years of your existence have never been part of your conscious life's history. Imagine then how much the years of your youth would mean to you if there were no links between them and the moment when you suddenly became an old man. A senile D'Alembert would not retain the slightest recollection of the youthful D'Alembert.

MLLE. DE L'ESPINASSE. It's just as though you were a swarm of bees in which not a single one had had time to acquire any sense of belonging to the hive.

D'ALEMBERT. What do you mean by that?

MLLE. DE L'ESPINASSE. I mean simply that the monastic spirit persists only because the monastery replaces its members a few at a time, so that whenever a new monk enters the community he finds himself surrounded by a hundred old ones who influence him to think and feel as they do. If one bee leaves the swarm, the bee that takes his place very quickly gets into the swing of things.

D'ALEMBERT. Come, now—you're being silly with all this talk about monks, bees, hives and monasteries.

BORDEU. Not so silly as you might think. While there is only one center of consciousness in an animal, there are many, many different impulses. Every organ has impulses peculiar to itself.

D'ALEMBERT. How's that again?

BORDEU. I mean that the stomach may want food while the palate doesn't, and that the only difference between palate or stomach on one hand and the whole animal on the other is that the animal knows it wants something, while the palate and stomach have wants without knowing that they have them. You might say that palate and stomach stand in the same relation to the whole creature as the lower animals occupy in relation to man. As for the bees, they lose their individual identities, but keep their appetites and impulses. In the body each fiber is a simple animal, whereas a man is a compound animal—but let's save that theme for another occasion. At any rate, it takes much less than the sudden onset of senility to deprive a man of the consciousness of self. I have known a dying man, for example, to receive the last sacraments with deep piety, confess all his faults, ask forgiveness of his wife, embrace his children, call his friends to his bedside, talk with his physician, give instructions to his servants, dictate his last will, put all his affairs in order—all with the most sober judgment and the most complete presence of mind. Then, unexpectedly, he takes a turn for the better, regains his health, and has not the slightest recollection of anything he said or did during his illness—that interval, sometimes a very long period of time, has simply dropped out of his life. There are even cases where people have picked up the thread of the very same action or conversation that had been interrupted by a sudden attack of illness.

D'ALEMBERT. Well, I remember how a certain pedant in one of the colleges of the University, who was taking part in a public debate, and who was, as usual, all puffed up with a sense of his own omniscience, was tied up in knots, as the saying goes, by a Capuchin whom he had always held in contempt. He, tied up in knots! And by whom? By a Capuchin, of all people! And on what subject? On the contingency of future events! The very branch of theology he had been studying all his life! And in what circumstances? Before a large audience! Before a crowd of his own students! He felt utterly discredited and humiliated. His mind busied itself so well with these ideas that he sank into a lethargic condition, forgetting completely the vast fund of learning he had so painfully acquired.

MLLE. DE L'ESPINASSE. I'd call that a stroke of good fortune!

D'ALEMBERT. And you are right. He still had his common sense intact, but he had forgotten everything he had ever learned. It was possible to teach him reading and writing, but he died about the time he had become a tolerably good speller. And this man was not at all stupid; it was even generally agreed that he was rather gifted as an orator.

MLLE. DE L'ESPINASSE. Since you have told the doctor your story, I want to tell him one I know. There was a young man, about eighteen or twenty years old, whose name I don't recall——

BORDEU. It was Monsieur de Schellemberg of Winterthur, and he was only fifteen or sixteen at the time.

MLLE. DE L'ESPINALLE. Well, this young man took a tumble and had his head rather violently shaken up.

BORDEU. Violently shaken up, indeed! He fell from the roof of a barn. His skull was fractured and he was unconscious for six months.

MLLE. DE L'ESPINASSE. Have it your own way. But do you know what happened to him as a result of that accident? It was the same thing that happened to your pedantic professor—he forgot everything he had ever known; he behaved just like a little boy. He went through a second period of infancy. He was timid and apprehensive. He played with babies' toys. If he was scolded for doing something naughty, he would go hide in a corner. He would ask to be put on the toilet to do Number One or Number Two. He was taught to read and write, and I forgot to tell you that he had to learn to walk all over again. Eventually he grew up to be a man, and a very able one, too; he wrote a book about natural history.

BORDEU. You mean he made the engravings to illustrate Sulzer's book on insects, classified according to the Linnaean system. I am familiar with his case. It happened in the canton of Zurich in Switzerland, and there are a great many similar cases. If you disturb the center of the bundle of fibers, you change the whole creature whose entire being seems to be concentrated there, sometimes dominating the rest of the network of threads and sometimes dominated in turn by them.

MLLE. DE L'ESPINASSE. In other words, the creature is either despotically or anarchically governed?

BORDEU. Despotism is a very good term to apply. The center of the bundle gives orders and all the other parts obey. If that is the situation, then the creature is master of itself—*compos mentis*, of sound mind.

MLLE. DE L'ESPINASSE. Whereas if anarchy prevails, and all the threads of the network rise up in rebellion against their sovereign, then there is no longer any supreme authority.

BORDEU. Precisely. When a person is swept away by passion, when he is delirious, when he is threatened with great danger, if the master directs the whole strength of all his subjects toward a single end, the weakest of beings sometimes gives proof of unbelievable strength.

MLLE. DE L'ESPINASSE. Would you say that when ladies have the vapors they are suffering from a kind of anarchy that is peculiar to them?

BORDEU. It certainly resembles a weak administration in which each subordinate tries to arrogate to himself as much of the master's authority as possible. I know of only one remedy, and it is an infallible one, though difficult to apply. It can only work if the center of the sensitive web, that part that constitutes the real self, can be induced by some powerful motive to recover its authority.

MLLE. DE L'ESPINASSE. Well, what is the outcome, as a rule?

BORDEU. Either that the center successfully reasserts its authority or that the organism dies. If there were time, I would tell you about two odd cases of this sort.

MLLE. DE L'ESPINASSE. Well, Doctor, the hour of your visit in the suburbs is past and your patient no longer expects you.

BORDEU. Some day I will learn not to come here when I have any work to do, because once here I can never break away.

MLLE. DE L'ESPINASSE. Now that you have spoken so frankly and gotten that off your chest, suppose you tell us about those two cases.

BORDEU. This one should satisfy you for today. There was a woman who had just given birth to a child; as a result, she suffered a most alarming attack of the vapors—compulsive tears and laughter, a sense of suffocation, convulsions, swelling of the breasts, melancholy silence, piercing shrieks—all the most serious symptoms—and this went on for several years. Now this woman was passionately in love, and eventually she began to think she saw signs indicating that her lover had grown weary of her illness and complaints and was beginning to break off their affair. That was when she decided that she must either get well or make an end of herself. In this way there began a sort of civil war inside her own consciousness. Sometimes this war would turn to the advantage of the master; sometimes the subjects would get the upper hand. Whenever the two sides were equal, so that the force exerted by the fibers exactly counterbalanced that of the center of the bundle, she would fall to the ground as though dead. Then, when carried to her bed, she would lie for hours on end, entirely motionless and almost lifeless. On other occasions the effect would be only one of general lassitude or exhaustion or loss of consciousness from which it often seemed she would never recover. For six months she kept up the struggle. Whenever the rebellion began in her fibers she was able to feel it coming on. She would stand up, run about, busy herself with the most vigorous forms of physical exercise, climb up and down stairs, saw wood or shovel dirt. She would make the center of her network, the organ of will power, as rigid as possible by saying to herself: You must conquer or die. At the end of a long succession of victories and defeats the head finally won out, and the conquered "subjects" had been so thoroughly reduced to submission that, although this woman has had to contend with all sorts of domestic troubles and has suffered from various sorts of illness, she has never had the least tendency to the vapors since that time.

MLLE. DE L'ESPINASSE. Good for her! But I think that in her place I could have done as well as she did.

BORDEU. Yes, I think so, because you have a firm disposition, and if you were in love, you would not be lukewarm about it.

MLLE. DE L'ESPINASSE. I think I understand. A person will have a firm disposition if the center of the network is able, as a result of education, habit or organization, to dominate the various threads. If the center is dominated by the threads, the person has a weak disposition.

BORDEU. And from that proposition one could draw a whole series of further conclusions.

MLLE. DE L'ESPINASSE. First tell us your other case history, and then draw your conclusions.

BORDEU. There was a young woman who had been leading a rather loose life. One day she decided to turn over a new leaf and give up all her accustomed pleasures. No sooner was she alone than she started to have fits of melancholy and to suffer from the vapors. She sent for me. I advised her to go to the country and lead the life of a peasant, to dig with a shovel all day long, to sleep on a straw pallet and eat black bread. But she had no taste for that prescription. Well, then, said I, why not travel? So she set off for a tour of all the countries of Europe, and she regained her health along the way.

MLLE. DE L'ESPINASSE. That's not what you should have said, but never mind. Let's get to your conclusions.

BORDEU. There's no end to them.

MLLE. DE L'ESPINASSE. So much the better. Let's have them.

BORDEU. My courage fails me.

MLLE. DE L'ESPINASSE. Why should that be?

BORDEU. Because at the pace we are going we shall only be able to skim the surface of a lot of things without getting deeply into any of them.

MLLE. DE L'ESPINASSE. What's the harm in that? We are only having a conversation, not writing a treatise on the subject.

BORDEU. Well, for example—if the center of the network absorbs all the forces of the organism into itself, if the whole system functions, as it were, in reverse, as I believe happens in a man who meditates deeply, in a fanatic who sees the heavens open before his eyes, in the savage who sings in the midst of flames, in all cases of ecstatic frenzy or of insanity, whether involuntary or self-induced . . .

MLLE. DE L'ESPINASSE. Yes, what then?

BORDEU. Then the creature makes itself impervious to pain, for it exists only at a single point. I have never seen the priest of Calamo, of whom St. Augustine speaks, who carried the process of self-alienation to the point where he was insensitive to live coals. Nor have I seen those savages bound to the rack who laugh at their enemies and insult them by suggesting more exquisite forms of torment than the ones they are being made to undergo. Nor have I seen those dying gladiators in the arena who remember the graceful movements they learned in their gymnastic training. But I believe in the truth of all these things because I have seen with my own eyes a performance just as extraordinary as any of those I have mentioned.

MLLE. DE L'ESPINASSE. Please tell me about it, Doctor. I am as eager as any young child to hear stories that deal with unusual happenings. And, if these stories are to the credit of the human race, I am almost never inclined to quarrel with their truth.

BORDEU. In Langres, a small city in Champagne, there was a highly respected priest named Le Moni, or De Mony, who was deeply convinced of the truth of his religion—not to say saturated with it. He had a bad attack of gallstones, and had to undergo an operation to remove the stone. The date was arranged, and the surgeon, his assistants and I went to his house. He greeted us in a perfectly serene manner, undressed and stretched out on the bed. They wanted to tie him down, but he refused. "Just put me where you want me," he said. So they put his body in the right position. Then he asked for a big crucifix that hung at the foot of his bed. It was handed to him, and he clasped it tightly in his arms, holding his lips pressed firmly against it. He never moved a muscle all during the operation. Not once did he cry out, nor even groan, and when the stone was out he didn't even know it.

MLLE. DE L'ESPINASSE. Splendid. After that, who can doubt that the martyr who had his ribs broken when he was showered with rocks did not really see the heavens open before his eyes?

BORDEU. Have you had any experience with earache?

MLLE. DE L'ESPINASSE. No.

BORDEU. You're very fortunate. It is one of the most painful of all illnesses.

MLLE. DE L'ESPINASSE. I am very familiar with toothache, I regret to say. Is earache worse than that?

BORDEU. There's no comparison. A certain philosopher whom you know was tormented with one for two weeks. Finally one morning he said to his wife: "I don't think I have courage enough to get through the day." It seemed to him that the only thing to do was to get the better of the disease by trickery. He was able to immerse himself by degrees in some problem of metaphysics or geometry, and by that means succeeded in forgetting his ear. His dinner was brought to him, and he ate it without being aware of what he was doing. Bedtime arrived, and still he was unconscious to any pain. To be sure, the horrible throbbing began again the moment his mind ceased to be fully occupied, and its fury seemed to have redoubled, whether because the irritation itself was increased by fatigue or whether, because he was tired, he felt it more intensely.

MLLE. DE L'ESPINASSE. Such an agony as that must leave a person exhausted and lethargic. The same thing sometimes happens to that fellow over there in the bed.

BORDEU. He should be more careful. That condition can be dangerous.

MLLE. DE L'ESPINASSE. I tell him so time and time again, but he pays no attention.

BORDEU. He can't help doing as he does—that is the way he lives, and I suppose it will kill him eventually.

MLLE. DE L'ESPINASSE. Don't say such things—you terrify me.

BORDEU. Exhaustion and lethargy are indicative of something. They mean that the threads that make up the bundle have not been passive; on the contrary, the whole system has been subjected to powerful tension in the direction of the common center.

MLLE. DE L'ESPINASSE. And what if that tension or powerful striving should persist? What if it should get to be habitual?

BORDEU. Then the center of the bundle would develop a tic.

The creature would go mad, and such insanity is almost always incurable.

MLLE. DE L'ESPINASSE. Why?

BORDEU. Because there is a difference between a tic that affects one of the fibers and a tic that affects the center. The head can issue orders to the feet, but not the other way around. The center can command one of the fibers, but not vice versa.

MLLE. DE L'ESPINASSE. And how, if you please, do you account for the difference? Why, indeed, is it impossible that I should think with my whole body? That's a question I should have thought of asking you a long time ago.

BORDEU. You can be sure that there is only one center of consciousness.

MLLE. DE L'ESPINASSE. That's very easy to say.

BORDEU. It is physically impossible that it can be in more than one place, namely, at the center to which all sensations are transmitted, where the memory functions, where comparisons are made. Each thread is capable of detecting only a certain limited number of impressions, of successive, isolated sensations, none of which leaves any memory in the thread. The center can receive all kinds of sensations, can register them, can remember them—that is, retain a continuous impression. Besides, every animal is obliged, from the first moment of his existence, to refer himself to this center, to attach himself entirely to it, and to concentrate his whole existence in it.

MLLE. DE L'ESPINASSE. But what if my finger had a memory?

BORDEU. Then your finger would be able to think.

MLLE. DE L'ESPINASSE. And what, precisely, is memory?

BORDEU. It is a property of the center, the specific sense peculiar to the hub of the network, just as sight is the specific property of the eye. It is no reason for astonishment that the eye has no memory, any more than that the ear has no sense of vision.

MLLE. DE L'ESPINASSE. Doctor, I'm afraid you're evading my questions instead of really answering them.

BORDEU. No, I'm not trying to dodge anything. I'm only

telling you what I know, and I would know more if I were as well acquainted with the structure of the network's center as I am with the structure of the fibers, or if I had the same facilities for observing it. However, if I have to be vague about specific details, at least I can give a better account of myself when it comes to generalities.

MLLE. DE L'ESPINASSE. What generalities, for example?

BORDEU. Reason, judgment, imagination, insanity, idiocy, ferocity, instinct.

MLLE. DE L'ESPINASSE. All right, I see what you mean. All those things are nothing but consequences of the original or habitually acquired relation between the center of the web and its threads.

BORDEU. Exactly. The stock or trunk may be too vigorous in relation to its branches. In that case you get poets, artists, men of vivid imagination, cowards, fanatics, maniacs. If the trunk is too weak, you will get a thug, a savage brute. If the whole system is soft, loose and lacking in energy, you will have a fool. If the whole system is energetic, harmonious and well-ordered, you will get sound thinkers, philosophers or sages.

MLLE. DE L'ESPINASSE. Suppose one branch tyrannizes over the system. Then depending on which branch predominates you will have various kinds of instincts in the lower animals, special types of genius in men—a keen nose in the dog, acute hearing in fish, sight in eagles; D'Alembert will be a mathematician, Vaucanson a builder of machines, Grétry a musician, Voltaire a poet. All these aptitudes must be consequences of the fact that one thread of the network is more vigorous than the others, and more vigorous than the corresponding thread in other members of their species.

BORDEU. You will find a similar explanation for the traits that work to a person's disadvantage—the infatuation of an old man for a woman, or Voltaire's determination to go on writing tragedies.

(*Here the doctor falls into a pensive silence; presently Mlle. de L'Espinasse says to him:*)

MLLE. DE L'ESPINASSE. A penny for your thoughts, Doctor.

BORDEU. I was just thinking——

MLLE. DE L'ESPINASSE. About what?

BORDEU. About Voltaire.

MLLE. DE L'ESPINASSE. Well?

BORDEU. I was thinking of how a great man is put together.

MLLE. DE L'ESPINASSE. How is he put together?

BORDEU. How? Well, sensibility——

MLLE. DE L'ESPINASSE. Sensibility?

BORDEU. —or extreme mobility in certain threads of the network—that is the dominant attribute of mediocre people.

MLLE. DE L'ESPINASSE. Doctor! What a terrible thing to say!

BORDEU. I thought you'd find it shocking. But what exactly is a person who is said to have sensibility? He is a creature who is moved in all things by the behavior of his diaphragm. Just let a well-chosen word catch his ear, just let his eye light upon an odd situation, and—lo and behold—all of a sudden his insides are in a commotion, every fiber in his nervous system is agitated, he begins to tremble from head to foot, he may be struck dumb with terror, he weeps floods of tears, sighs and groans almost suffocate the poor fellow, his voice fails him—in short, the center of the bundle of fibers doesn't know what's going to become of it. It would be better to have a little more *sang-froid*, a little more reason, more judgment, more instinct, more self-reliance.

MLLE. DE L'ESPINASSE. I recognize myself in your description.

BORDEU. In the event that a great man has unfortunately inherited that type of disposition, he must work unceasingly to overcome it, to dominate his sensibility, to make himself the master of his impulses and to safeguard the center of the bundle in all its rights. If successful, he will be wholly self-possessed in the midst of the gravest dangers; his judgment will be calm and sound. He will overlook nothing that might serve his purposes or further his ends; he will not be easily astonished; at the age of forty-five he will be a great king, a great statesman, a great political leader, a great artist—especially a great actor—a great philosopher, a great musician, poet or physician; he will dominate himself and everyone around him. He will have no fear of death, for the fear of death, as the Stoic philosopher has said, is a halter which the strong man grasps so as to lead the weak wherever he pleases—the great man will have broken the halter and will thus have liberated himself from all the tyrannies of this world. The fools and the people of excessive sensibility will be on the stage; he will be observing them from the pit, for he is a wise man.

MLLE. DE L'ESPINASSE. May the Lord preserve me from the company of your wise man!

BORDEU. The reason you will always be flying back and forth like a shuttlecock between violent pleasures and violent pains is that you have never tried to behave as he does. So you will be condemned to spend your whole life laughing or weeping, and you will never be anything but a child.

MLLE. DE L'ESPINASSE. I accept my fate.

BORDEU. Do you think that's the best way to happiness?

MLLE. DE L'ESPINASSE. I really don't know.

BORDEU. My dear friend, this much-touted sensibility is a quality that never leads to anything great, and it almost never is strongly indulged in without causing distress. Moderately indulged in, it produces boredom. The victim is either yawning or intoxicated. Abandon yourself without restraint to the delicious strains of a choice piece of music, or let the charm of some pathetic scene in a play absorb your attention completely, and what happens? Your diaphragm gets tense all of a sudden, and there's an end to your pleasure! You are left with a suffocated feeling that bothers you all the rest of the evening.

MLLE. DE L'ESPINASSE. But what if that is the price I have to pay for enjoying the music or being touched by the tragic situation?

BORDEU. You're mistaken. I know how to enjoy myself as well as the next man, and I can admire something if it's well done, but I never feel distress as a result. Only when I have the colic. I think my pleasure is more pure for that reason, and that I am both a more severe critic and a person whose applause should be more flattering because it is more deliberate. Is there any such thing as a bad play for people who

have minds as volatile as yours? How many times have you
blushed as you have read a play and remembered how you
had been swept off your feet on hearing the same verses re-
cited in the theater? Or the other way around?

MLLE. DE L'ESPINASSE. I admit it has happened to me.

BORDEU. That's why cold, serene people like me—and not
sensitive creatures like yourself—are the only ones who have
the right to say: This or that is true, good or beautiful. . . .
We must strengthen the center of the network—it's the very
best thing we can do for ourselves. Did you know that life
itself may depend on it?

MLLE. DE L'ESPINASSE. Life itself! That's a serious matter.

BORDEU. Yes indeed. Almost everyone at some time or other
has been in deep depression. It takes only some chance event
to make this condition involuntary and habitual. Then, no
matter what distractions you go in for, no matter how many
types of amusement you try, no matter what friendly advice
you try to follow, no matter what efforts you make on your
own hook, the fibers stubbornly keep on transmitting harmful
messages to the center of the web. The unlucky sufferer may
bestir himself as much as he will, but he will continue to
look at the world through dark glasses, he is obsessed wherever
he goes with a swarm of gloomy thoughts, and in the end he
does away with himself.

MLLE. DE L'ESPINASSE. Doctor, you scare me.

D'ALEMBERT. (who has gotten up with his nightcap on and
put on his dressing gown). What do you have to say about
sleep, Doctor? I say it's a good thing.

BORDEU. Sleep is the condition in which, whether because
of fatigue or habit, the whole network relaxes and becomes
immobile. It is the condition in which, as in some illnesses,
each thread of the web moves, vibrates and so transmits to
the center a whole series of sensations that are often ill-
assorted, incoherent, or confused; at other times these sensations may be so unified, consistent and well-ordered that the
man in question would display no greater rationality, no
greater imagination and no greater eloquence if he were wide-

awake. Sometimes, too, the sensations are so lively or even violent that the sleeper can't be wholly sure afterward whether he has been waking or dreaming.

MLLE. DE L'ESPINASSE. So we would say, then, that sleep——

BORDEU. —Is a condition in which the animal ceases to exist as a whole entity. Co-operation and subordination among his various faculties are lacking. The master is thrown on the mercy of his vassals or, one might also say, is abandoned to the energy of his own uninhibited activity. Perhaps something impinges on the optic thread—the center of the web will see something. If the auditory thread is sending it a message, it will hear something. Nothing else need occur beyond these actions and reactions. All this is merely the result of the specific property of the center and it all follows from the law of continuity and habit. If the process should begin in one of the voluptuary fibers, destined by nature to serve the pleasures of love and the propagation of the race, then the image evoked will be that of the object of one's passion—this will be the reaction at the center of the web. If, on the other hand, the image should appear initially at the center of the bundle of fibers, then the reaction in the voluptuary fibers will take the form of tension, erection and emission of seminal fluid.

D'ALEMBERT. Hence you might say that there are dreams that go upstairs and dreams that go downstairs. I seem to have had one of the kind you mention last night, though I'm not sure whether it started at the top or at the bottom.

BORDEU. When we are wide-awake the network is governed by the impressions made on it by external objects. When we are asleep, it is the activity of our own consciousness that originates all the sensations we are aware of. Because we are free from all distractions when we sleep, our dreams are correspondingly vivid. A dream is almost always the result of sensory stimulation; it is a transitory form of illness. The center of the web is active and passive by turns and in a great variety of ways—hence the sense of disorder that is characteristic of dreams. Or, the ideas may be very logically connected on occasion—fully as distinct as they would be if we were awake and staring at the thing in question. In that case we are merely looking at a picture of that thing as it has been recomposed in the mind—this accounts for the faithfulness of the image and for our difficulty in telling whether we are waking or sleeping. We have no evidence for drawing either conclusion, and no way of correcting our error except through experience.

MLLE. DE L'ESPINASSE. Is it always possible to check with experience?

BORDEU. No, not always.

MLLE. DE L'ESPINASSE. What if I should see in a dream, clearly and vividly, the image of some friend I have lost, just as though he were alive, what if he should speak to me and I should understand, what if I should touch him and have the impression of something solid at my fingers' ends? What if, when I wake up, I am filled with tenderness and sorrow so that tears well up in my eyes? What if my arms are still outstretched toward where I seemed to see him? What can convince me that I did not really see, hear and touch my friend?

BORDEU. His absence should convince you. But if it is impossible to distinguish sleep from wakefulness, how much more difficult it is to estimate the length of time one has been asleep! When we lie perfectly still, it is only on interval sandwiched in between the instant we go to bed and the instant we wake up. If our sleep is troubled, on the other hand, it seems to last for years on end. In the former case, at any rate, one's awareness of himself is completely suspended. Can you tell me what dream it is that no one has ever had or ever will have?

MLLE. DE L'ESPINASSE. Yes. One in which the dreamer thinks he is someone else.

D'ALEMBERT. Don't forget that in troubled sleep one has not only an awareness of being oneself, but in addition one has the sense of free will. What about this free will that a dreamer seems to be conscious of?

BORDEU. What about it? It's no different from the sense of free will in a man who is awake—it is simply the most recent impulse of desire or aversion, the most recent result of all that he has been and done since the moment of his birth. I defy the most captious critic to discover the slightest difference between the two.

D'ALEMBERT. You really believe that?

BORDEU. You of all people ask me that question! You are a fellow much given to deep speculation, and you have spent two-thirds of your life dreaming with your eyes wide open. In that state you do all sorts of involuntary things—yes, involuntary—much less deliberately than when you are asleep. While you are dreaming about mathematics, you are also giving orders and handing out instructions, and you are obeyed. You are alternately satisfied and dissatisfied. You are contradicted, you run up against obstacles, you get irritated, you have amorous impulses, you indulge some of your dislikes, you confer blame, you approve of something, you laugh, you weep, you come and go. In the midst of your meditations, your eyes are scarcely open in the morning before you are deep in the idea that was on your mind the previous evening. You get dressed, you sit down at the table, you keep on meditating, tracing figures on the cloth; all day long you pursue your calculations; you sit down to dinner; afterwards you pick up your combinations again; sometimes you even get up and leave the table for a moment in order to verify them. You speak with other people, you give orders to your servants, you have a bite of supper, you go to bed and you drop off to sleep without having done a single act of your own free will the whole livelong day. You live concentrated in a single point, and you act continually, but not with deliberation. And anyhow, what can one will, all on one's own hook? A deliberate act of will always originates in some internal or external motive, from some present impression or from some memory of the past, from some passionate impulse, or from some plan for the future. All that being so, I have only one thing to say about freedom of the will—a so-called voluntary act is nothing but the most recent of our actions and the necessary effect of one single cause: ourselves. This is a very complex cause, but it is a single cause just the same.

MLLE. DE L'ESPINASSE. But are you sure it's a necessary one?

BORDEU. Certainly. Try to conceive of some other action taking place, supposing that the actor remains the same person.

MLLE. DE L'ESPINASSE. He's right. Since I am the one who does thus and so, anyone who could act otherwise wouldn't be me. To maintain that at the very moment when I do or say a certain thing, I could just as well do or say something else, is the same thing as maintaining that I am both myself and somebody different. But Doctor, how does all this relate to virtue and vice? Virtue! The word that is so holy in all languages! The idea that is so sacred among all nations!

BORDEU. We shall have to transform it into the notion of doing good and change its opposite into the idea of doing ill. A person has either a good or a bad heredity, and once born he is insensibly drawn into the general current that carries one person along to glory and another to a shameful end.

MLLE. DE L'ESPINASSE. And how about self-respect, modesty and guilt?

BORDEU. Childish notions with no foundation but the vanity and ignorance of a creature who takes the credit or the blame for one link in the chain of necessity.

MLLE. DE L'ESPINASSE. And the theory of rewards and punishments?

BORDEU. Useful for correcting a malleable creature whom we call bad and for encouraging one whom we call good.

MLLE. DE L'ESPINASSE. But isn't that a dangerous thing to go around saying?

BORDEU. Is it true or is it not?

MLLE. DE L'ESPINASSE. I think it's true.

BORDEU. Then you mean that you think a lie may have some usefulness and the truth some inconveniences.

MLLE. DE L'ESPINASSE. That's what I believe.

BORDEU. So do I. But the advantages that can arise from a lie are only momentary, and those that spring from the truth are eternal. The troublesome consequences of telling the truth, if there should be any, pass quickly away, while the evils that follow from a lie end only with its destruction. Just consider for a moment what effects a lie produces inside a man's mind and in his conduct. Inside his mind either the lie gets mixed up with the truth in some helter-skelter fashion, so that he can't think straight, or the lie is logically and consistently linked up with the truth, and the mind is full of error. Tell me, what kind of behavior can you expect from a mind that is either inconsistent in its true reasoning or consistent in its mistakes?

MLLE. DE L'ESPINASSE. The latter of the two vices, although less often condemned, is perhaps more to be feared than the former.

D'ALEMBERT. Hear, hear! Now you have reduced everything to mere sensitivity, memory and organic functions. I don't object to that. But what about imagination? What about abstract ideas?

MLLE. DE L'ESPINASSE. Just a moment, Doctor. Let's go over the ground again briefly, if you don't mind. According to your principles, I gather that by a series of purely mechanical operations I could reduce the greatest genius on earth to a mass of unorganized pulp. This pulp would be deprived of everything except a momentary sensitivity. Now you tell us that this shapeless mass could be brought back from the most abject stupidity imaginable to the condition of a man of genius. The first operation would consist of mutilating a certain number of the threads in the original embroidery frame and thoroughly snarling the rest. The opposite process is one of restoring to the frame the threads that have been detached and leaving the rest to be repaired by the healing powers of nature. For instance, let's suppose that I remove from Newton the two auditory threads—he'd have no more perceptions of sounds. Then I take away the olfactory threads—no more smells. I detach the optical threads—no more sense of color. The taste threads—no more flavors. I eliminate or tangle up the others— and it's good-by to the structure of the brain. No more memory, judgment, desires, aversions, passions, will power, self-awareness. We are left with nothing but a shapeless mass that retains only life and sensitivity.

BORDEU. Two properties that are practically identical. Life is the whole, of which the different kinds of sensitivity form the elementary parts.

MLLE. DE L'ESPINASSE. Now I take the shapeless mass and put back the olfactory threads—now it can smell again; the auditory threads, and it can hear; the optical threads, and it can see; the taste threads, and it can taste. By unsnarling the rest of the embroidery frame I allow the other threads to grow into place again, and under my eyes are reborn memory, the ability to make comparisons, judgment, reason, desires, aversions, the passions, natural aptitudes, talent—and I have recovered my man of genius, all without the intervention of any unintelligible outside agency.

BORDEU. Splendid! Put that under your hat and hang onto it, because anything else they may tell you is poppycock. . . . But you were asking me about imagination and abstract thought. Well, imagination is memory of shapes and colors. The visual impression of a scene or object necessarily winds up the sensitive instrument in a certain way; either it winds itself up, or it is wound up by some external circumstance. Afterwards it either hums inside or buzzes outside. It records silently the impressions it receives; then it gives them out again in the form of conventional sounds.

D'ALEMBERT. But its rendition usually exaggerates, omits details or adds them, disfigures the fact or else embellishes it, so that the nearby instruments receive impressions that are in truth those of the instrument that is speaking, but hardly those corresponding to the thing that actually happened.

BORDEU. All very true. The recital can be either historical or poetic.

D'ALEMBERT. But how did the poetry, that is, the element of untruth, get into the story?

BORDEU. By the process whereby one idea calls up another; and they evoke' one another because they have always been connected. Since you have made free to compare animals to clavichords, you must allow me to compare a poet's narrative to a melody.

D'ALEMBERT. Fair enough.

BORDEU. Well, for every melody there is an octave. This octave has its intervals, and each string that corresponds to these notes has its harmonic strings which, in turn, have harmonic strings of their own. Thanks to this arrangement it is possible to introduce modulated passages into the melody, embellishing and lengthening the song. The actual happening we were talking about is a set theme which every musician interprets in his own style.

MLLE. DE L'ESPINASSE. But why do you becloud the question with your figurative language? I would simply say that because everyone has his own pair of eyes, everyone sees and reports things differently. I would say that every idea awakens others and that each person, depending on the way he has his head screwed on—his character—either sticks to the ideas that represent the happening faithfully, or else mingles these with other ideas that have been evoked. I would say that there is a wide field of choice when it comes to these latter ideas. And I would say . . . but if one were to treat the subject exhaustively he would have to write a big, fat book.

D'ALEMBERT. You're right. But I'm not going to let that stop me from asking the doctor whether he really believes that the imagination never gives birth to some shape that has no relation to anything at all, and whether the poet might not put such a shape into his description.

BORDEU. I really believe it never happens. The fevered imagination is no more than on a level with the skill of those charlatans who cut several different animals in pieces and stick them together so as to make a weird creature never seen in nature.

D'ALEMBERT. And how about abstract ideas?

BORDEU. There's no such thing. There are only habitual omissions of detail, ellipses that make propositions more general and so enable us to speak more rapidly and conveniently. The abstract sciences arose out of the signs of language. The fact that a number of actions have some one thing in common has given rise to words like "vice" and "virtue." "Ugliness" and "beauty" came into being because several objects were found to have a common property. At first people said one man, one horse, two animals; later they simply said one, two, three, and the whole science of numbers was born. There is no particular mental image that corresponds to an abstract word. People noticed that all solid bodies have three dimensions—length, breadth and thickness—then they set their minds to work on each of the three dimensions, and from that activity all the mathematical sciences have been derived. Every abstraction is only a symbol from which all particular notions have been removed. All the abstract sciences are merely combinations of symbols. The specific notions were excluded when the symbol was detached from the physical object. A scientific procedure can only become a science of particulars when the symbols are joined up once more with the physical objects they represent. This accounts for the necessity of appealing to examples in conversation, and even in serious works. When, after you have waded through a long series of symbols, you ask for an example, what you are doing is to require of the person speaking that he give some body, some shape, some reality, some particular content, to the successive noises he has been making by connecting them up with familiar sensations.

D'ALEMBERT. Is all that clear enough for you to follow, Mademoiselle?

MLLE. DE L'ESPINASSE. Not altogether. But I imagine the doctor will make it clearer as he goes along.

BORDEU. It's good of you to say so. It's not that there may not be a number of points that need to be corrected and a great number that need to be added to what I have said. But it's half-past eleven, and I must make a call in the Marais quarter at noon.

D'ALEMBERT. "To make language more rapid and convenient!" Doctor, do we really understand ourselves? Do we really make ourselves understood?

BORDEU. Nearly all conversations are like reckonings that have been drawn up . . . Where the devil did I put my cane? . . . One seldom has an idea clearly in mind. . . . And now, my hat. . . . And for the simple reason that no one man is exactly like any other, we never understand one another exactly; there is always an element of more-or-less; our language always overshoots or falls short of the actual sensation. We are very well aware of how much judgments differ, and there are a thousand

times more differences than we are aware of—which, fortunately, it is impossible to be aware of. . . . Well, I'll be on
my way. Good-by.

MLLE. DE L'ESPINASSE. Please, Doctor, just one more question.

BORDEU. All right, let's have it.

MLLE. DE L'ESPINASSE. You remember those leaps you were
telling me about?

BORDEU. Yes.

MLLE. DE L'ESPINASSE. Well, do you suppose that idiots and
men of genius may have leaps of that sort in their heredity?

BORDEU. Why not?

MLLE. DE L'ESPINASSE. So much the better, then, for our
grandchildren! Perhaps one of them will be a second Henry IV.

BORDEU. Perhaps there has already been a second one.

MLLE. DE L'ESPINASSE. Doctor, why don't you come back and
have dinner with us?

BORDEU. I will if I can, but I make no promises. You'll
have to expect me when you see me coming.

MLLE. DE L'ESPINASSE. We'll wait for you until two o'clock
if need be.

BORDEU. It's a bargain.

Sequel to the Conversation

SPEAKERS: MADEMOISELLE DE L'ESPINASSE
AND BORDEU.

*The doctor returned as two o'clock was striking. D'Alembert
had gone to dine elsewhere, and the doctor sat down to table
alone with Mlle. de L'Espinasse. Dinner was brought in. They
spoke about this and that until the dessert arrived, but the
moment the servants were out of the room, Mlle. de L'Espinasse said to the doctor:*

MLLE. DE L'ESPINASSE. Now, then, Doctor, let me pour you
a glass of this Malaga, and then answer a question that has

run through my head a hundred times. It's something I wouldn't think of speaking of to anyone but yourself.

BORDEU. Hm! This Malaga is really first-class. . . . Now, what was your question?

MLLE. DE L'ESPINASSE. What do you think about the possibility of successful mating between members of different species?

BORDEU. I declare, that's a good question, too. Well, I think that human beings have attached a great deal of importance to the act of procreation, and they are right. But I don't think very much of their laws, both civil and religious, on the subject.

MLLE. DE L'ESPINASSE. How would you rewrite them?

BORDEU. They have been written without regard for equity, for the purpose to be served, for the nature of things, or for the public welfare.

MLLE. DE L'ESPINASSE. I wish you'd explain yourself more at length.

BORDEU. I'll try. . . . But hold on a moment. . . . (He looks at his watch.) Good, I have a whole hour to give you; then I'll have to leave on the run, and that will be that. All right, then. We are alone, and you are no prude, so you won't imagine that I want to seem lacking in the respect I ought to show a lady. Hence, whatever opinion you may have of my theories, I, for my part, hope that at least you won't infer anything to the detriment of my good moral reputation.

MLLE. DE L'ESPINASSE. Most assuredly not. But your preamble rubs me the wrong way.

BORDEU. In that case, let us talk of something else.

MLLE. DE L'ESPINASSE. No, no. Follow your fancy. One of your friends who was looking for husbands for me and my two sisters managed to provide a sylph for the youngest, a strapping Angel of the Annunciation for the eldest, and one of Diogenes' disciples for me—he understood all three of us to perfection. But all the same, Doctor, don't be too specific! Leave a few things under wraps, if you please!

BORDEU. That goes without saying, at least to the extent that my profession and the nature of the subject permit.

MLLE. DE L'ESPINASSE. I am sure it will cost you no great effort. . . . But here's your coffee. . . . Don't forget to drink your coffee. . . .

BORDEU. Your question concerns physical science, morality and esthetics.

MLLE. DE L'ESPINASSE. Esthetics?

BORDEU. Undeniably. The art of creating new human beings in imitation of those that already exist is certainly part of esthetics. In this instance, however, allow me to cite Horace rather than Hippocrates. This poet, or maker, says somewhere: *Omne tulit punctum, qui miscuit utile dulci*—the supreme merit is to have mingled the pleasant with the useful. Perfection consists in reconciling these two requirements. Hence those actions which are both pleasant and useful ought to occupy the apex of the esthetic hierarchy. We would have to grant second place to what is only pleasant, and the third place belongs to what is merely useful. We relegate those things that yield neither pleasure nor profit to the very bottom of the heap.

MLLE. DE L'ESPINASSE. So far, so good. Up to this point, at least, I can share your opinions without having to blush. But where do we go from here?

BORDEU. Be patient and you'll see. Mademoiselle, can you tell me what pleasure or profit anyone can get out of total chastity and continence—or society either, when it comes to that?

MLLE. DE L'ESPINASSE. None at all, upon my word.

BORDEU. Therefore, despite the magnificent praise that the fanatics have lavished on chastity and continence, and despite the civil laws that encourage them, we shall strike them out of the catalogue of virtues, and we shall agree that nothing could be more childish, ridiculous, absurd, harmful and despicable —nothing worse short of positive evil—than these two rare attributes.

MLLE. DE L'ESPINASSE. I'll grant you that.

BORDEU. Keep your eyes open, now, I warn you—pretty soon you're going to find the going too rough!

MLLE. DE L'ESPINASSE. I shan't draw back no matter how rough it gets.

BORDEU. How about secret pleasures?

MLLE. DE L'ESPINASSE. Well!

BORDEU. Well. At least they give pleasure to the individual. So either our principle is false, or——

MLLE. DE L'ESPINASSE. Doctor!

BORDEU. Why, yes, Mademoiselle, of course that's how it is, and for the reason that they do no harm and are actually useful in some degree. They satisfy a need, and even if one were not urged on by the need, they would still be a source of pleasure. I want people to be healthy—don't misunderstand me, I think it's the most important thing in the world. I condemn all excess, but in a society such as ours, the case is open and shut, even leaving aside the individual's temperament and the injurious consequences of strict continence, especially for young people. Poverty, a young man's fear of doing something he would repent bitterly of in after years, a young woman's fear of losing her honor—all these bugbears prey on the miserable creatures' minds and drive them, perishing as they are from languor and boredom, to take the cynic's way out. Cato, who saw a young man on the point of going in to visit a courtesan and who said to him, "Courage, my boy," might not give him the same advice today. If on the other hand he should surprise the young man alone, *in flagrante delicto,* would he not tell him: What you are doing is better than corrupting someone else's wife or risking your health and reputation. What the devil! Just because circumstances conspire to deprive me of the greatest joy imaginable, that of mingling my senses, my intoxication, my soul, with those of a companion whom my heart has chosen, and of reproducing myself through and with her—must I deny myself a necessary and delicious pleasure just because I can't consecrate my action with the seal of utility? We have ourselves bled to relieve a plethoric condition—what difference does it make what kind of fluid is in excess supply? Who cares what color it is or how it is gotten rid of? There is too much fluid, no matter which of the two complaints one suffers from. The seminal fluid may just as well be drawn up from its reservoirs and distributed through the whole blood system, then evacuated from the body by the longest, most dangerous and most painful route, but isn't it lost just the same? Nature doesn't put up with anything useless, and why should I not take it upon myself to help her when she cries out to me for aid by the most unmistakable symptoms? To be sure, we should never force her, but let us be ready to lend her a hand on occasion. I can see nothing but laziness and imbecility in the refusal to do so—that, and loss of pleasure. They tell you, live soberly and exhaust yourself by physical exertion. I take this to mean: Deprive yourself of a little pleasure, give yourself a little pain in order to ward off an equal enjoyment. A fine piece of reasoning!

MLLE. DE L'ESPINASSE. But your doctrine shouldn't be taught to children.

BORDEU. Nor to grownups, for that matter. Still, will you allow me to assume something for the sake of argument? Let's say that you have a well-behaved daughter—a little too proper; innocent—a little too innocent. She has just reached the age at which the character starts to form. Well, she develops a case of the vapors, and it fails to clear up in the normal course of events, so you call me. I see at once that all the symptoms that worry you are traceable to a superabundance of repressed sexual desire. I warn you that she may be threatened with the loss of her sanity, perhaps without hope of recovery, but that this tragedy would be easy to prevent. I explain the remedy to you. What would you do?

MLLE. DE L'ESPINASSE. Well, to tell you the truth, I think . . . But such a thing could never happen. . . .

BORDEU. Don't you believe it. It isn't at all uncommon, and it would happen a lot more often than it does if the laxity of our morals didn't help to prevent it. . . . Still, whatever the truth of the matter may be, anyone who taught my doctrine to young people would be trampling all decency under foot, would draw down on himself the most odious suspicions, and would commit a crime against society. What are you dreaming about?

MLLE. DE L'ESPINASSE. Oh. I was making up my mind whether or not to ask you if an occasion had ever arisen when you had to divulge this secret of yours to a young girl's mother.

BORDEU. Certainly.

MLLE. DE L'ESPINASSE. And what reply did you get?

BORDEU. I have always met with a sensible attitude. . . . I admit that I wouldn't take my hat off in the street to a man suspected of practicing my theory; I would even be pleased to hear him called infamous. But we are speaking between ourselves and with no practical implications, and I would say of my philosophy what Diogenes, stark naked, said to the modest Athenian youth with whom he was about to wrestle. "Don't be afraid, my boy, I'm not such a scum as that fellow over there."

MLLE. DE L'ESPINASSE (putting her hands over her eyes). Doctor, I see what you are leading up to, and I'll wager——

BORDEU. I won't bet with you because you'd win. Well, you asked for my opinion, Mademoiselle, and there you have it.

MLLE. DE L'ESPINASSE. But can you really believe that it makes no difference whether one limits oneself to the members of one's own species or whether one doesn't?

BORDEU. No difference at all.

MLLE. DE L'ESPINASSE. You're a monster!

BORDEU. It's not I that's monstrous. It's either nature or society. Listen, Mademoiselle. I don't judge things according to the words by which they are called, and I let my tongue run all the more freely because I can call a spade a spade and because the well-known purity of my morals makes me secure against malicious attacks. I ask you, therefore, what will be the verdict of common sense as between two acts, both equally limited to the satisfaction of lust, both capable only of giving a wholly non-utilitarian pleasure, but of which one gives pleasure only to the one that does it and the other gives pleasure both to him and to a being of the same or of the opposite sex? In this matter, you see, it makes no difference which sex does what, with which, and to whom.

MLLE. DE L'ESPINASSE. These questions are too abstruse for me.

BORDEU. You see, after having behaved like a man for four minutes, now you put on your boudoir cap and your petticoats again, and you're talking like a woman. All right for you! I'll have to treat you like a woman in that case. . . . No sooner said than done. . . . Today nobody any longer has a word to say about Madame du Barry. . . . You see how nicely everything works itself out? People were sure that her advent was going to turn the Court upside down. Not a bit of it. The master has acted like a sensible fellow—*omne tulit punctum*—he has kept the woman who gives him a good time together with the minister who makes himself useful. . . . But you aren't paying attention. . . . What are you thinking about?

MLLE. DE L'ESPINASSE. I'm thinking about all the various combinations that I consider contrary to nature.

BORDEU. Nothing that exists can be either against nature or outside of nature, and I don't even make an exception of chastity or voluntary continence, which would be the most heinous of crimes against nature if it were possible to sin against nature or commit crimes against it, and they would be the worst possible crimes against the civil laws of a nation where human behavior was weighed in scales other than those of fanaticism and prejudice.

MLLE. DE L'ESPINASSE. I keep getting back to your horrid syllogisms, and the trouble is that I can find no middle ground. I have either to agree with everything you say or deny it flatly. But see here, Doctor, the quickest and best method would be to jump right over the ditch and go straight back to my original question: What do you think about the possibility of mating between different species?

BORDEU. For that there's no need to jump anywhere. We had already gotten to that point. Do you want an answer from the scientific or the moral standpoint?

MLLE. DE L'ESPINASSE. The scientific, by all means.

BORDEU. So much the better. The moral issue takes priority, so I'm glad you have decided it and got it out of the way. That being the case——

MLLE. DE L'ESPINASSE. We agree. . . . Of course the moral question comes first. But I want you to . . . to separate the effect from the cause. Let's leave the ugly cause aside.

BORDEU. That's giving me orders to put the cart before the horse, but since that's the way you want it, I shall simply say that because of our chicken-heartedness, our skittishness, our laws and our prejudices, precious few experiments have ever been made. Hence we do not know what copulations might be totally unfruitful or what different ways there may be of combining the pleasant with the useful. We don't know what sort of species we might expect to produce as the result of varied and sustained experimentation. We don't know whether the fauns were real or legendary. For all we know, there may be a hundred ways of producing hybrids like the mule, and we aren't sure that the known hybrids are really barren. Still, there is a striking instance of hybridization, which any number of well-educated people will vouch for, but which is false nonetheless, and that is that they have seen in the barnyard of His Highness the Archduke an infamous rabbit who did the rooster's duty for a score of shameless hens who seemed to be enjoying it; these people add that they have had shown to them a number of chicks covered with fur who were the fruit of this bestiality. You may well believe that they have let themselves in for a lot of ribbing.

MLLE. DE L'ESPINASSE. But what do you mean by sustained experimentation?

BORDEU. I mean that there are many gradations that separate each animal species from the one next to it. Therefore you would have to make careful preparations for assimilating one to another. In order to succeed in this sort of experiment you would have to go about it over a long period of time, working at first to bring the two animals close to each other by making them follow a similar diet.

MLLE. DE L'ESPINASSE. You'll have quite a job on your hands if you try to get a man to browse in a pasture.

BORDEU. But no difficulty in getting him to drink a lot of goat's milk, and it's easy to get the nanny goat used to eating bread. I have picked a nanny goat for good and sufficient reasons of my own.

MLLE. DE L'ESPINASSE. And what might those reasons be?

BORDEU. You're really getting your courage up now! The reason is—well, the reason is that the mixture would give us a vigorous, intelligent, tireless and swift-footed race of animals of which we could make excellent domestic servants.

MLLE. DE L'ESPINASSE. Bravo, Doctor! I can see in my mind's eye already a picture of five or six great, insolent satyrs riding out behind the carriage of one of our duchesses, and the notion pleases my fancy enormously.

BORDEU. If my idea should work out, we would no longer have to degrade our fellow men by making them perform functions that are unworthy of them and of ourselves.

MLLE. DE L'ESPINASSE. This gets better every minute.

BORDEU. And in the colonies we would no longer have to reduce the natives to the condition of beasts of burden.

MLLE. DE L'ESPINASSE. Hurry, hurry, Doctor. Get to work and produce a lot of satyrs for us.

BORDEU. But wouldn't you have any moral scruples about allowing the experiment?

MLLE. DE L'ESPINASSE. Wait a moment! I've just thought of one—your satyrs would be dissolute rascals.

BORDEU. I couldn't promise you anything about their morals.

MLLE. DE L'ESPINASSE. Then honest women wouldn't feel safe for a single instant with them around. The satyrs would multiply endlessly, and in the long run we would either have to do away with them or knuckle under to them. No, I don't like your idea, I don't want them any more. Spare yourself the trouble.

BORDEU (getting ready to take his leave). And then there would be the question of whether to baptize them.

MLLE. DE L'ESPINASSE. It would throw the whole Sorbonne into a furor.

BORDEU. Have you ever seen in the Jardin du Roi, under a glass cage, that orangutan who looks so much like St. John preaching in the wilderness?

MLLE. DE L'ESPINASSE. Oh yes, I've seen him.

BORDEU. Well, Cardinal de Polignac said to him one day, "Just speak to me, my lad, and I'll baptize you."

MLLE. DE L'ESPINASSE. Well, good-by for now, Doctor. Don't desert us again for ages at a time, as you have been doing, and remember occasionally that I am madly in love with you. If people only knew what horrible things you have been telling me about!

BORDEU. I have no fear that you will let them in on it.

MLLE. DE L'ESPINASSE. Don't you be too sure of that. I only listen so as to have the pleasure of passing on what I hear. But tell me one thing more, and I promise I won't ever bring the subject up again as long as I live.

BORDEU. What do you want to know?

MLLE. DE L'ESPINASSE. What's at the bottom of these sexual perversions?

BORDEU. Invariably they are traceable to a weakness in the nervous organization of young persons or to the rotting of the brain in old people. In Athens they were brought about by the seductive power of beauty, in Rome by the scarcity of women, and in Paris they are caused by fear of the pox. Good-by, good-by.

3

PREFACE

Written early in 1772, the *Supplement* grew out of a book review probably intended for Grimm's *Correspondance Littéraire*, but not in fact used there. The occasion was Louis-Antoine de Bougainville's published account of his voyage around the world in 1766–69. Bougainville's book created a considerable stir because he was the first Frenchman to circumnavigate the globe and also because it touched upon two questions that were very much in dispute at the time. These were the expulsion of the Jesuits from Paraguay, where they had established a communistic society conducted on strongly authoritarian principles, and the not less controversial problem of the actual size of the natives of Tierra del Fuego. Bougainville, though he had witnessed the expulsion of the Jesuits from Paraguay in 1768, was laconic and noncommittal on that subject, but he categorically denied the truth of the venerable tradition (stemming from the account of Magellan's subordinate Pigafetta and "confirmed" as late as 1764 by Maty and Byron, two explorers accredited by the Royal Society of London) that the Patagonians were giants. Grimm had earlier used hard words about Bougainville's veracity on this point, and he may well have been reluctant to reverse himself by allowing Diderot's review refuting the existence of these giants to go to his subscribers.

The review itself has survived, and contains most of the main ideas of the *Supplement* in embryo. Diderot evidently made extensive use of it when he wrote the longer work, taking over large portions of the text verbatim. One passage of this review that was not used in the *Supplement* does have some independent interest, for it shows that Diderot was not swept off his feet by the fashionable tendency of the period to

178 DENIS DIDEROT

idealize the primitive: "Monsieur de Bougainville's book several times portrays the savage man as a being who is generally so stupid that a masterpiece of human industry makes no more impression on him than the great phenomena of nature; he has always seen those phenomena; he has ceased to think about them; he no longer marvels at them; and he lacks the necessary fund of elementary ideas that would lead him to a true estimation of great works of art. . . ." It is obviously, therefore, a serious error—though unfortunately not an infrequent one—to read the *Supplement to Bougainville's "Voyage"* as evidence of Diderot's "primitivism." It should be noted, too, that much of Diderot's idyllic account of life in Tahiti was drawn directly from Bougainville's account, not invented by him, and that none of the sources accessible to him pointed out the less attractive features of Tahitian existence such as the widespread practice of infanticide.

There is a certain irony in the fact that the manuscript of the *Supplément* would not, in all probability, have come down to us if a certain Abbé Bourlet de Vauxcelles, an acquaintance of Julie de L'Espinasse and D'Alembert, had not saved a copy that somehow came into his hands and published it in 1796 after the fall of Robespierre with the object of discrediting Jacobinism as well as the eighteenth-century ideas that had inspired it. In his preface the Abbé accused Diderot, the author of "this precious morsel of philosophy," of having been "the true founder of *sans-culotterie*, the name of which is most appropriate to the thing itself, though it was invented only after the fact." He also took Diderot to task for having "taught men like Chaumette and Hébert how to declaim against the three masters of the human race: the Great Workman, the magistrate, and the priest"—though it is difficult to see how those atheistic agitators of the Revolutionary period could have learned much from a manuscript that was presumably tucked safely away in the Abbé's portfolio until 1796. Diderot had, of course, allowed his manuscript to circulate among close friends—otherwise the Abbé could never have gotten his hands on it—but this audience must have been a very restricted one, and there is no evidence that any of them ever preached atheism during the Revolution.

SUPPLEMENT TO
BOUGAINVILLE'S "VOYAGE"

*Or, a Dialogue between A and B on the undesirability
of attaching moral values to certain physical acts which
carry no such implications.*

> *At quanto meliora monet, pugnantiaque istis,*
> *Dives opis naturae suae: tu si modo recte*
> *Dispensare velis, ac non fugienda petendis*
> *Immiscere; tuo vitio rerumne labores,*
> *Nil referre putas?**

HORACE, *Satires*

Critique of Bougainville's "Voyage"

A. The weather has played a trick on us. When we returned
home yesterday evening the sky was like a splendid vault
studded with stars. But evidently its promise of fine weather
was false.

B. How can you be so sure?

A. The fog is so thick that you can't see the tops of those
trees over there.

B. True enough. But the fog only hangs low because the
atmosphere near the ground is already filled with moisture.

---

* How much better it is, and how contrary to certain other precepts,
that you, a rich man, should be willing to allot your resources correctly
according to their own nature, so as not to mingle desirable things with
those that should be avoided! Do you count it as a matter of indifference
that you must toil because of your own shortcomings and those of your
subject matter?

Perhaps the fog will condense and its moisture fall to the ground.

A. Or, conversely, it may rise higher, past this layer of moist air, into the upper levels where the air is less dense. Up there it may not be saturated, as the chemists say.

B. Nothing for it but to wait and see.

A. And what do you plan to do while we are waiting?

B. I have a book to read.

A. Still Bougainville's account of his voyage?

B. Still at it.

A. I can't make head or tail out of that man. When he was young, he went in for mathematics, which implies a sedentary life. And now, suddenly, he deserts his meditations and takes up the active, difficult, wandering, dissipated life of an explorer.

B. Not at all. A ship, after all, is only a floating house, and the sailor who traverses enormous distances is shut up in a narrow little space in which he can scarcely move about. Look at it this way, and you will see how he can go around the globe on a plank, just as you and I can make a tour of the universe on your floor.

A. And another thing that's very odd—the disparity between the man's character and his exploit. Bougainville has a taste for the amusements of polite society; he loves women, the theater, fine meals. He takes as easily to the social whirl as to the inconstancy of the elements that have buffeted him about so much. He is gay and genial; he is a real Frenchman, ballasted on the port side with a treatise on integral and differential calculus, and to starboard with a voyage around the world.

B. He's only doing what everybody does—after a period of strenuous application he looks for distraction, and vice versa.

A. What's your opinion of the "Voyage"?

B. Well, so far as I can judge after a rather superficial reading, I should say that its chief merits are three: it affords us better knowledge of our old globe and its inhabitants, greater safety on the seas, which he sailed with sounding line in hand, and more correct information for the use of our map makers. When he undertook his voyage, Bougainville possessed the necessary scientific preparation and he had the requisite personal qualities—a philosophic attitude, courage and veracity; he had a quick eye for taking things in without having to waste time in making his observations; he had caution, patience, and a real desire to see, to learn and to enlighten himself; he knows the sciences of mathematics, mechanics, geometry, astronomy; he has a sufficient acquaintance with natural history.

A. How is his style?

B. Simple and direct, just right for the subject, unpretentious and clear, especially when one is familiar with the way sailors talk.

A. Was it a long voyage?

B. I've marked his course on this globe. Do you see that line of red dots?

A. Which starts at Nantes?

B. Yes, and runs down to the Straits of Magellan, enters the Pacific Ocean, twists among the islands of the great archipelago extending from the Philippines to New Holland, touches Madagascar, the Cape of Good Hope, continues into the Atlantic, follows the coast of Africa, and finally ends up where it began.

A. Did he have a very hard time of it?

B. All sailors take risks, and accept the need to expose themselves to the hazards of air, fire, earth and water. But the worst hardship is that when he finally makes port somewhere after wandering for months between the sea and the sky, between life and death, after being battered by storms, after risking death from shipwreck, disease, hunger and thirst, after having his ship all but torn apart under his feet—when he falls exhausted and destitute at the feet of a brazen monster of a colonial government he is either refused the most urgent relief or made to wait interminably for it—it is very hard!

A. It's a crime and it ought to be punished.

B. It's one of the disasters our explorer failed to take into account.

A. And he shouldn't have had to. I had thought that the

European powers were careful to send out to their overseas possessions only men of upright character and benevolent disposition, humane and sensitive to other people's distress. . . .

B. Oh, yes, you may be sure they worry a lot about that!

A. Have you come across any striking pieces of new information in this book of Bougainville's?

B. A great many.

A. Doesn't he report that wild animals often come right up to a human being, and that birds even fly down and perch on a man's shoulder, wherever they have had no chance to learn the danger of such familiarity?

B. He does, but others have said the same thing before.

A. How does he explain the presence of certain animals on islands that are separated from any continent by stretches of impassable sea? Who could have brought wolves, foxes, dogs, deer or snakes to such places?

B. He doesn't explain it; he only confirms the fact.

A. Well, how do you explain it?

B. Who knows anything about the early history of our planet? How many pieces of land, now isolated, were once pieces of some continent? The general shape of the bodies of water between them is the only clue on which to base some theory of what might have happened.

A. How do you mean?

B. You would have to reason from the shape of the pieces that are missing. Some day we can have a good time working that problem out, if the idea appeals to you. But for the moment, do you see this dot on the map called Lancer's Island? Looking at the position it occupies on the globe, who is there who wouldn't wonder how men came to be there? What means of communication were there between them and the rest of mankind? What will become of them if they go on multiplying on a little spit of land that is less than three miles across?

A. Probably they thin themselves out by eating each other. Perhaps you have there—in the very condition of island life— the origins of a very ancient and very natural form of cannibalism.

B. Or they may limit the growth of population by some superstitious law—perhaps babies are crushed under the feet of a priestess while still in their mothers' wombs.

A. Or perhaps grown men have the edge of a priest's knife put to their throats. Or perhaps some males are castrated. . . .

B. Or some women undergo infibulation, and there you would have the origin of many, many strange customs as cruel as they are necessary, the reasons for which have been lost in the darkness of the past and still torment philosophers. One rule that seems fairly universal is that supernatural and divine institutions seem to grow stronger the longer they remain in effect, and are eventually transformed into national constitutions or civil laws. Similarly, national or civil institutions acquire sanctity and degenerate into supernatural or divine precepts.

A. The worst sort of palingenesis.

B. It is just one more skein woven into the rope with which we are bound hand and foot.

A. Wasn't Bougainville in Paraguay just at the time when the Jesuits were expelled from there?

B. Yes, he was.

A. What does he say about it?

B. Less than he might have said. But he does say enough to make it clear that those cruel sons of Sparta in black robes treated their Indians slaves quite as badly as the ancient Spartans treated their helots. They forced them to work incessantly, grew rich on their sweat, deprived them of all property rights, kept them under the brutalizing influence of superstition, exacted the most profound veneration from them, and strode among them whip in hand, beating them without regard for age or sex. Another century, and it would have been impossible to get rid of them, or else the attempt would have touched off a long war between the monks and the sovereign, whose authority they had little by little been undermining.

A. And what about those Patagonian giants about whom Dr. Maty and La Condamine, the academician, made such a fuss?

B. They are good fellows who come running up to you
and shout "Chaoua!" as they embrace you. They are strong
and energetic, but the tallest of them stands no higher than
five feet five or six inches—there is nothing gigantic about
them except their fatness, the largeness of their heads and
the thickness of their limbs. Man is born with a taste for
the marvelous, with a tendency to magnify everything he
sees, so how should one be able to maintain a just proportion among the things he has seen, especially when one must,
as it were, justify the long trip he has made and the trouble
he has taken to go to some remote place to look at them?

A. Well, what in general is Bougainville's opinion of
savages?

B. Apparently they acquire their cruel ways from the daily
necessity of defending themselves against wild animals—at
least this may explain what many travelers have observed.
Whenever his peace and safety are not disturbed, the savage
is innocent and mild. All warfare originates in conflicting
claims to the same bit of property. The civilized man has a
claim which conflicts with the claim of another civilized man
to the possession of a field of which they occupy respectively
the two ends, so the field becomes the object of a dispute
between them.

A. And the tiger has a claim, which conflicts with that of
the savage, to the possession of a forest. This must be the
first instance of conflicting claims as well as the most ancient
cause of war. . . . Did you happen to see the Tahitian that
Bougainville took on board his vessel and brought back to
this country?

B. Yes, I saw him. His name was Aotourou. When they
first sighted land after leaving Tahiti, he mistook it for the
voyagers' native country, whether because they had misrep-
resented the length of the voyage to him or because, being
naturally misled by the smallness of the apparent distance
from the seashore where he lived to the point at which the
sky seemed to touch the horizon, he had no idea of the
actual size of the earth. The Tahitian custom of having all
women in common was so firmly ingrained in his mind that
he threw himself upon the first European woman who came

near him, and he was getting ready, in all seriousness, to render her one of the courtesies of Tahiti. He soon got bored, though, living among us. Because the Tahitian alphabet has no b, c, d, f, g, q, s, y or z, he was never able to learn to speak our language, which demanded too many strange articulations and new sounds from his inflexible organs of speech. He grew more and more disconsolate from a desire to be back in his own country, and I can understand his feelings. This account of Bougainville of his voyage is the only book that has ever made me hanker after another country than my own. Up to now, I had always thought that a person was never so well off as when at home. Consequently I thought that everyone in the world must feel the same. All this is a natural result of the attraction of the soil, and this is an attraction that is bound up with all the comforts one enjoys at home and is not so sure of finding away from it.

A. What? Don't you find that the average inhabitant of Paris is just as sure that grain grows in the fields of the Roman Campagna as in those of Beauce?

B. Heavens, no! Bougainville finally sent Aotourou back to Tahiti, after having provided for his expenses and made certain that he would arrive safely.

A. Well, friend Aotourou! And weren't you pleased to see your father and mother, your brothers and sisters, your lady loves, your fellow countrymen—and what things you must have had to tell them about us!

B. Precious few things, you may be sure, and they didn't believe a single one of them.

A. Why do you say he had only a few things to tell them?

B. Because he couldn't have taken in very many, and because he wouldn't have been able to find the words in his language to talk about those things he had gained some notion of.

A. And why shouldn't they have believed him?

B. Because when they came to compare their customs with ours they would prefer to think that Aotourou was a liar rather than that we are so crazy.

A. Are you serious?

B. I have no doubt of it. The life of savages is so simple,
and our societies are such complicated machines! The Tahitian is close to the origin of the world, while the European is close to its old age. The contrast between them and
us is greater than the difference between a newborn baby
and a doddering old man. They understand absolutely
nothing about our manners or our laws, and they are bound
to see in them nothing but shackles disguised in a hundred
different ways. Those shackles could only provoke the indignation and scorn of creatures in whom the most profound feeling is a love of liberty.

A. Do you mean to go on and spin out the whole fable
about how wonderful life is in Tahiti?

B. It isn't a fable at all. And you would have no doubt
about Bougainville's sincerity if you had read the supplement to his account of his voyage.

A. Well, how can one get hold of this supplement?

B. It's right over there, on that table.

A. Will you let me borrow it to read at home?

B. I'd rather not. But if you would like to, we can read
it over together.

A. Of course I should like to. Look over there—the fog is
starting to settle, and you can see a few patches of blue sky.
It seems that it's my fate to be on the wrong side of any
argument with you, even when it's over trifles. I must have
a very good disposition to be able to forgive you for being
so consistently superior!

B. Here, take the manuscript and read it aloud. Skip over
the preamble, which doesn't amount to anything, and start
with the farewell speech made by one of the island's chiefs
to the travelers. That will give you some notion of how
eloquent those people can be.

A. But how was Bougainville able to understand this oration if it was spoken in a language he didn't know?

B. You'll find out. The speaker is an old man.

The Old Man's Farewell

He was the father of a numerous family. At the time of the Europeans' arrival, he cast upon them a look that was filled with scorn, though it revealed no surprise, no alarm and no curiosity. They approached him; he turned his back on them and retired into his hut. His thoughts were only too well revealed by his silence and his air of concern, for in the privacy of his thoughts he groaned inwardly over the happy days of his people, now gone forever. At the moment of Bougainville's departure, when all the natives ran swarming onto the beach, tugging at his clothing and throwing their arms around his companions and weeping, the old man stepped forward and solemnly spoke:

"Weep, wretched Tahitians, weep—but rather for the arrival than for the departure of these wicked and grasping men! The day will come when you will know them for what they are. Someday they will return, bearing in one hand that piece of wood you see suspended from this one's belt and in the other the piece of steel that hangs at the side of his companion. They will load you with chains, slit your throats and enslave you to their follies and vices. Someday you will be slaves to them, you will be as corrupt, as vile, as wretched as they are. But I have this consolation— my life is drawing to its close, and I shall not see the calamity that I foretell. Oh Tahitians, Oh my friends! You have the means of warding off a terrible fate, but I would die before I would advise you to make use of it. Let them leave, and let them live."

Then, turning to Bougainville, he went on: "And you, leader of these brigands who obey you, take your vessel swiftly from our shores. We are innocent and happy, and you can only spoil our happiness. We follow the pure instinct of nature, and you have tried to efface her imprint from our hearts. Here all things are for all, and you have preached to us I know not what distinctions between mine and thine.

Our women and girls we possess in common; you have shared this privilege with us, and your coming has awakened in them a frenzy they have never known before. They have become mad in your arms; you have become ferocious in theirs. They have begun to hate one another; you have cut one another's throats for them, and they have come home to us stained with your blood.

"We are free—but see where you have driven into our earth the symbol of our future servitude. You are neither a god nor a devil—by what right, then, do you enslave people? Orou! You who understand the speech of these men, tell every one of us, as you have told me, what they have written on that strip of metal—'This land belongs to us.' This land belongs to you! And why? Because you set foot in it? If some day a Tahitian should land on your shores, and if he should engrave on one of your stones or on the bark of one of your trees: 'This land belongs to the people of Tahiti,' what would you think? You are stronger than we are! And what does that signify? When one of our lads carried off some of the miserable trinkets with which your ship is loaded, what an uproar you made, and what revenge you took! And at that very moment you were plotting, in the depths of your hearts, to steal a whole country! You are not slaves; you would suffer death rather than be enslaved, yet you want to make slaves of us! Do you believe, then, that the Tahitian does not know how to die in defense of his liberty? This Tahitian, whom you want to treat as a chattel, as a dumb animal— this Tahitian is your brother. You are both children of Nature—what right do you have over him that he does not have over you?

"You came; did we attack you? Did we plunder your vessel? Did we seize you and expose you to the arrows of our enemies? Did we force you to work in the fields alongside our beasts of burden? We respected our own image in you. Leave us our own customs, which are wiser and more decent than yours. We have no wish to barter what you call our ignorance for your useless knowledge. We possess already all that is good or necessary for our existence. Do we merit

your scorn because we have not been able to create superfluous wants for ourselves? When we are hungry, we have
something to eat; when we are cold, we have clothing to
put on. You have been in our huts—what is lacking there,
in your opinion? You are welcome to drive yourselves as
hard as you please in pursuit of what you call the comforts
of life, but allow sensible people to stop when they see they
have nothing to gain but imaginary benefits from the continuation of their painful labors. If you persuade us to go
beyond the bounds of strict necessity, when shall we come
to the end of our labor? When shall we have time for enjoyment? We have reduced our daily and yearly labors to
the least possible amount, because to us nothing seemed
more desirable than leisure. Go and bestir yourselves in
your own country; there you may torment yourselves as
much as you like; but leave us in peace, and do not fill our
heads with a hankering after your false needs and imaginary
virtues. Look at these men—see how healthy, straight and
strong they are. See these women—how straight, healthy,
fresh and lovely they are. Take this bow in your hands—it
is my own—and call one, two, three, four of your comrades
to help you try to bend it. I can bend it myself. I work the
soil, I climb mountains, I make my way through the dense
forest, and I can run four leagues on the plain in less than
an hour. Your young comrades have been hard put to it to
keep up with me, and yet I have passed my ninetieth year. . . .

   "Woe to this island! Woe to all the Tahitians now living,
and to all those yet to be born, woe from the day of your
arrival! We used to know but one disease—the one to which
all men, all animals and all plants are subject—old age. But
you have brought us a new one: you have infected our blood.
We shall perhaps be compelled to exterminate with our own
hands some of our young girls, some of our women, some of
our children, those who have lain with your women, those
who have lain with your men. Our fields will be spattered
with the foul blood that has passed from your veins into
ours. Or else our children, condemned to die, will nourish
and perpetuate the evil disease that you have given their

fathers and mothers, transmitting it forever to their descendants. Wretched men! You will bear the guilt either of the
ravages that will follow your baneful caresses, or of the
murders we must commit to arrest the progress of the poison!
You speak of crime! Can you conceive of a greater crime than
the one you have committed? How do they punish, in your
country, the man who has killed his neighbor? Death by the
headsman's ax! How do you punish the man who has poisoned
his neighbor? Burning at the stake! Compare the second
crime with your own, and then tell us, you poisoner of whole
nations, what tortures you deserve!

"But a little while ago, the young Tahitian girl blissfully
abandoned herself to the embraces of a Tahitian youth and
awaited impatiently the day when her mother, authorized
to do so by her having reached the age of puberty, would
remove her veil and uncover her breasts. She was proud of
her ability to excite men's desires, to attract the amorous
looks of strangers, of her own relatives, of her own brothers.
In our presence, without shame, in the center of a throng
of innocent Tahitians who danced and played the flute,
she accepted the caresses of the young man whom her young
heart and the secret promptings of her senses had marked
out for her. The notion of crime and the fear of disease have
come among us only with your coming. Now our enjoyments,
formerly so sweet, are attended with guilt and terror. That
man in black, who stands near to you and listens to me, has
spoken to our young men, and I know not what he has said
to our young girls, but our youths are hesitant and our girls
blush. Creep away into the dark forest, if you wish, with the
perverse companion of your pleasures, but allow the good,
simple Tahitians to reproduce themselves without shame
under the open sky and in broad daylight.

"What more noble or more wholesome feelings could you
put in the place of the ones we have nurtured in them and by
which they live? When they think the time has come to enrich the nation and the family with a new citizen, they
glorify the occasion. They eat in order to live and grow; they
grow in order that they may multiply, and in that they see

neither vice nor shame. Listen to the consequences of your crimes. Scarcely had you shown yourselves among our people than they became thieves. Scarcely had you set foot upon our soil than it began to reek of blood. You killed the Tahitian who ran to greet you, crying 'Taïo—friend!' And why did you kill him? Because he was tempted by the glitter of your little serpent's eggs. He gave you his fruit; he offered you his wife and daughter; he gave you his hut to live in—and you killed him for taking a handful of those little glass beads without asking your permission. And the others? At the sound of your murderous weapons they fled to the hills. But you should know that had it not been for me they would soon have come down again to destroy you. Oh, why did I appease their anger? Why did I calm their fury? Why do I still restrain them, even at this moment? I do not know, for you surely have no claim to pity. Your own soul is hard and will never feel any.

"You and your men have gone where you pleased, wandered over the whole island; you have been respected; you have enjoyed everything: no barrier nor refusal has been placed in your path. You have been invited into our homes; you have sat down at our tables; our people have spread before you the abundance of our land. If you wanted one of our young women, her mother presented her to you all naked, unless she was one of those who are not yet old enough to have the privilege of showing their faces and breasts. Thus you have enjoyed possession of these tender sacrificial victims to the duty of hospitality. For the girl and for you we have strewn the ground with leaves and flowers, the musicians have put their instruments in tune; nothing has troubled the sweetness nor interfered with the freedom of her caresses and yours. We chanted the hymn, the one that urges you to be a man, that urges our child to be a woman, a compliant and voluptuous woman. We danced around your couch. Yet you had hardly left this girl's embrace, having experienced in her arms the sweetest intoxication, than you killed her brother, her friend, or perhaps her father.

"And you have done worse still—look yonder at that enclosure, bristling with arrows, with weapons that heretofore
have threatened only our foes—see them now turned against
our own children. Look now upon the unhappy companions
of your pleasures! See their sorrow! See the distress of their
fathers and the despair of their mothers! That is where they
are condemned to die at our hands or from the disease you
gave them. So leave this place, unless your cruel eyes delight
in the spectacle of death! Go! And may the guilty sea, that
spared your lives when you came here, now absolve itself
and avenge our wrongs by swallowing you up on your home-
ward way! And you, Tahitians, go back to your huts, go in-
doors, all of you, so that these unworthy strangers, as they
depart, may hear nothing but the growling of the waves and
may see nothing but the white spray dashing in fury on a
desert coast!"

He finished speaking, and in an instant the throng of
natives disappeared. A vast silence reigned over the whole
extent of the island, and nothing was to be heard but the
dry whistling of the wind and the dull pounding of the waves
along the whole length of the coast. It was as though the
winds and waters had heard the old man's voice and obeyed
him.

B. Well, what do you think of that?

A. The oration strikes me as forceful enough, but in the
midst of so much that is unmistakably abrupt and savage I
seem to detect a few European ideas and turns of phrase.

B. You must remember that it is a translation from Tahitian into Spanish and from Spanish into French. The
previous night, the old man made a visit to Orou, the one to
whom he appealed while speaking, in whose family the
knowledge of Spanish had been preserved for several generations. Orou wrote down the old man's harangue in Spanish,
and Bougainville had a copy of it in his hand while the old
man was speaking.

A. Now I understand only too well why Bougainville suppressed this fragment. But I see there is more, and I have more than a mild curiosity to know what's in the rest.

B. Quite possibly you will find the next part less interesting.

A. Never mind.

B. It is a conversation between the ship's chaplain and a native of the island.

A. Orou?

B. The very same. When Bougainville's ship hove in sight of Tahiti, a great swarm of hollowed-out tree trunks put out from the shore. In an instant his vessel was surrounded by them. In whatever direction he turned his eyes he saw demonstrations of surprise and good will. The natives threw food to the sailors, welcomed them with outstretched arms, clambered up the ship's ropes and clung to its sides. They filled the captain's gig, shouting back and forth between ship and shore. More natives came running down to the beach. As soon as the Europeans had set foot on land, dozens of pairs of friendly arms were thrown around the members of the expedition, who were passed about from group to group and finally led off, each to the hut of a different family. The men kept on embracing their guests around the waist, while the women stroked and patted their hands and cheeks. Imagine what it must have been like to have been there! As a witness of this hospitable scene, at least in thought, tell me what you think of the human race.

A. It's very fine.

B. But I was almost forgetting to tell you about a most peculiar thing. The friendly and generous spectacle I have described was suddenly marred by the cries of a man calling for help. It was the servant of one of Bougainville's officers. Several Tahitian lads had laid hold of him, stretched him out flat on the ground, removed his clothes, and were getting ready to render him the customary politeness of the country.

A. What! Do you mean that those simple people, those good decent savages . . . ?

B. You're jumping to false conclusions. The servant was a woman disguised as a man. Her sex had been kept secret from the crew during the whole voyage, but the Tahitians recognized it at the first glance. She was born in Burgundy and her family name was Barré; she was neither beautiful nor ugly, and twenty-six years old. She had never undressed outside her hammock. She had suddenly got the urge to travel, and her first idea was to circumnavigate the globe. She showed courage and good sense at all times.

A. Those frail constitutions sometimes contain strong characters.

Conversation Between the Chaplain and Orou

B. When the members of Bougainville's expedition were shared out among the native families, the ship's chaplain fell to the lot of Orou. The Tahitian and the chaplain were men of about the same age, that is, about thirty-five years old. At that time, Orou's family consisted of his wife and three daughters, who were called Asto, Palli and Thia. The women undressed their guest, washed his face, hands and feet, and put before him a wholesome though frugal meal. When he was about to go to bed, Orou, who had stepped outside with his family, reappeared and presented to him his wife and three girls—all naked as Eve—and said to him:

"You are young and healthy and you have just had a good supper. He who sleeps alone, sleeps badly; at night a man needs a woman at his side. Here is my wife and here are my daughters. Choose whichever one pleases you most, but if you would like to do me a favor, you will give your preference to my youngest girl, who has not yet had any children."

The mother said: "Poor girl! I don't hold it against her. It's no fault of hers."

The chaplain replied that his religion, his holy orders, his moral standards and his sense of decency all prevented him from accepting Orou's invitation.

Orou answered: "I don't know what this thing is that you call 'religion,' but I can only have a low opinion of it because it forbids you to partake of an innocent pleasure to which Nature, the sovereign mistress of us all, invites everybody. It seems to prevent you from bringing one of your fellow creatures into the world, from doing a favor asked of you by a father, a mother and their children, from repaying the kindness of a host, and from enriching a nation by giving it an additional citizen. I don't know what it is that you call 'holy orders,' but your chief duty is to be a man and to show gratitude. I am not asking you to take my moral standards back with you to your own country, but Orou, your host and your friend, begs you merely to lend yourself to the morality of Tahiti. Is our moral code a better or a worse one than your own? This is an easy question to answer. Does the country you were born in have more people than it can support? If it does, then your morals are neither better nor worse than ours. Or can it feed more people than it now has? Then our morals are better than yours. As for the sense of propriety that leads you to object to my proposal, that I understand, and I freely admit that I am in the wrong. I ask your pardon. I cannot ask you to do anything that might harm your health; if you are too tired, you should by all means go to sleep at once. But I hope that you will not persist in disappointing us. Look at the distress you have caused to appear on the faces of these four women— they are afraid you have noticed some defect in them that arouses your distaste. But even if that were so, would it not be possible for you to do a good deed and have the pleasure of honoring one of my daughters in the sight of her sisters and friends? Come, be generous!"

THE CHAPLAIN. "You don't understand—it's not that. They are all four of them equally beautiful. But there is my religion! My holy orders!"

OROU. "They are mine and I offer them to you; they are all of age and they give themselves to you. However clear a conscience may be demanded of you by this thing, 'religion,' or by those 'holy orders' of yours, you need have no scruples about accepting these women. I am making no abuse of my paternal authority, and you may be sure that I recognize and respect the rights of individuals to their own persons."

At this point in his account, the truthful chaplain has to admit that up to that moment Providence had never exposed him to such strong temptation. He was young, he was excited, he was in torment. He turned his eyes away from the four lovely suppliants, then let his gaze wander back to them again. He lifted his hands and his countenance to Heaven. Thia, the youngest of the three girls, threw her arms around his knees and said to him: "Stranger, do not disappoint my father and mother. Do not disappoint me! Honor me in this hut and among my own family! Raise me to the dignity enjoyed by my sisters, for they make fun of me. Asto, my eldest sister, already has three children; Palli, the second oldest of. us, has two; and Thia has none! Stranger, good stranger, do not reject me! Make me a mother! Give me a child whom I can some day lead by the hand as he walks at my side, to be seen by all Tahiti—a little one to nurse at my breast nine months from now, a child of whom I can be proud, and who will be part of my dowry when I go from my father's hut into that of another. Perhaps I shall be more fortunate with you than I have been with our Tahitian young men. If you will only grant me this favor, I will never forget you; I will bless you all my life; I will write your name on my arm and on that of my child; we will always pronounce it with joy; and when you leave this shore, my prayers will go with you across the seas all the way to your own country."

The poor chaplain records that she pressed his hands, that she fastened her eyes on his with the most expressive and touching gaze, that she wept, that her father, mother and sisters went out, leaving him alone with her, and that despite his repetition of "But there is my religion and my holy orders," he awoke the next morning to find the young girl lying at his side. She overwhelmed him with more caresses, and when her father, mother and sisters came in, she called upon them to add their gratitude to hers.

Asto and Palli, who had left the room briefly, soon returned bearing native food, drink and fruits. They embraced their sister and wished her good fortune. They all ate breakfast together; then, when Orou was left alone with the chaplain, he said to him:

"I see that my daughter is pleased with you, and I thank you. But would you be good enough to tell me the meaning of this word, 'religion,' which you have spoken so frequently and so mournfully?"

After considering for a moment what to say, the chaplain replied:

"Who made your hut and all the furnishings in it?"

OROU. I did.

THE CHAPLAIN. Well, we believe that this world and everything in it is the work of a maker.

OROU. Then he must have hands and feet, and a head.

THE CHAPLAIN. No.

OROU. Where is his dwelling place?

THE CHAPLAIN. Everywhere.

OROU. In this place too?

THE CHAPLAIN. In this place too.

OROU. But we have never seen him.

THE CHAPLAIN. He cannot be seen.

OROU. He sounds to me like a father that doesn't care very much for his children. He must be an old man, because he must be at least as old as the things he made.

THE CHAPLAIN. No, he never grows old. He spoke to our ancestors and gave them laws; he prescribed to them the way in which he wishes to be honored; he ordained that certain actions are good and others he forbade them to do as being evil.

OROU. I see. And one of these evil actions which he has forbidden is that of a man who goes to bed with a woman or girl. But in that case, why did he make two sexes?

THE CHAPLAIN. In order that they might come together—but only when certain conditions are satisfied and only after certain initial ceremonies have been performed. By virtue of these ceremonies one man belongs to one woman and only to her; one woman belongs to one man and only to him.

OROU. For their whole lives?

THE CHAPLAIN. For their whole lives.

OROU. So that if it should happen that a woman should go to bed with some man who was not her husband, or some man should go to bed with a woman that was not his wife . . . but that could never happen because the workman would know what was going on, and since he doesn't like that sort of thing, he wouldn't let it occur.

THE CHAPLAIN. No. He lets them do as they will, and they sin against the law of God (for that is the name by which we call the great workman) and against the law of the country; they commit a crime.

OROU. I should be sorry to give offense by anything I might say, but if you don't mind, I'll tell you what I think.

THE CHAPLAIN. Go ahead.

OROU. I find these strange precepts contrary to nature, and contrary to reason. I think they are admirably calculated to increase the number of crimes and to give endless annoyance to the old workman—who made everything without hands, head or tools, who is everywhere but can be seen nowhere, who exists today and tomorrow but grows not a day older, who gives commands and is not obeyed, who can prevent what he dislikes but fails to do so. His commands are contrary to nature because they assume that a thinking being, one that has feelings and a sense of freedom, can be the property of another being like himself. On what could such a right of ownership be founded? Do you not see that in your country you have confused things that have no feelings, thoughts, desires or wills —things one takes or leaves, keeps or sells, without them suffering or complaining—with things that can neither be bought nor sold, which have freedom, volition, and desires of their own, which have the ability to give or to withhold themselves for a moment or forever, which suffer and complain? These latter things can never be treated like a trader's stock of goods unless one forgets what their true character is and does violence to nature. Furthermore, your laws seem to me to be contrary to the general order of things. For in truth is there anything so senseless as a precept that forbids us to heed the changing impulses that are inherent in our being, or commands that require a degree of constancy which is not possible, that violate the liberty of both male and female by chaining them perpetually to one another? Is there anything more unreasonable than this pefect fidelity that would restrict us, for the enjoyment of pleasures so capricious, to a single partner—than an oath of immutability taken by two individuals made of flesh and blood under a sky that is not the same for a moment, in a cavern that threatens to collapse upon them, at the foot of a cliff that is crumbling into dust, under a tree that is withering, on a bench of stone that is being worn away? Take my word for it, you have reduced human beings to a worse condition than that of the animals. I don't know what your great workman is, but I am very happy that he never spoke to our forefathers, and I hope that he never speaks to our children, for if he does, he may tell them the same foolishness, and they may be foolish enough to believe it. Yesterday, as we were having supper, you told us all about your "magistrates" and "priests." I do not know who these characters are whom you call Magistrates and Priests and who have the authority to govern your conduct—but tell me, are they really masters of good and evil? Can they transform justice into injustice and contrariwise? Is it within their power to attach the name of "good" to harmful actions or the name of "evil" to harmless or useful deeds? One can hardly think so because in that case there would no longer be any difference between true and false, between good and bad, between beautiful and ugly—only such differences as it pleased your great workman, your magistrates or your priests to define as such. You would then have to change your ideas and behavior from one moment to the next. One day you would be told, on behalf of one of your three masters: "Kill," and in all good conscience you would be obliged to kill. Another day they might say: "Steal," and you would be bound to steal. Or: "Do not eat of this fruit," and you would not dare to eat of it; "I forbid you to eat this vegetable or this meat," and you would be careful never to touch them. There is not a single good thing they could not forbid you to enjoy, and no wickedness they could not order you to commit. And where would you be if your three masters, dis-

agreeing among themselves, took it into their heads to permit,
enjoin and forbid you to do the same thing, as I am sure must
occasionally happen? Then, in order to please your priest, you
would have to get yourself into hot water with the magistrate;
to satisfy the magistrate, you would have to risk the displeasure
of the great workman; and to make yourself agreeable to the
great workman, you would have to fly in the face of your own
nature. And do you know what will finally happen? You will
come to despise all three, and you will be neither man, nor
citizens nor pious believer; you will be nothing at all; you will
be at odds with all the authorities, at odds with yourself, malicious, disturbed by your own conscience, persecuted by your
witless masters, and miserable, as you were yesterday evening
when I offered you my wife and daughters and you could only
wail: "What about my religion? What about my holy orders?"
Would you like to know what is good and what is bad in all
times and places? Pay close attention to the nature of things
and actions, to your relations with your fellow creatures, to the
effect of your behavior on your own well-being and on the
general welfare. You are mad if you believe that there is anything in the universe, high or low, that can add or subtract
from the laws of nature. Her eternal will is that good shall
be chosen rather than evil, and the general welfare rather
than the individual's well-being. You may decree the opposite,
but you will not be obeyed. By threats, punishment and guilt,
you can make more wretches and rascals, make more depraved
consciences and more corrupted characters. People will no
longer know what they ought or ought not to do. They will
feel guilty when they are doing nothing wrong and proud of
themselves in the midst of crime; they will have lost the North
Star that should guide their course. Give me an honest answer
—in spite of the express commands of your three legislators, do
the young men in your country never go to bed with a young
woman without having received permission?

THE CHAPLAIN. I would be lying if I said they never do.

OROU. And the women, once they have sworn an oath to
belong to only one husband, do they never give themselves to
another man?

THE CHAPLAIN. Nothing happens more often.

OROU. And are your legislators severe in handing out punishment to such disobedient people, or are they not? If they are, then they are wild animals who make war against nature; if they are not severe, they are fools who risk bringing their authority into contempt by issuing futile prohibitions.

THE CHAPLAIN. The guilty ones, if they escape the rigor of the laws, are punished by public opinion.

OROU. That's like saying that justice is done by means of the whole nation's lack of common sense, and that public folly is the substitute for law.

THE CHAPLAIN. A girl who has lost her honor cannot find a husband.

OROU. Lost her honor! And for what cause?

THE CHAPLAIN. An unfaithful woman is more or less despised.

OROU. Despised! Why should that be?

THE CHAPLAIN. And the young man is called a cowardly seducer.

OROU. Coward? Seducer? Why that?

THE CHAPLAIN. The father and mother and their dishonored child are desolate. An erring husband is called a libertine; a husband who has been betrayed shares the shame of his wife.

OROU. What monstrous foolishness you're talking! And still you must be holding something back, because when people take it upon themselves to rearrange all ideas of justice and propriety to suit their own whims, to apply or remove the names of things in a completely arbitrary manner, to associate the ideas of good and evil with certain actions or to dissociate them for no reason save caprice—then of course people will blame each other, accuse each other, suspect each other, tyrannize, become jealous and envious, deceive and wound one another, conceal, dissimulate, and spy on one another, catch each other out, quarrel and tell lies. Girls will deceive their parents, husbands their wives and wives their husbands. Unmarried girls—yes, I am sure of it—unmarried girls will suffocate their babies; suspicious fathers will neglect or show contempt for their own rightful children; mothers will abandon their infants and leave them to the mercy of fate. Crime

DENIS DIDEROT

and debauchery will appear in every imaginable shape and form. I see all that as plainly as if I had lived among you. These things are so because they must be so, and your society, whose well-ordered ways your chief boasts to you about, can't be anything but a swarm of hypocrites who secretly trample the laws under foot, or a multitude of wretched beings who serve as instruments for inflicting willing torture upon themselves; or imbeciles in whom prejudice has utterly silenced the voice of nature, or ill-fashioned creatures in whom nature cannot claim her rights.

THE CHAPLAIN. That is a close likeness. But do you never marry?

OROU. Oh yes, we marry.

THE CHAPLAIN. Well, how does it work?

OROU. It consists only of an agreement to occupy the same hut and to sleep in the same bed for so long as both partners find the arrangement good.

THE CHAPLAIN. And when they find it bad?

OROU. Then they separate.

THE CHAPLAIN. But what becomes of the children?

OROU. Oh Stranger! That last question of yours finally reveals to me the last depths of your country's wretchedness. Let me tell you, my friend, that the birth of a child is always a happy event, and its death is an occasion for weeping and sorrow. A child is a precious thing because it will grow up to be a man or a woman. Therefore we take infinitely better care of our children than of our plants and animals. The birth of a child is the occasion for public celebration and a source of joy for its entire family. For the hut it means an increase in wealth, while for the nation it signifies additional strength. It means another pair of hands and arms for Tahiti—we see in the newborn baby a future farmer, fisherman, hunter, soldier, husband or father. When a woman goes from her husband's hut back to that of her family, she takes with her all the children she had brought with her as her dowry; those born during the marriage are divided equally between the two spouses, and care is taken to give each an equal number of boys and girls whenever possible.

THE CHAPLAIN. But children are a burden for many years before they are old enough to make themselves useful.

OROU. We set aside for them and for the support of the aged one part in six of all our harvests; wherever the child goes, this support follows him. And so, you see, the larger the family a Tahitian has, the richer he is.

THE CHAPLAIN. One part in six!

OROU. Yes. It's a dependable method for encouraging the growth of population, for promoting respect for our old people and for safeguarding the welfare of our children.

THE CHAPLAIN. And does it ever happen that a couple who have separated decide to live together again?

OROU. Oh, yes. It happens fairly often. Also, the shortest time any marriage can last is one month.

THE CHAPLAIN. Assuming, of course, that the wife is not with child, for in that case, wouldn't the marriage have to last at least nine months?

OROU. Not at all. The child keeps the name of its mother's husband at the time it was conceived, and its paternity, like its means of support, follows it wherever it goes.

THE CHAPLAIN. You spoke about the children that a wife brings to her husband as dowry.

OROU. To be sure. Take my eldest daughter, who has three children. They are able to walk, they are healthy and attractive, and they promise to be strong when they are grown up. If she should take it into her head to get married, she would take them along, for they belong to her, and her husband would be extremely happy to have them in his hut. He would think all the better of his wife if she were carrying still a fourth child at the time of her wedding.

THE CHAPLAIN. *His* child?

OROU. His or another's. The more children our young women have had, the more desirable they are as wives. The stronger and lustier our young men are, the richer they become. Therefore, careful as we are to protect our young girls from male advances, and our young boys from intercourse with women, before they reach sexual maturity, once they have passed the age of puberty we exhort them all the more strongly

to have as many children as possible. You probably haven't
fully realized what an important service you will have rendered
my daughter Thia if you have succeeded in getting her with
child. Her mother will no longer plague her every month by
saying, "But Thia, what is the matter with you? You never get
pregnant, and here you are nineteen years old. You should
have had at least a couple of babies by this time, and you have
none. Who is going to look after you in your old age if you
throw away your youth in this way? Thia, I begin to think
there is something wrong with you, some defect that puts men
off. Find out what it is, my child, and correct it if you can. At
your age, I was already three times a mother!"

THE CHAPLAIN. What precautions do you take to safeguard
your boys and girls before they reach maturity?

OROU. That's the main object of our children's education
within the family circle, and it's the most important point in
our code of public morality. Our boys, until the age of twenty-
two, that is for two to three years after they reach maturity,
must wear a long tunic that covers their bodies completely,
and they must wear a little chain around their loins. Before
they reach nubile age, our girls would not dare to go out without white veils. The two misdeeds of taking off one's chain or
of raising one's veil are rarely met with because we teach our
children at a very early age what harmful results will ensue.
But when the proper time comes—when the male has attained
his full strength, when the principal indication of virility lasts
for a sufficient time, and when we are confirmed in our judgment by the quality and by the frequent emission of the seminal fluid—and when the young girl seems wilted and suffers
from boredom, when she seems mature enough to feel passion,
to inspire it and to satisfy it—then the father unfastens his
son's chain and cuts the nail on the middle finger of the boy's
right hand. The mother removes her daughter's veil. The
young man can now ask a woman for her favors or be asked by
her to grant his. The girl may walk about freely in public
places with her face and breast uncovered; she may accept or
reject men's caresses. All we do is to point out in advance to the
boy certain girls and to the girl certain boys that they might

well choose as partners. The day when a boy or girl is emancipated is a gala holiday. In the case of a girl, the young men assemble the night before around her hut and the air is filled all night long with singing and the sound of musical instruments. When the sun has risen, she is led by her father and mother into an enclosure where dancing is going on and where games of wrestling, running and jumping are in progress. A naked man is paraded in front of her, allowing her to examine his body from all aspects and in all sorts of attitudes. For a young man's initiation, the young girls do the honors of the occasion by letting him look at the nude female body unadorned and unconcealed. The remainder of the ceremony is enacted on a bed of leaves, just as you saw it on your arrival here. At sunset the girl returns to her parents' hut or else moves to the hut of the young man she has chosen and remains there as long as she pleases.

THE CHAPLAIN. But is this celebration a marriage ceremony or is it not?

OROU. Well, as you have said . . .

A. What do I see written there in the margin?

B. It is a note in which the good chaplain says that the parents' advice on how to choose wives and husbands was full of common sense and contained many acute and useful observations, but that he could not bring himself to quote the catechism itself because it would have seemed intolerably licentious to corrupt, superstitious people like us. He adds, nevertheless, that he was sorry to have left out certain details that would have shown, in the first place, what vast progress a nation can make in some important matter without the assistance of physics and anatomy, if it busies itself continually with it, and in the second place, the different ideals of beauty that prevail in a country where one judges forms in the light of momentary pleasures, as contrasted with a nation where they are appreciated for their usefulness over a longer period of time. To be considered beautiful in the former country a woman must have a high color, a wide forehead, a small mouth, large eyes, finely modeled features, a narrow waist, and small hands and feet. . . . With the Tahitians, however, scarcely one of these things is of any account. The woman who attracts the most admirers and the most lovers is the one who seems most likely to bear many children (like the wife of Cardinal d'Ossat) and whose children seem likely to be active, intelligent, brave, healthy and strong. The Athenian Venus has next to nothing in common with the Venus of Tahiti—the former is a flirtatious Venus, the latter a fertile Venus. A woman of Tahiti said scornfully one day to a woman of her acquaintance: "You are beautiful enough, but the children you bear are ugly; I am ugly, but my children are beautiful, so the men prefer me."

Following this note by the chaplain, Orou continues:

OROU. What a happy moment it is for a young girl and her parents when it is discovered that she is with child! She jumps up and runs about, she throws her arms around her father's and mother's necks. She tells them the wonderful news amidst outcries of mutual joy. "Mother! Father! kiss me! I am pregnant!" "Is it really true?" "Really and truly!" "And who got you with child?" "Such-and-such a one."

THE CHAPLAIN. How can she know who the father of her child is?

OROU. How could she not know? With us the same rule that applies to marriage applies also to love affairs—each lasts at least from one moon to the next.

THE CHAPLAIN. And is the rule strictly observed?

OROU. You can judge for yourself. First, the interval between two moons isn't long, but when it appears that two men have well-founded claims to be the father of a child, it no longer belongs to the mother.

THE CHAPLAIN. To whom does it belong?

OROU. To whichever of the two men the mother chooses to give it. This is the only right she has, and since a child is an object of both interest and value, you can understand that among us loose women are rare and that our young men keep away from them.

THE CHAPLAIN. Then you do have a few licentious women? That makes me feel better.

OROU. Yes, we have some, and more than one kind—but that is another subject. When one of our girls gets pregnant, she is twice as pleased with herself if the child's father is a handsome, well-built, brave, intelligent, industrious young man, because she has reason to hope that the child will inherit its father's good qualities. The only thing a girl would be ashamed of would be a bad choice. You have no idea how much store we set by good health, beauty, strength, industry and courage; you have no notion what a tendency there is, even without our having to pay any particular attention to it, for good physical inheritance to be passed on from generation to generation among us. You are a person who has traveled in all sorts of countries—tell me if you have seen anywhere else so many handsome men and beautiful women as in Tahiti. Look at me. What do you think of me? Well, there are ten thousand men on this island who are taller than I am and just as strong; but there is none braver, and for that reason mothers very often point me out to their girls as a good father for their children.

THE CHAPLAIN. And out of all these children you have sired outside your own hut, how many fall to your share?

OROU. Every fourth, be it a boy or a girl. You see, we have developed a kind of circulation of men, women and children— that is, of able-bodied workers of all ages and occupations— which is much more important than trade in foodstuffs (which are only the products of human labor) in your country.

THE CHAPLAIN. I can easily believe it. What is the significance of those black veils that I have seen a few persons wearing?

OROU. They indicate barrenness, either congenital or that which comes with advanced age. Any woman who lays aside such a veil and mingles with men is considered dissolute, and so is any man who raises such a veil and has commerce with a barren woman.

THE CHAPLAIN. And the gray veils?

OROU. That shows that the woman is having her monthly period. Failure to wear this veil when it should be worn also stigmatizes a woman as dissolute if she has relations with men during that time, and likewise the man who has relations with her.

THE CHAPLAIN. Do you punish this libertinism?

OROU. Only with public disapproval.

THE CHAPLAIN. May a father sleep with his daughter, a mother with her son, a brother with his sister, a husband with someone else's wife?

OROU. Why not?

THE CHAPLAIN. Well! To say nothing of the fornication, what of the incest, the adultery?

OROU. What do you mean by those words, *fornication*, *incest*, and *adultery?*

THE CHAPLAIN. They are crimes, horrible crimes for which people are burned at the stake in my country.

OROU. Well, whether they burn or don't burn in your country is nothing to me. But you cannot condemn the morals of Europe for not being those of Tahiti, nor our morals for not being those of Europe. You need a more dependable rule of judgment than that. And what shall it be? Do you know a better one than general welfare and individual utility? Well, now, tell me in what way your crime of *incest* is contrary to the two aims of our conduct; if you think that everything is settled once and for all because a law has been promulgated, a derogatory word invented, and a punishment established. Why don't you tell me what you mean by *incest*.

THE CHAPLAIN. Why, incest . . .

OROU. Yes, incest . . . ? Has it been a long time since your great workman without hands, head or tools made the world?

THE CHAPLAIN. No.

OROU. Did he make the whole human race at one time?

THE CHAPLAIN. No, he made only one man and one woman.

OROU. Had they children?

THE CHAPLAIN. Of course.

OROU. Let's suppose that these two original parents had no sons—only daughters—and that the mother was the first to die. Or that they had only sons and that the wife lost her husband.

THE CHAPLAIN. You embarrass me. But in spite of anything you may say, incest is a horrible crime, so let's talk about something else.

OROU. That's all very well for you to say. But as for me, I won't speak another word until you tell me why incest is such a horrible crime.

THE CHAPLAIN. All right, I'll grant you that perhaps incest does not offend nature, but isn't it objection enough that it threatens the political order? What would happen to the security of the chief of state, and what would become of a nation's tranquillity, if millions of people should come to be under the thumbs of fifty or so fathers of families?

OROU. That would be the lesser of two evils: There would be no single great society but fifty or so little ones, more happiness and one crime the less.

THE CHAPLAIN. I should think, though, that even here, it must not be very common for a son to sleep with his mother.

OROU. No, not unless he has a great deal of respect for her, or a degree of tenderness that makes him forget the disparity in their ages and prefer a woman of forty to a girl of nineteen.

THE CHAPLAIN. What about intercourse between fathers and daughters?

OROU. Hardly more frequent, unless the girl is ugly and little sought after. If her father has a great deal of affection for her, he helps her in getting ready her dowry of children.

THE CHAPLAIN. What you say suggests to me that in Tahiti the women on whom nature has not smiled have a rather hard time of it.

OROU. What you say only shows that you haven't a high opinion of the generosity of our young men.

THE CHAPLAIN. As for unions between brothers and sisters, I imagine they are very common.

OROU. Yes, and very strongly approved of.

THE CHAPLAIN. According to you, the same passion that gives rise to so many evils and crimes in our countries is completely innocent here.

OROU. Stranger, you have poor judgment and a faulty memory. Poor judgment, because whenever something is forbidden, it is inevitable that people should be tempted to do that thing, and do it. Faulty memory, because you have already forgotten what I told you. We do have dissolute old women who sneak out at night without their black veils and offer themselves to men, even though nothing can come of it. If they are recognized or surprised, the punishment is either exile to the northern tip of the island or slavery. There are precocious girls who lift their white veils without their parents' knowledge—for them we have a locked room in the hut. There are young boys who take off their chain before the time established by nature and our laws—in that case the parents get a strong reprimand. There are women who find the nine months of pregnancy a long time; women and girls who are careless about wearing their gray veils—but as a matter of fact we attach little importance to all these lapses. You would find it hard to believe how much our morals have been improved on these points by the fact that we have come to identify in our minds the idea of public and private wealth with the idea of increasing the population.

THE CHAPLAIN. But don't disturbances ever arise when two men have a passion for the same woman, or when two girls desire the same man?

OROU. I haven't seen as many as four instances. The choice of the woman or man settles the matter. If a man should commit any act of violence, that would be a serious misdemeanor, but even then no one would take any notice unless the injured party were to make a public complaint, and it is almost unheard of for a girl or woman to do so. The only thing I have noticed is that our women are a little less considerate of homely men than our young men are of ill-favored women; but no one is worried with this state of affairs.

THE CHAPLAIN. So far as I can see, jealousy is practically unknown here in Tahiti. But tenderness between husband and wife, and maternal love, which are strong, beautiful emotions —if they exist here at all, they must be fairly lukewarm.

OROU. We have put in their place another impulse, which is more universal, powerful and lasting—self-interest. Examine your conscience in all candor, put aside the hypocritical parade of virtue which is always on the lips of your companions, though not in their hearts, and tell me, if there is anywhere on the face of the earth a man who, if he were not held back by shame, would not prefer to lose his child—a husband who would not prefer to lose his wife—rather than lose his fortune and all the amenities of life? You may be sure that if ever a man can be led to care as much about his fellow men as he does about his own bed, his own health, his leisure, his house, his harvests or his fields, he can be depended upon to do his utmost to look out for the well-being of other people. Then you will see him shedding tears over the bed of a sick child or taking care of a mother when she is ill. Then you will find fruitful women, nubile girls and handsome young men highly regarded. Then you will find a great deal of attention paid to the education of the young, because the nation grows stronger with their growth, and suffers a material loss if their well-being is impaired.

THE CHAPLAIN. I am afraid there is some reason in what this savage says. The poor peasant of our European lands wears out his wife in order to spare his horse, lets his child die without help, and calls the veterinary to look after his ox.

OROU. I didn't quite hear what you were just saying. But when you get back to your own country where everything is so well managed, try to teach them how well our method works. Then they will begin to realize how precious a newborn baby is and how important it is to increase the population. Shall I tell you a secret? But take care that you don't let it out. When you came, we let you do what you liked with our women and girls. You were astonished and your gratitude made us laugh. You thanked us, even though we were levying the heaviest of all taxes on you and your companions. We asked no money of you; we didn't loot your ship; we didn't give a hang for any of your stores of food—but our women and girls came to draw the blood out of your veins. When you go away, you will leave with us a brood of children. Do you think we could have extracted a more valuable tribute from you than this tax collected from your own bodies and from your own substance? If you would care to try and estimate its value, imagine that you have yet to sail along two hundred leagues of coastline, and that every twenty miles they collect the same tribute from you! We have vast areas of land yet to be put under the plow; we need workers, and we have tried to get you to give them to us.

We have epidemics from time to time, and these losses must be made up; we have sought your aid to fill up the gaps in our population. We have external enemies to deal with, and for this we need soldiers, so we have allowed you to give them to us. We have a surplus of women and girls over men, and we have enlisted your services to help us out. Among these women and girls there are some with whom our men have thus far been unable to beget any children, and these were the ones we first assigned to receive your embraces. A neighboring nation holds us in vassalage, and we have to pay an annual tribute to them in men; you and your friends have helped us to pay off this debt, and in five or six years we shall send them your sons if they turn out to be inferior in some way to our own. Although we are stronger and healthier than you, we have observed that you have the edge on us when it comes to intelligence. So we immediately marked out some of our most beautiful women and girls to collect the seed of a race superior to ours. This is an experiment we have tried, and that we hope will succeed. We have taken from you and your fellows the only thing we could get from you. Just because we are savages, don't think we are incapable of calculating where our best advantage lies. Go wherever you will, and you will always find a man as shrewd as you are. He will give you what he has no use for, and he will always ask for something he has need of. If he offers to trade you a piece of gold for a scrap of iron, that is because he doesn't care a hang for gold, and desires iron. By the way, why is it that you are not dressed like the others? What is the significance of the long robe that covers you from head to foot, and what is that pointed bag that you let hang over your shoulders and sometimes draw up around your ears?

THE CHAPLAIN. The reason I dress as I do is that I am a member of a society of men who are called monks in my country. The most sacred of their vows is never to have intercourse with any woman and never to beget any children.

OROU. Then what kind of work do you do?

THE CHAPLAIN. None.

OROU. And your magistrates allow that sort of idleness—the worst of all?

THE CHAPLAIN. They more than allow it: they honor it and make others do the same.

OROU. My first thought was that nature, or some accident, or some cruel form of sorcery, had deprived you of the ability to reproduce your kind, and that out of pity they had let you go on living instead of killing you. But my daughter tells me that you are a man as robust as any Tahitian and that she has high hopes of getting good results from your repeated caresses. Well, at last I know why you kept mumbling yesterday evening, "But there's my religion, my holy orders!" Could you explain to me why it is that your magistrates show you such favor and treat you with so much respect?

THE CHAPLAIN. I don't know.

OROU. Still, you must know why it was that, although you are a man, you have condemned yourself of your own free will to be one no longer?

THE CHAPLAIN. That's hard to explain, and it would take too long.

OROU. Are monks faithful to their vows of sterility?

THE CHAPLAIN. No.

OROU. I was sure of it. Do you also have female monks?

THE CHAPLAIN. Yes.

OROU. As well behaved as the male monks?

THE CHAPLAIN. They are kept more strictly in seclusion, they dry up from unhappiness and die of boredom.

OROU. So nature is avenged for the injury done to her! Ugh! What a country! If everything is managed the way you say, you are more barbarous than we are.

The good chaplain tells us that he spent the rest of the day wandering about the island, visiting a number of huts, and that in the evening, after supper, the father and mother begged him to go to bed with Palli, the second eldest daughter. She offered herself in the same undress as Thia's, and he tells us that several times during the night he cried out, "My religion! My holy orders!" The third night he suffered the same guilty torments in the arms of Asto, the eldest, and the fourth night, not to be unfair, he devoted to his hostess.

A. Before you go on with his remarks, I have a favor to ask

of you, which is to remind me of what happened in New England.*

B. This is the story. A prostitute, Miss Polly Baker, upon becoming pregnant for the fifth time, was brought before the high court of Connecticut, near Boston. The law condemns all women of loose life who become mothers when they are unable to pay a fine. Miss Polly, on coming up before her judges for a hearing, delivered herself of the following speech:

"Allow me, gentlemen, to address you briefly. I am a girl who is both wretched and poor and I lack the means to pay lawyers for my defense. But I shall not detain you long. I do not flatter myself that in handing down your sentence upon me you will deviate from the law. What I dare to hope is that you will deign to petition the government on my behalf and relieve me of the fine. This is the fifth time, gentlemen, that I appear before you for the same cause. Twice I have paid heavy fines, twice I have suffered the shame of punishment in public because I was unable to pay. This may be in conformity with the law—I do not argue the point. But there may sometimes be unjust laws which should be abrogated. There may be some that are too severe, and the legislative power should suspend the sentences rendered. I say that the law which condemns me is at once unjust in itself and too severe upon me.

"I have never offended anybody in the place where I live and I defy my enemies—if I have any—to prove that I have ever done the slightest injury to man, woman, or child. Allow me to forget for a moment that the law exists, in which case I cannot imagine what my crime may be. I have, at the peril of my life, brought five handsome children into the world; I have nourished them at my breast, I have reared them by my toil,

---

* The story that follows has of course no basis in fact. It has been shown to be an invention of Benjamin Franklin's and is reprinted in the 1905 edition of his *Writings* (vol. I, 172 and II, 463–67). In Franklin's day it was reproduced in two British periodicals and translated, with some variations, by both Diderot and the Abbé Raynal. It does not occur in any of the printed versions of Diderot's *Supplément* before that edited in 1935 by Gilbert Chinard, who supplied these bibliographical details. The wording here given is not Franklin's but a translation of Diderot's French, which departs in important ways from the original.

and I would have done even more for them had I not had to pay the fines that deprived me of the means.

"Is it a crime to increase the number of His Majesty's subjects in a new country which is short of inhabitants? I took away no woman's husband; I seduced no young man; never have I been accused of any evil deed. If any man can complain of me, it can only be the minister who has been deprived of the fee paid him for marriages. But even that is not my fault. I appeal to you, gentlemen, and ask whether you do not think me sensible enough to prefer the honorable status of wife to the shameful condition in which I have lived hitherto.

"I have always wanted, and still want, to get married, and I make bold to say that I would give as strong evidence of the good conduct, industry, and economy, which befit a woman, as I have so far given of fertility. I defy anybody to say that I have refused to enter that state. The first and only offer of it that was made me, I accepted while still a virgin. I was simple enough to entrust my honor to a man who had none. He gave me my first child and left me. That man is one known to you all; he is actually a judge like yourselves and sits on the same bench. I had hoped that he would appear today in court and that he would have enlisted your interest and pity in my favor, that is, in favor of a poor wretch whom he has made such.

"I should have been incapable of exposing him and making him blush for what passed between us. Am I then wrong to complain of the injustice of the law? The first cause of my error, my seducer, is raised to power and honors by the same government which punishes my distress with whips and infamy. I shall be told that I have transgressed the precepts of religion. If I have offended God, leave Him the task of punishing me. You have already excommunicated me from His church: is that not enough? Why add to the torments of Hell which you think are awaiting me in the next world the pain of a fine and a whipping in this one?

"Forgive these remarks, gentlemen. I am no theologian, but I find it hard to believe that it is a great crime to have brought into the world some handsome children to whom

God has given a soul and who adore Him. If you make laws to change the nature of human actions, make some against bachelors, whose numbers grow larger every day. They seduce and bring dishonor into family life, deceive young girls like me and then compel them to live in the shameful state in which I find myself, in the midst of a society that rejects and despises them. It is they who break the public peace; theirs are the crimes that deserve reprobation far greater than mine."

This strange speech had the effect hoped for by Miss Baker. The judges remitted the fine and the punishment that replaces. it. Her seducer, informed of what had occurred, felt remorse for his behavior and sought to make amends. Two days later he married Miss Baker and made an honest woman of her whom five years earlier he had made a prostitute.

A. And all this is no invention of yours?

B. No.

A. I am very glad to hear it.

B. I am not sure whether the Abbé Raynal does not also report the facts in his *History of Trade in the Two Indies.*

A. An excellent work and so different in tone from his previous ones that the Abbé has been suspected of having pressed other hands into service.

B. That is unfair to him.

A. Malicious gossip, rather.* People will pluck at the laurel leaves that bind a great man's brow and the plucking goes so far that he is left without a single leaf.

B. But time gathers them up again and restores the crown.

A. Yes, but the man is dead then. He has suffered from his contemporaries' buffetings, and he is insensible to his rehabilitation by posterity.

Continuation of the Dialogue

A. I like this courteous chaplain.

B. And I have formed a high opinion of the manners and customs of Tahiti, and of Orou's speeches.

* This is a handsome compliment of Diderot's, who had himself been one of Raynal's collaborators in that large work.

A. Yes, even though they are cast somewhat in a European mold.

B. I suppose they are. But now, to continue, the good chaplain complains that his visit to Tahiti was too short. He says that it is very difficult to form a just estimate of the customs of a people that is wise enough to stop when it has attained a golden mean, happy enough to inhabit a part of the world where the fertility of the soil guarantees a long and languid life, industrious enough to provide for the most pressing needs, and indolent enough so that their innocence, repose and felicity are not endangered by a too rapid advance of knowledge. They have no laws and hold no opinions that would stigmatize as evil something that is not by its nature evil. Their plowing and their harvesting are done in common. Their sense of property is very limited. The passion of love, reduced to simple physical appetites, produces none of the disturbances that we connect with it. The whole island lives like one large family, in which each hut is like a single apartment in one of our big houses. The chaplain ends by assuring us that he will never forget the Tahitians, and confesses that he was tempted to throw his vestments into the ship and spend the rest of his days with them. And he fears that he will have more than one occasion to be sorry he didn't.

A But despite this eulogy, what practical conclusions can you draw from the strange morals and picturesque customs of an uncivilized people?

B. As I see it, human progress began when certain physical causes—for example, the necessity of winning a livelihood from stony soil—brought man's cunning into play. This first push was enough to carry him forward some distance beyond his original goal. When once the aim of satisfying his elementary needs was achieved, he was swept on into the boundless ocean of imagination, with no means of returning. May the happy Tahitians stop where they are now! I see that except in that remote corner of the earth, there has never been any morality and that perhaps in no other part of the world will there ever be any.

A. What do you mean by morality?

B. I mean a general obedience to, and a conduct arising from, the laws, whether they be good or bad. If the laws are good, morals are good; if the laws are bad, morals are bad. If the laws, good or bad, are not observed, the worst possible condition for a society, there are no morals. Now what chance is there of getting people to observe the laws when the laws are contradictory? Read the history of centuries and nations, ancient and modern, and you will find that there are three codes of law under which men have lived—the code of nature, the civil code, and the laws of religion. They have been obliged to violate each of these codes in turn because they have never been in harmony. The result has been that nowhere do we find anyone (as Orou suspected in speaking of our own country) who can be called at once a man, a citizen, and a believer.

A. From which you conclude that if morality were to be based on the eternal, universal relations of men with one another, the religious law would perhaps become superfluous, and the civil law should become nothing more than an explicit statement of the laws of nature.

B. Exactly; otherwise the penalty will be that we shall increase the numbers of the wicked instead of multiplying the good.

A. Or else, if it is considered necessary to preserve all three sets of laws, civil and religious law should be strictly patterned on the law of nature, which we carry with us, graven on our hearts, wherever we go, and which will always be the strongest.

B. What you say is not wholly true. When we are born we bring nothing into the world with us except a constitution similar to that of other human beings—the same needs, an impulsion toward the same pleasures, a common dislike for the same pains: that is what makes man what he is, and the code of morality appropriate to men should rest on no other foundations than these.

A. Yes, but it's not easy to work out in detail.

B. Nothing could be more difficult. Indeed, I believe that the most backward nation in the world, the Tahitians, who have simply held fast to the law of nature, are nearer to having a good code of law than is any civilized nation.

A. For the reason that it would be easier for them to get rid of some of their rustic ways than for us to turn the clock back and reform our abuses.

B. Especially those connected with the relations between men and women.

A. You may be right. But let's begin at the beginning. Let us put nature resolutely to the question and see, without prejudice, what answers she will give on this question.

B. A good idea.

A. Is marriage part of the natural order?

B. If, by marriage, you mean the preference the female has for one male over all others, or that a male has for one female as over against other females—in other words, a mutual preference, leading to the formation of a more or less durable union that perpetuates the species by reproducing individuals—if you mean no more than that, then yes, marriage is part of the natural order.

A. I think so, and for the same reason, because the preference you speak of can be observed not only among human beings but also in various other animal species. You have only to think of the large number of stallions that go chasing after the same mare in our pastures every spring. Only one of them finally gets himself accepted as her mate. But how about courtship?

B. If, by courtship, you mean the vast and varied assortment of expedients, both subtle and forceful, that passion inspires in both male and female when one of them is trying to obtain that preference which leads to the sweetest, most important and most universal of enjoyments—then yes, courtship is part of the natural order.

A. I think so too. Witness the whole variety of small attentions the male renders the female in order to please her, and the countless ways females of all species have of stirring up the passion and attracting the preference of the male. But what about flirtation?

B. That is nothing but deception, for it consists of simulating a passion that one doesn't feel at all and promising favors that one has no intention of conferring. The male flirt is mak-

ing sport of the female, and vice versa. It's a perfidious game
that often ends in the most deplorable fiasco imaginable; a
ridiculous sort of jumping through the hoop, in the course of
which both the deceiver and the deceived are punished alike
by the waste of the most precious part of their lives.

A. So you would say that flirtation is not a part of nature?

B. I wouldn't say that.

A. What about constancy in love?

B. Nothing I could say on that subject would equal what
Orou told the chaplain; it is a vain delusion that two children
may have at the age when they know nothing about themselves, or when they are blinded by a moment of ecstasy to the
transitory character of everything in nature.

A. And that rare phenomenon, marital fidelity?

B. In our part of the world it is the punishment for stub-
bornness which an honest man and an honest woman must
suffer. In Tahiti it is a will-o'-the-wisp.

A. And jealousy?

B. It's the passion of a starved, miserly creature who is afraid
of being deprived. In man it is an unjust attitude produced
by our false moral standards and the extension of property
rights to a free, conscious, thinking being that has a will of its
own.

A. Then, according to you, jealousy has no place in nature?

B. I didn't say that. Nature includes both vices and virtues
along with everything else.

A. A jealous man is gloomy.

B. For the same reason that tyrants are gloomy—they know
what they are up to.

A. And modesty?

B. Now you're asking me to give a course on the principles
of love-making. A man does not want to be disturbed or distracted while he is taking his pleasure. The delights of love are
followed by a condition of lassitude that would put a man at
the mercy of his enemy if the latter attacked him at such a
moment. Apart from this there is nothing natural in modesty
—all the rest is social convention. The chaplain himself, in a
third fragment that I haven't yet read to you, notes that the

Tahitians are not embarrassed by certain involuntary actions that the nearness of a woman excites in them; and the women and girls are never flustered—though they are sometimes stirred —by the sight of such things. As soon as a woman came to belong to a certain man, and as soon as another man's furtive enjoyment of that girl's favors came to be considered robbery, then the words *modesty, demureness,* and *propriety* were born, along with a whole retinue of imaginary vices. In a word, people tried to build up between the sexes a barrier that would hinder them from tempting one another to violate the laws imposed upon them—but these barriers often produce the contrary effect, since they serve to heat up the imagination, and provoke desires. I have sometimes thought of all the trees planted around our kings' palaces—the sight of a bodice that both reveals and conceals a woman's breasts suggests the same idea—and in both instances I seem to detect a secret wish to escape into the forest, a suppressed impulse to recapture the freedom of our old habitat. The Tahitians would say, "Why do you hide your body? What are you ashamed of? Is it wrong to yield to the noblest urges of one's nature? Man, show yourself frankly if you are well-liked. Woman, if this man is attractive to you welcome his advances with the same frankness."

A. Don't get angry. Though we may begin by acting like civilized people, it is seldom that we don't wind up acting like the Tahitians.

B. Yes, but the preliminaries required by convention waste half the lifetime of a man of genius.

A. True enough, but what's the harm in it? It merely slows down by that much the pernicious impetuosity of the human spirit against which you were inveighing not so long ago. Someone once asked one of our most eminent living philosophers why it is that men court women and not the other way around, to which he replied that it is logical, when you want something, to ask someone who is always in a position to give it.

B. That explanation has always struck me as more ingenious than correct. Nature—indecently, if you like—impels both sexes toward each other with equal force, and in the dreary wild state of nature, which one may imagine, although it probably doesn't exist anywhere . . .

A. Not even in Tahiti?

B. No . . . the gap which divides a man from a woman would be crossed first by the more amorously inclined of the two. If one of them hesitates or runs away or pursues or avoids the other or attacks him or puts up a defense against him, the reason is simply that passion, which flares up more abruptly in the one than in the other, does not impel them with equal force. Hence it happens that sexual desire is aroused, consummated and extinguished on one side while it is scarcely developed on the other, and both are disappointed. This is a realistic account of what might happen between two young people who were perfectly free and innocent of sophistication. But after women have learned through experience and education what more or less painful consequences can follow a blissful interlude, their hearts tremble at a man's approach. The man's heart is far from trembling; he is urged on by his senses and he obeys. The woman's senses cry out for gratification, but she is afraid to listen to them. It's up to the man to find ways of putting her fears to rest, to sweep her off her feet and overwhelm her with ecstasy. Men have kept all of their natural desire for women, whereas, as a geometrician might say, the natural attraction that women feel toward men is directly proportional to the passion they feel and inversely proportional to their fears. This ratio is complicated by a multitude of elements which reflect the usages of our society, and these elements work together to augment the timidity of one sex and the length of time the other sex spends in pursuit. It is a kind of problem in tactics, as when the means of defense and the power of the offense have kept exactly abreast. We have consecrated the woman's resistance, we attach blame to the man's violence—violence that would be only a slight injury in Tahiti, but becomes a crime in our cities.

A. But how did it come about that an act so solemn in its purpose, an act to which nature invites us by so powerful a summons—how did it come about that this act, the greatest, the sweetest and the most innocent of pleasures, has become the chief source of our depravity and bad conduct?

B. Orou explained it ten times over to the chaplain. Listen once more to what he said, and try to remember it:

It is owing to the tyranny of men, who have converted the possession of a woman into a right of property.

It is owing to the development of morality and custom, which have burdened the conjugal state with too many conditions.

It is owing to our civil laws, which have subjected the institution of marriage to endless formalities.

It is owing to our form of society, in which the disparity of rank and of wealth has given rise to notions of propriety and impropriety.

It is owing to a strange contradiction that is found in all existing societies—the birth of a child, although it is always considered an increase in the national wealth, is usually even more certain to mean more abject poverty for the family into which it is born.

It is owing to our rulers' political philosophy which teaches them to subordinate everything to their own interests and their own security.

It is owing to religious institutions, because their teachings have attached the labels "vice" and "virtue" to actions that are completely independent of morality.

How far we have departed from nature and happiness! Yet nature's sovereignty cannot be destroyed; it will persist in spite of all the obstacles raised in its way. Men may write as much as they like on tablets of bronze—to borrow the saying of Marcus Aurelius—that it is criminal to rub two intestines together voluptuously—the human heart will only be torn between the threats contained in the inscription and the violence of its own impulses. But the untamed heart will not cease to cry out against its oppressors, and in the course of a lifetime the terrible inscription will be ignored a hundred times by the average person. You may engrave on marble: Thou shalt not eat of the ixion nor of the wild vulture; thou shalt have carnal knowledge of no woman save only thy wife; thou shalt not take thy sister in marriage—but you must not forget to increase the severity of the penalties in proportion as your prohibitions become more arbitrary. Indeed, you may make them as ferocious as you please; still you will never be able to root out my natural impulses.

A. How concise the legal codes of nations would be if they only conformed strictly to the law of nature! How many errors and vices would be spared to man!

B. Shall I outline for you the historical origin of nearly all our unhappiness? It is simply this: Once upon a time there was a natural man; then an artificial man was built up inside him. Since then a civil war has been raging continuously within his breast. Sometimes the natural man proves stronger; at other times he is laid low by the artificial, moral man. But whichever gains the upper hand, the poor freak is racked and torn, tortured, stretched on the wheel, continually suffering, continually wretched, whether because he is out of his senses with some misplaced passion for glory or because imaginary shame curbs and bows him down. But in spite of all this, there are occasions when man recovers his original simplicity under the pressure of extreme necessity.

A. Poverty and sickness are two great exorcists.

B. Yes, you've put your finger on it. What, in fact, becomes of all our conventional virtues under such circumstances? A man in dire need is without scruples, and grave illness makes a woman forget her modesty.

A. So I have noticed.

B. And there's another thing that has probably not escaped you—the gradual reappearance of the moral, artificial man follows step by step during one's progress from illness to convalescence and from convalescence to full recovery. The internal warfare breaks out again as soon as the illness is cured, although the invader is almost always at a temporary disadvantage.

A. That's very true. I have had occasion to learn from my own experience that during a period of convalescence the natural man seems to manifest a vigor that is downright damaging to the artificial, moral man. But tell me, in a word, is it better to civilize man or allow him to follow his instincts?

B. Must I be frank?

A. Certainly.

B. If you want to become a tyrant, civilize him; poison him as best you can with a system of morality that is contrary to nature. Devise all sorts of hobbles for him, contrive a thousand obstacles for him to trip over, saddle him with phantoms which terrify him, stir up an eternal conflict inside him, and arrange things so that the natural man will always have the artificial, moral man's foot upon his neck. Do you want men to be happy and free? Then keep your nose out of his affairs— then he will be drawn toward enlightenment and depravity, depending on all sorts of unforeseeable circumstances. But as for our celebrated lawgivers, who have cast us in our present rigid and awkward mold, you may be sure that they have acted to serve their interests and not ours. I call to witness all our political, civil and religious institutions—examine them thoroughly: unless I am very much mistaken, you will see how, through the ages, the human race has been broken to the halter that a handful of rascals were itching to slip over its head. Watch out for the fellow who talks about putting things in order! Putting things in order always means getting other people under your control. The Calabrians are just about the only ones who have refused to be taken in by the flattery of lawgivers.

A. You are an admirer of the state of anarchy in Calabria?

B. I am only appealing to experience, and I'll wager that their barbarous society is less vicious than our "polite society." You hear a great deal about their spectacular crimes, but how many of our everyday rascalities do you suppose it would take to even up the score? I look upon uncivilized people as a number of separate, isolated springs. Naturally these springs occasionally slip loose and snap against each other, and then one or two of them may get broken. In order to prevent this, some sublime genius endowed with profound wisdom fitted all the little springs together into a complicated machine called society. All the springs are wound up in such a way that they are always pushing against each other, and more get broken in a single day in the state of civilization than would have in a whole year if they had been left in their natural anarchy. What a mess! What wreckage! And what wholesale destruction

of little springs when two, three or four of these gigantic machines happen to run smack into each other!

A. So you would prefer to live in the raw, wild state of
nature?

B. In truth, it's a difficult choice to make. Still, I have heard
that on more than one occasion city people have set to plunder-
ing each other and then taken to the woods to live, and I've
never heard that any forest dwellers ever put on proper
clothes and went to live in the city.

A. I have often thought that for every individual the sum
total of good and bad was different, but that for any species of
animals there was a definite aggregate of happiness and unhappiness that was not subject to change. So perhaps, for all
our striving, we do ourselves as much harm as good. Perhaps
we have only tormented ourselves in order to make both sides
of the equation a little larger without disturbing in the least
the eternally necessary balance between its two sides. On the
other hand, it isn't to be doubted that the average civilized
man lives longer than the average uncivilized native.

B. Well, but what conclusion can you draw from that, seeing
that the length of time a machine lasts is no true measure of
the stresses and strains that are put on it?

A. I see that you are inclined, on the whole, to believe that
men become more wicked and unhappy the more civilized
they become.

B. Without going through the list of all the countries in
the world, I can only assure you that you won't find the human
condition perfectly happy anywhere but in Tahiti. And in
only one little spot on the map of Europe will you find it even
tolerable—there a set of haughty rulers, anxious about their
own safety, have found ways and means of reducing man to
what you would have to call a state of bestiality.

A. Are you talking about Venice?

B. Possibly. At least you won't deny that there's no place
where enlightenment has made so little headway, where there
is less artificial morality, or where there are fewer imaginary
vices and virtues.

A. I didn't expect you to sing the praises of the Venetian Republic.

B. No, I'm not singing its praises. I am only pointing out to you one of the ways slavery can be compensated for, a way that all visitors to Venice have noticed and commented on.

A. A poor compensation!

B. Perhaps so. The Greeks proscribed the man who added one string to Mercury's lyre.

A. And that prohibition in itself is the most biting satire on their early lawgivers. They should have cut the first string instead of adding a new one.

B. You see what I'm driving at. Wherever there is a lyre you may be sure it has strings. Wherever natural appetites are brought under regulation you can be sure there will be loose women.

A. Just like La Reymer.

B. And abominable men.

A. Just like Gardeil.

B. And people who get into trouble through no fault of their own.

A. Like Tanié, Mademoiselle de la Chaux, the Chevalier Desroches and Madame de La Carlière.* There's no doubt that in Tahiti you would search in vain for a parallel to the depravity of the first two or to the misfortunes of the last three. So what should we do—go back to the state of nature or obey the laws?

B. We should speak out against foolish laws until they get reformed, and meanwhile we should obey them as they are. Anyone who takes it upon himself, on his private authority, to break a bad law, thereby authorizes everyone else to break the good ones. There is less harm to be suffered in being mad among madmen than in being sane all by oneself. We should say to ourselves—and shout incessantly too—that shame, dishonor and penalties have been erroneously attached to actions that are in themselves perfectly harmless. But let us not do

---

* All the persons referred to are characters in Diderot's short story, *"Ceci n'est pas un conte."*

those things, because shame, dishonor and penalties are the greatest evils of all. Let us follow the good chaplain's example —be monks in France and savages in Tahiti.

A. Put on the costume of the country you visit, but keep the suit of clothes you will need to go home in.

B. But especially, be scrupulously honorable and truthful in our dealings with those frail creatures who can only gratify our desires by putting in jeopardy the most precious advantages of society.

. . . Well, what has become of that thick fog?

A. It seems to have settled.

B. So when we've had our dinner, we'll have a choice between staying inside and going for a stroll?

A. I suppose that will depend more on the ladies' inclination than ours.

B. The women again! You can't take a step in any direction without running straight into them.

A. What do you say, shall we read them the chaplain's account of his talk with Orou?

B. What do you suppose they would say if we did?

A. I haven't the faintest notion.

B. Well, what would they think of it?

A. Probably the opposite of what they would say.

4

PREFACE

Soon after returning from the country to Paris in October 1770, Diderot showed *The Two Friends from Bourbonne* to Grimm and made a few revisions suggested by the latter. The story then appeared, with a witty but misleading introduction by Grimm—which most subsequent editors have followed too literally in their discussions of the genesis of the piece—in the *Correspondance Littéraire* of December 15, 1770.

Diderot continued to take an interest in the piece, asking for the return of his manuscript early in 1771, and again later in the year, so he could correct, among other things, an inconsistency that was perhaps pointed out to him by the Neapolitan economist and diplomat, Abbé Galiani. At this stage the text still lacked any mention of the Sicilian bandit Testalunga or of the actor Caillot, and Galiani may have contributed one or both of these bits as well.

As with *Rameau's Nephew* and *Jacques le fataliste*, the first printed version of *The Two Friends from Bourbonne* was in German translation. It appeared in 1772, together with another short piece of Diderot's (*A Conversation between a Father and His Children*) as part of the *Moralische Erzählungen und Idyllen von Diderot und S. Gessner*, at Zurich. Gessner was a Swiss artist and writer with whom Diderot was friendly, and it was hoped by both men that the inclusion of two works by a more eminent writer would increase the sale of Gessner's book. Early in 1773 a French translation of Gessner's stories, accompanied by the original French text of Diderot's, was brought out by the same Swiss publisher; at Diderot's request, however, the title page mentioned only Gessner and "Monsieur D***," partly because Diderot was afraid he might be thought presumptuous if he put his name on a book that was almost entirely by another author and partly, perhaps, because he was not sure how his pieces would be appraised by the French censorship. Only fifty copies of the de luxe format were at first sent to Paris since there was a chance that the work would be condemned and seized by the police. The latter did, in fact, object to *The Two Friends from Bourbonne* and refused permission to reprint it in France on the ground that it would not do to allow smugglers to read Diderot's rather complaisant account of the career of a member of their fraternity. On the assumption, apparently, that French smugglers were poor, the authorities did allow the expensive quarto edition of 1773 to be imported and sold discreetly, but they refused to extend this tolerance to the cheaper Zurich edition of the same year.

The most nearly authentic French text of *The Two Friends from Bourbonne* was published in 1795 by Renouard in his edition of Gessner's collected works; this editor claimed to have used a manuscript corrected and somewhat augmented by Diderot himself just before his death, and the Renouard text does include some seemingly genuine material that had not been included in earlier editions. The conclusion from this fact, together with what is known from other sources, is that Diderot cared enough for this story to revise it at least three times in the course of fourteen years.

THE TWO FRIENDS
FROM BOURBONNE

There used to be two men here who might be called the Damon and Pythias of Bourbonne. One was named Olivier and the other Felix. They were born on the same day in the same house, and their mothers were sisters. They were even nursed on the same milk, for one of the sisters died in childbirth and the other took charge of the two children. They were brought up together and had little to do with other children. They loved each other spontaneously, without thinking about it, any more than one thinks about breathing or living. They were aware of their friendship at all times, yet they probably never spoke of it. Once Olivier saved Felix from drowning when he almost went under, right after boasting what a fine swimmer he was, but neither boy remembered the incident for very long. On numerous occasions Felix got Olivier out of the scrapes his impetuous nature was always landing him in, but it never occurred to Olivier to say "Thank you." They would just go home together, either in silence or talking about something else along the way.

When the time came for the young men of the town to draw lots to see which two would be drafted into the army the first unlucky ticket was drawn by Felix. Olivier spoke up and said, "I'll take the other one." They did their military service together and came home together, but whether they were dearer to each other than they had been before, I would not take it upon myself to say. For if, dear brother, deliberate friendships are made more solid by mutual help, perhaps the latter has no effect on those friendships which I am tempted to call animal or domestic.

While in the army they were in a skirmish. Olivier was in danger of having his head split open by a saber blow; as

231

a matter of course Felix threw himself in front of his friend and carried away a huge, livid scar. Some have said that he was proud of this wound, but as for myself I don't think so for a moment. At the battle of Hastembeck Olivier managed to pull Felix out of a heap of corpses under which he was covered. If questions were asked, one of them would sometimes speak of the aid he had received from the other, but never of what he had done for his friend. Olivier would talk about Felix and Felix about Olivier, but neither would praise himself.

Some time after returning home they both fell in love, and, as luck would have it, it was with the same girl. Still there was no rivalry between them. Felix was the first to be aware of how things stood with his friend, so he retired from the field. Olivier married the girl. Felix, who had lost his taste for life without quite realizing why, took up one dangerous occupation after another and finally became a smuggler.

You surely know, dear brother, that there are in France four tribunals—at Caen, Reims, Valence and Toulouse—where smugglers are brought to justice, and of these the most severe is that at Reims where a certain Coleau presides, a man whose temperament is perhaps the most savage that nature has ever formed. Felix was seized, arms in hand, taken before this terrible Coleau and condemned to death like the five hundred others who had preceded him there.

Olivier soon learned of his friend's fate. One night he crept out of bed, leaving his wife asleep, and without saying a word to her, went off to Reims. There he got an audience with the judge, Coleau. Throwing himself at the magistrate's feet he begged the favor of being allowed to see Felix once more in order to embrace him for the last time. For a moment, Coleau looked at him without speaking and then motioned him to a chair. Olivier sat down. At the end of half an hour, Coleau pulled out his watch and said to Olivier, "If you want to see your friend while he is still alive, you had better hurry. He is already on his way to the gallows, and, if my watch is keeping good time, he will be swinging before ten minutes are up."

Olivier, who was beside himself with rage, leaped to his feet and threw at the judge a great stick of stove wood which struck him in the nape of the neck and stretched him out on the floor nearly lifeless. He ran to the place of execution, shouting at the top of his voice, struck down the hangman and began beating up the men-at-arms. The populace, who were full of indignation at the large number of recent executions, joined in the fight. Stones flew; Felix was set free and took to his heels. Olivier was beginning to think about his own escape when a soldier of the Maréchaussée jabbed him in the side with a bayonet. Olivier did not notice this at the time, but on reaching the city gates he fell to the ground from exhaustion. Some kindhearted teamsters picked him up, threw him in their wagon and unloaded him at the door of his own house barely a moment before he died. He had only enough time to tell his wife, "Come here, girl, and let me kiss you. I am dying, but that fellow with the scar is safe."

One evening when some friends and I were out for a walk, as we are in the habit of doing, we noticed a tall woman standing in front of a cottage with four children at her feet. Her sad but firm expression attracted our attention, and she soon became aware that we were looking at her. After a moment of silence, she spoke to us. "Do you see these four children here? I am their mother, and I don't have a husband any more." This rather haughty way of asking for sympathy was exactly calculated to touch our hearts. We offered her some money and she accepted it gratefully. She went on to tell us the story of her husband Olivier and his friend Felix. Since that time we have put in a good word for her with several people, and I hope that our recommendation has done her some good. From which you see, dear brother, that largeness of spirit and the other high qualities are to be found in all stations of life and in all countries. A man may die in obscurity simply because he lacked a more conspicuous scene of action, and you do not have to go as far as the home of the Iroquois to find two friends.

In the days when the brigand Testalunga was terrorizing Sicily with his band, Romano, his friend and henchman, was captured. Romano was Testalunga's lieutenant and his second-in-command. The father of this Romano was then arrested and put in prison for his own crimes. He was promised his liberty and a pardon, if Romano would agree to betray his chief, Testalunga, and hand him over to justice. For Romano the struggle between filial love and sworn friendship was a violent one. But Romano's father persuaded his son to give the preference to friendship because he would have been ashamed to owe his life to a betrayal. Romano gave in and accepted his father's decision. The father was put to death and not even the most cruel torture could wring from the son the least bit of information about his accomplices.

You ask me, dear brother, what became of Felix. Your curiosity is so natural and the reason for it so praiseworthy, that we were a little annoyed with ourselves for neglecting to ask the question. With the idea of repairing this fault we thought at first of Monsieur Papin, doctor of theology and curé of the parish of Sainte-Marie at Bourbonne. But then Mother had a second thought, and we decided to ask the Sub-Delegate, Aubert, who is a jolly fellow, round and roly-poly, and he has sent us the following account, of which the veracity is not to be doubted:

"Felix is still alive. After his escape from the hands of justice, he went into hiding in the forests of this province. He had, of course, learned all the paths and bypaths of these parts while he was plying the smuggler's trade. He tried to work his way little by little to the vicinity of Olivier's house in order to find out what had become of him.

"In the middle of the forest, where you have sometimes gone walking, lives a charcoal maker whose hut serves as a shelter for men of this stripe. It is also a place where they store their goods and their weapons. Felix made his way there, though at the risk of falling into the clutches of the Maréchaussée, who were on his trail. The news of his imprisonment at Reims had already reached the hut, thanks to some of his friends. So the charcoal maker and his wife thought he had already been executed when suddenly he appeared.

"I will tell you exactly what happened, according to the charcoal maker's wife, who died a short time ago.

"The children, who were playing around the hut, were the first to see him. While he stopped to fondle the youngest, whose godfather he was, the others burst into the hut shouting, 'It's Felix! It's Felix!' The father and mother ran out, also shouting for joy; but the poor fellow was so weak from exhaustion and hunger that he had no strength left to speak to them and fell almost unconscious into their arms.

"These good people gave him what refreshment they had, which was only some bread, a little wine, and a few vegetables. He soon finished eating and immediately fell asleep.

"When he woke up, the first word he spoke was 'Olivier! Good friends, do you know what's happened to Olivier?' 'No,' they replied. He told them what had taken place at Reims, and they prevailed upon him to stay with them that night and the following day. At intervals he would heave a great sigh as he pronounced Olivier's name, for he thought his friend must be in jail at Reims. He spoke of going back there to die with him. The charcoal maker and his wife had a hard time talking him out of this plan.

"About midnight on the second night he picked up a musket, slung a saber under his arm, and spoke in a low voice to the charcoal maker. 'My friend!'

" 'Yes, Felix!'

" 'Get your ax and let's be on our way.'

" 'Where to?'

" 'What a question! To Olivier, of course.'

"They started out, but they had no sooner reached the edge of the forest than they were surrounded by a patrol of mounted police.

"I am only reporting what the charcoal maker's wife told me, and it seems incredible that two men on foot could have put up resistance against twenty cavalrymen; but apparently the soldiers were spread out widely, or perhaps they had orders to take their prisoners alive. However this may be, there was some hot fighting, during which five horses were put out of action and seven horsemen cut down or sabered. The poor charcoal maker was killed in the midst of the battle by a pistol shot in the temple. Felix got away and reached the forest. Being uncommonly quick on his feet, he began running from one thicket to another, reloading as he ran, pausing to fire, and letting out a shrill whistle from time to time. These whistles, together with the succession of shots coming from different points of the compass, made the soldiers of the Maréchaussée think that they had blundered into a whole nest of smugglers, and they retired in haste.

"As soon as Felix saw them disappear in the distance, he returned to the field of battle, threw the charcoal maker's body over his shoulders and made his way back to the hut where the charcoal maker's wife and children were still sleeping. In front of the door he halted, laid the corpse on the ground, and sank down with his back against a tree trunk, his face turned toward the door of the hut. That was the spectacle that met the wife's eyes when she came out.

"As soon as she awoke, she saw that her husband was not at her side, she looked around for Felix, but he was gone too. She sprang from the bed, ran to the door, and saw what lay on the doorstep. She screamed and fell down in a faint. The children came running, saw the body and began to cry all at once, trying to clutch first their father and then their mother. The wife, restored to her senses by the children's noise and tumult, fell to tearing her hair and lacerating her cheeks with her nails. Felix sat motionless all the while at the foot of the tree, his eyes closed and head tilted back. Finally he said in a muffled voice, 'Kill me.' There was a moment of silence, then the cries and the sobbing began again, and Felix repeated, 'Kill me, dear friends—have pity on me and kill me.'

"And so for three days and nights the little hut was filled with sounds of grief. On the fourth day Felix said to the charcoal maker's wife, 'Woman, take your knapsack, put some bread in it and come with me.' After a long roundabout journey on foot through the mountains and forests of our province they came to Olivier's house, which is situated, as you know, on the very edge of town at the place where the main highway splits into two roads, one fork leading to Franche-Comté and the other to Lorraine.

"It was there that Felix was to learn of the death of Olivier in the presence of the widows of two men who had lost their lives on his account. He opened the door and spoke abruptly to Olivier's wife. 'Where is Olivier?' Then, when the woman did not reply, and when he saw the condition of her clothing and the tears coming to her eyes, he understood that Olivier was dead. Suddenly he felt ill. He staggered and fell, striking his head violently against the trough for kneading bread. The two widows managed to pick him up, half unconscious, his blood pouring over them. As they tried to stop the bleeding with their aprons he said to them, 'To think that you are their wives, and still you are so kind to me!' Then he lost consciousness. A moment later he came to his senses again and said with a sigh, 'Why didn't he let me hang? Why did he go to Reims? Why did you let him go? . . .' Then his speech became confused, he groaned and tossed like a madman, rolling his head about and tearing his clothing to pieces. At the height of one of these fits he drew his saber and was about to plunge it into his vitals when the two women threw themselves upon him, crying out for help. Several neighbors came running, and at last they got him tied securely with rope. After he had been bled seven or eight times his fury began to subside owing to the weakening of his physical strength, and he lay still as a corpse for three or four days. At the end of this time his sanity was restored.

"At first he looked all around the room like a man who has just awakened from a deep sleep, and said, 'Where am I? Who are you, you women there?' The charcoal maker's wife answered, 'I am the wife of the charcoal maker . . .' He repeated, 'Oh, yes. The wife of the charcoal maker. . . . And you . . . ?' Olivier's wife was silent. At this he began to weep. He turned his face to the wall and said, sobbing, 'I am in Olivier's house. . . . This is his bed. . . . And that woman over there—she was his wife! . . .'

"The two women took care of him so anxiously, they filled him so with pity, they begged him so earnestly to go on living, and they insisted so poignantly that he was the only means of support left them, that finally he let himself be convinced.

"But for the rest of his stay in that house he could not bring himself to sleep in the bed. At night he would go outdoors, wander through the fields, often throwing himself to the ground and crying out Olivier's name as he rolled about in torment. One of the women would follow at a distance and lead him home at daybreak.

"Several people knew of his presence in Olivier's house, and among these were a few malicious gossips. The two widows finally warned him of the risks he was running. It was one afternoon while he was sitting on a bench, his saber laid across his knees, his elbows on the table and his two fists pressed into the hollows of his eyes. At first he made no reply.

"Olivier's wife had a son of seventeen or eighteen; the charcoal maker's wife had a daughter of fifteen. Suddenly he said to the charcoal maker's wife, 'Good friend, please go and bring your daughter from where she is staying.' He still had a few bits of land; these he sold for cash. A little later the widow of the charcoal maker returned with her daughter and it was arranged that she would marry Olivier's son. Felix gave them the proceeds from the sale of his land, embraced them both and with tears streaming down his cheeks asked their forgiveness. Then the young couple went back to set up housekeeping in the little hut; they still live there and have taken it upon themselves to be a father and mother to the charcoal maker's younger children. The two widows decided to live together, so Olivier's children had one father and two mothers.

"The charcoal maker's wife has been dead now for about a year and a half, and Olivier's wife still weeps for her every day.

"One evening when the two women were watching Felix (they had agreed that one of them would keep an eye on him at all times) they saw him suddenly burst into tears. Without saying anything he stretched out his arms toward the doorway that separated the room he was in from the one in which they were sitting. Then he began to pack his knapsack. They made no effort to stop him, for they well understood how necessary his departure was. The three of them ate supper in silence. Late that night he got up from the table and walked on tiptoe toward the door. Both women were wide-awake. At the door he paused, looked back at the bed where the two women were lying, wiped his eyes with the back of his hand, and went out. The two women wept together the rest of the night, locked in each other's arms. No one knew where Felix had gone into hiding, but scarcely a week went by without his sending them a little money.

"The forest where the charcoal maker's daughter had gone to live with Olivier's son belonged to a gentleman named Leclerc de Rançonnières, a man of great wealth who was the seigneur of another village in the neighborhood called Courcelles. One day when Monsieur de Rançonnières, or De Courcelles if you prefer his other title, was hunting in the woods he came upon the hut belonging to Olivier's son. He went in, got to playing with the children, who were very attractive, and began to ask all sorts of questions. Afterward he remembered the wife's face, which was far from ugly, and he had been favorably impressed by the straightforward manner of the young husband who strongly resembled his father. He learned of the parents' misfortunes and promised to try to secure a pardon for Felix. His efforts were successful.

"Felix entered the service of Monsieur de Rançonnières as a gamekeeper.

"After he had been living for two years at the Château de Rançonnières, sending most of his wages to the two widows, he got mixed up in a fracas—thanks to his strong sense of personal dignity and on account of his loyalty to his master—which was trivial in origin but disastrous in its consequences.

"Monsieur de Rançonnières had a neighbor in Courcelles, a certain Fourmont, a councillor at the presidial court of Chaumont. The two houses were separated only by a boundary marker. This stone obstructed the driveway leading to Monsieur de Ranconnières' front door and made it awkward for carriages to turn in from the street. So Monsieur de Rançonnières had it moved over a few feet toward Fourmont's house. The latter had it moved back the same distance onto Monsieur

de Rançonnières property. Then followed the usual sequence
of hatred, insults, and finally a lawsuit between two neighbors.
The litigation over the boundary stone provoked several others
of a more serious nature.

"This is where matters stood when Monsieur de Rançonnières returned one evening from hunting, accompanied
by his gamekeeper, and happened to meet Fourmont the
magistrate and his brother, who was an officer, on the high
road. The latter said, 'Brother, what do you say we cut off the
nose of that old rascal over there?' Monsieur de Rançonnières
did not hear this remark, but Felix unfortunately did. Addressing himself with dignity to the younger man, Felix said,
'Captain, I doubt that you have courage enough even to begin
to do what you have just said.' As he spoke he laid his musket
on the ground and rested his hand on the grip of his saber,
for he never went out without it. The young soldier drew his
sword and advanced on Felix; Monsieur de Rançonnières ran
to throw himself between the two men and pinned Felix's
arms to his side. Nevertheless the soldier seized the musket
that was lying on the ground and fired at Felix, but the shot
missed him. Felix defended himself with his saber and was able
to strike the young man's sword to the ground, along with half
the arm that had been holding it.

"Now there was a criminal prosecution in addition to the
three or four civil suits already in progress. Felix was thrown
into various jails; the trial was a gruesome affair that ended
with one magistrate stripped of his office, one officer cashiered,
Monsieur de Rançonnières dead of remorse, and Felix still
languishing in prison, the object of the vindictive machina-
tions of the whole Fourmont tribe. He would surely have come
to a miserable end if love had not come to his rescue;
fortunately the turnkey's daughter conceived a violent passion
for him and helped him escape—this may not be the exact
truth, but at least it is what people say. He was able to get
away to Prussia, where he is now in service with the Guards
Regiment. They say he even is very popular with his comrades,
and that he has even come to the King's attention. He has
taken a *nom de guerre*—they call him 'Le Triste.' Olivier's

widow tells me that he still sends her money regularly by post. "This information, Madame, is all I have been able to gather about Felix's career. I am enclosing with this account a letter written by Monsieur Papin, our curé. I do not know what it may contain, but I am a little fearful that our worthy priest, whose mind is a little narrow and whose heart is not the warmest in the world, may very well allow his prejudices to color the story he will tell you about Felix and Olivier. Therefore I beg you, Madame, to rely only on those facts of which the authenticity is above question, and to be guided thereafter only by the goodness of your own nature, which will advise you better than the most celebrated casuist of the Sorbonne (and I do not mean Monsieur Papin)."

A LETTER FROM MONSIEUR PAPIN, DOCTOR OF THEOLOGY,
AND CURÉ OF THE PARISH OF SAINTE-MARIE
AT BOURBONNE

"I do not know, Madame, what the Sub-Delegate has written you about the affairs of Felix and Olivier, nor do I understand what interest you can possibly have in a pair of brigands whose every footstep in this world has been soaked in blood. Providence, which has already punished one of them, has granted the other a reprieve of a few moments from which I greatly fear he will not be able to profit very much. But may God's will be done! I know that there are some persons here —and I would not be surprised to learn that the Sub-Delegate is one of them—who talk as though these two men were rare models of pure friendship. But of what value in God's eyes is even the most sublime virtue if it is not clothed with pious feelings, with respect for the Church and its ministers, and with submission to the majesty of the law? Olivier died on his own threshold, without the sacraments; and when I was summoned to visit Felix, then living with the two widows, the only word I could get them to speak was Olivier's name—not a sign of religion, not a trace of repentance! I cannot recall that this

Olivier ever so much as once presented himself at the con-
fessional. His wife has always been an arrogant woman who
has failed me on numerous occasions. On the pretext that she
knows how to read and write she thinks herself qualified to
look after the education of her children; hence we never see
them in the parish school or at my lessons on the catechism.
You may judge from all this, Madame, whether persons of this
description are indeed worthy of your charity! The Gospel unceasingly teaches us to pity the sufferings of the poor; but we
double the merit that attaches to our charity when we choose
wisely among the poor to find out which are truly deserving,
and no one can know better which are the deserving poor
than the common pastor of rich and poor. If you will be so
good as to honor me with your confidence, Madame, I shall
perhaps be able to distribute the signs of your beneficence in
a manner more useful to the unfortunate and more meritorious
to yourself.

"I am, with all due respect, etc."

Madame de *** thanked the Sub-Delegate, Aubert, for his
good intentions, and sent her charitable gift to Monsieur Papin
with the following note:

"I am greatly obliged to you, Sir, for your sound advice. I
confess that the story of these two men had moved me deeply;
surely you will agree that such a rare example of true friendship was well calculated to mislead a candid and sensitive soul.
But you have enlightened me, and I see now that it is better
to give one's alms to the poor who have Christian virtue rather
than to those whose virtue is merely natural and pagan. Therefore I beg you to accept the modest sum which I enclose, and
to distribute it according to those principles of charity which
you understand so much better than I do.

"I have the honor to be, etc."

You may well believe that Felix and Olivier's widow did
not get very much of the donation from Madame de ***
Felix eventually died, and the poor widow and her children
would also have died of want if she had not taken refuge in
the forest in the house of her eldest son. There she did her
full share of the work, despite her advanced age, and kept

body and soul together as best she could in the midst of her children and grandchildren.

To bring matters to a conclusion, there are three kinds of stories. . . . Many more than that, you may tell me. . . . All right; have it your own way. But I distinguish first of all stories in the manner of Homer, of Virgil and of Tasso, and I would prefer to call these the stories of the marvelous or miraculous. In them nature is exaggerated, and their truth is always hypothetical. If the storyteller has kept his recital in the same key throughout, and if everything harmonizes—I mean the actions and the dialogue—then he will have achieved the highest degree of perfection that the nature of his work permits, and you cannot ask anything more of him. When you begin to read his poem you enter unknown territory where nothing happens the way it would in the real world you are familiar with. Instead, everything is projected, as it were, on a much grander scale, while all everyday things seem to shrink almost to insignificance.

Then there is the agreeable tale in the manner of La Fontaine, Vergier, Ariosto and Hamilton, where the author is not trying to imitate nature, nor to tell the exact truth, nor to create an illusion; instead, he carries you off to an imaginary realm. You tell him: Be gay, ingenious, full of variety, eccentric or even extravagant—I agree to everything in advance; only you must hold my interest with details and you must always divert attention from the plot's lack of plausibility by the charms of language and form. Now if this storyteller has done all that you required of him he has done all he can do.

In the third place, there is the story about real people, such as you will find in the novels of Scarron, Cervantes and Marmontel. . . .

"The devil take the so-called 'realistic' story and its author! He is a dull and platitudinous liar . . ."

Of course, if he does not know his trade. Such and such a one sets out to deceive you; he sits down at your fireside; he says he is going to tell you nothing but what is absolutely true; he wants you to believe him; he wants to arouse your interest,

your sympathy; he wants to get you involved, to stir you up
in your deepest feelings, to give you goose-pimples and make
tears stream from your eyes—and all these effects can only be
produced by eloquence and poetic skill. But eloquence is a
kind of lie, and there is nothing more inappropriate than
poetry for giving the illusion of real speech; both the one and
the other exaggerate, overdo, amplify, and inspire mistrust.
How, then, will the storyteller go about deceiving you? In the
following way. He will scatter throughout his story so many
little details intimately connected with the subject in hand, so
many touches that are so simple and so natural, and above all
so difficult to make up out of whole cloth, that you will be
compelled to say to yourself: Upon my word, this is the
truth—such things can't be invented. In this way he will
achieve the necessary heightening of reality without eloquence
and without poetry, and the truth of nature will hide the
pretense of art. In short, he will be able to satisfy two requirements which at first seem contradictory—to be at the same
time a historian and a poet, both veracious and mendacious.

An example borrowed from another field of art will perhaps
make my meaning easier to grasp. A painter executes a head on
his canvas. The outlines are all strong, bold and regular; it is
a collection of the most rare and the most perfect traits. Looking at it, I feel respect, admiration and awe. I seek its model
in nature, and do not find it there; in comparison with the
picture everything natural seems weak, petty and mediocre.
This, I feel, and I tell myself, is an imaginary head. But let the
artist show me a small scar on the forehead of this portrait, a
mole on one of the temples, a barely perceptible cut on the
lower lip, and although it seemed an imaginary portrait only
a moment before, now it becomes the likeness of a real person. Add a pockmark at the corner of the eye, or beside the
nose, and this woman's face is no longer that of Venus; it is the
portrait of one of my neighbors.

And so I say to our purveyors of "real life" tales: Your
figures are handsome, if you like that sort of thing, but they
lack the mole on the temple, the cut on the lip, the pockmark
beside the nose—all the touches that would make them seem

genuine. As my friend Caillot used to say, "Put a little dust on my shoes, and I have just returned from the country, not just stepped out of my box at the Opera."

> *Atque ita mentitur, sic veris falsa remiscet,*
> *Primo ne medium, medio ne discrepet imum.*
> HORACE, *De Arte Poetica*, V, 151

And this is another way to tell lies—one mixes a false thing with the true so that the middle will fit well with the beginning and the end with the middle.

And finally, after this little discussion of literature, let us have a little morality—how well the two things go together! Felix was a poor devil who had not a sou to his name, and Olivier was another poor devil who had not a sou to his name; the same can be said of the charcoal maker and his wife, and of the other people in this story. Our general conclusion must be that there can hardly be any such thing as pure, solid friendship except among people who have not a sou to their names. For under those conditions a man's friend is his whole fortune, and the friend is in the same predicament. Whence we derive the truth that experience has always taught—that poverty brings people closer to one another. All these demonstrations might give [my friend Helvetius] the material for one more paragraph in the next edition of his book *On the Mind*.

5

A CONVERSATION BETWEEN A FATHER AND HIS CHILDREN

Or, The Danger of Putting Oneself above the Law
(First published in 1772.)

My father, though a very pious man, had excellent judgment and was known throughout our province for his strict honesty. More than once he was chosen by his fellow citizens to arbitrate their disputes. Sometimes total strangers entrusted to him the carrying out of their last wishes. When he died, all the poor people in town wore mourning for him. When he fell sick, both great and humble took occasion to show how much they had his recovery at heart. When it was known that he had not much longer to live, the whole town grieved. His image will always be vivid in my memory—it seems almost as though I can see him now, sitting at ease in his armchair and wearing his habitually serene expression. It seems to me that I still hear his voice. Here is an account of one of the evenings we spent together—and it was but one of many evenings that passed after the same fashion.

It was winter. My brother, Abbé Diderot, my sister, and I were seated with him in front of the fire. We had been talking about some of the disadvantages of being famous. He said to me: "My son, you and I have both made a certain amount of noise in the world, but there is a difference between us— the noise you have made with your tools has cost you your own peace of mind, while the noise I've made with mine has de-

246

prived other people of their rest." After the old smith had made this little joke—good or bad according to one's taste—he grew pensive and looked at us more closely than before. Finally the abbé said "Father, what are you thinking about?"

"I was just thinking," he replied, "that to enjoy a reputation as an upright man, though it is the most precious thing in the world, can have certain dangers, even for a person who deserves to have that reputation." Then, after a brief pause, he added, "I tremble even now whenever I think about it! . . . Would you believe it, children—there was one time in my life when I came within an inch of losing everything we possess! Yes, I almost made beggars of you all."

THE ABBÉ. How do you mean?

MY FATHER. I'll tell you. Listen——But before I begin (he said to his daughter), put my cushion back up here where it belongs, Sister, it has slipped down too far. (Then to me:) And you, Denis, pull the skirts of my dressing gown together, the fire is roasting my shins. . . . Well, do all of you remember the old priest at Thivet?

MY SISTER. The kind old priest who still walked his four leagues every morning at the age of one hundred?

THE ABBÉ. And who died at a hundred and one upon learning of the death of the brother who shared his house—and who was only ninety-nine?

MY FATHER. That's the one.

THE ABBÉ. Well, what about him?

MY FATHER. His heirs were all very poor—none of them had a roof over his head, and all of them had to beg for a living on the public highway, in the countryside, or at the church door. They sent me a power of attorney authorizing me to enter the late curé's house and to provide for the security of their relative's personal property. How could I have refused to do for those poor ragamuffins the same favor I have so often done for wealthy families? So I went to Thivet, where I set the legal machinery in motion. I had the authorities put seals on all the locks; then I sat down to wait for the heirs to arrive. They lost no time in coming. There were ten or a dozen of them. The women had no stockings or shoes, you might almost say that they had no clothes at all. Several had babies in their arms, all of whom were wrapped in threadbare bits of discarded smocks. There were old men, dressed in rags, who had barely found strength enough to drag themselves thither, each carrying on a stick over his shoulder a parcel of odds and ends tied up in a scrap of cloth—the very image of poverty at its worst. With that picture in mind, imagine, if you can, the delight of those heirs at the prospect of laying hands on the ten thousand francs or so that each one stood to inherit, for local opinion had it that the old priest's estate might easily amount to a hundred thousand francs.

The seals were removed, and I went to work making an inventory of personal effects, a job that took the whole day. I was still at it when darkness fell and the poverty-stricken heirs went off to bed, leaving me alone. I was hoping to wind things up quickly so as to put them in possession of their several legacies, bid them good-by and get back to my own affairs. At last I had looked at everything but an old chest, minus its cover, that had been pushed under a desk. It was filled to the brim with all sorts of old scraps of paper—letters dating from many years back, rough drafts of the curé's replies to them, ancient receipts and stubs of receipts he had given to others, household accounts, and other waste paper of the same kind. In such circumstances, though, you have to read everything; you mustn't overlook anything, no matter how trivial it may seem. Well, I was just about done with that tedious job of inspection, when I chanced to put my hand on a rather bulky document—and what do you suppose it was? A will! A will signed by the old priest! A will bearing a date so remote that none of the executors named in it had been alive for twenty years past! A will in which he disinherited all the relatives who were at that moment sleeping soundly in the adjoining rooms and named as his only heirs the Frémin family—those wealthy publishers in Paris whom you must know (speaking to me).

I leave it to you to judge what a painful shock it was to find that will—but what the devil was I to do with it? Burn it? Why not? Didn't all the signs point to the old priest's having decided to throw it away? I mean the place where I found it, the fact that it was in the midst of all those worthless papers—didn't these indications point clearly enough to its having been canceled—to say nothing of the revolting injustice of its terms? That's what I thought to myself, at the same time as I let my mind dwell on the prospective despair of the wretched heirs who would all be robbed of their anticipated legacies if this will was allowed to take effect. I held the will a little closer to the fire in front of which I was sitting. Then there came into my head a whole swarm of ideas that contradicted my earlier reasoning—an indescribable fear of making an irreparable mistake in a matter so delicate, doubts as to the sufficiency of my own knowledge, the thought that perhaps I was in danger of letting the voice of pity, which cried out from the bottom of my heart, drown out the promptings of equity. All these reflections made me suddenly stop short. I sat there wide-awake the rest of that night, pondering the iniquitous document— which I several times brought within a hand's breadth of the flames—unable to make up my mind whether to burn it or not.

At last I decided not to burn it. Had I stopped deliberating a minute sooner or had I gone on a minute longer, it would have come out the other way. Perplexed as I was, I came to the conclusion that my wisest course of action would be to seek the advice of someone more enlightened than myself. So at daybreak I saddled my horse and posted off at top speed to Langres. I rode straight past my own front door, not stopping to go in, and went on to the seminary, occupied at that time by the Brothers of the Oratory, among whom there was one in particular who was famous for his huge fund of precise information as well as for the holiness of his life. This was a certain Father Bouin, who has left behind him in this diocese a very great reputation as an adviser on matters of conscience.

My father had gotten only as far as this point in his story when he was interrupted by the arrival of Dr. Bissei, our family physician and an old friend. He asked after my father's health, took his pulse, added some items to his diet and eliminated some others, settled himself in a chair, and joined our conversation.

Some of the doctor's patients were known to my father, who, of course, wanted to hear the latest news about them. Among others, there was a certain scoundrel who had been employed as chief steward by M. de La Mésangère, formerly mayor of our town. This steward had made a total wreck of his master's affairs, had borrowed money fraudulently in his name, had lost or destroyed many of his title deeds, embezzled his funds, and had perpetrated a whole series of similar felonies, most of which he had freely confessed to. He was at that moment waiting to have the judges pronounce sentence upon him; in all likelihood he would either get death on the gallows or be sent to the galleys for life. The whole province was all agog over his misdeeds. The doctor told my father that the prisoner was seriously ill at the moment, but that he had by no means given up hope of pulling him through.

MY FATHER. You won't be doing him any great favor.

MYSELF. It would be a great mistake to save his life.

DR. BISSEI. A great mistake! Why do you call it that, if you please?

MYSELF. Because there are already so many wicked men in this world that we ought not to cling to the coattails of one who has been taken with an urgent desire to leave it for good.

DR. BISSEI. My job is to cure them, not to pass judgment on them. I intend to cure him if I can because that's my trade; afterwards the judge can send him to the gallows because that's *his* trade.

MYSELF. But Doctor, there is one obligation that rests on all good citizens—on you, on me, and on all the rest; it is our duty to work with might and main for the public welfare, and it strikes me that the public interest is badly served when you restore a desperate criminal to health, especially a man about to be legally prevented from committing fresh outrages against society.

DR. BISSEI. Tell me this: Who has the right to declare him a criminal? Have I any such right?

MYSELF. His deeds have already branded him guilty.

DR. BISSEI. Who is qualified to determine the truth or falsehood of what has been alleged against him? Am I qualified?

MYSELF. No. But allow me, Doctor, if you will, to change my line of argument a little. Suppose that you have as a patient some fellow whose crimes are a matter of common knowledge. He calls you and you come running. You pull aside the curtains of his bed and you recognize Cartouche or Nivet.* Would you save Cartouche's life or put Nivet back on his legs again?

Dr. Bissei hesitated for a moment or two and then replied in a very firm tone of voice that he would save them both, trying to forget the sick man's name and to pay attention only to the symptoms of his illness, inasmuch as these were the only facts he had a right to take cognizance of. If he were to take one single step beyond that line, he added, there would soon be no way of telling where to stop. Every human life would be completely at the mercy of ignorance, passion and prejudice from the moment it was once admitted that a doctor's prescription ought to depend upon the outcome of an inquiry into the morals or mode of life of the patient. "What you say about Nivet, a Jansenist will say about a Molinist,† or a Catholic about a Protestant. If you drive me away from Cartouche's bedside, some religious fanatic will be authorized to pull me away from an atheist's bed. Really, it is difficult enough to measure out medicine needed to cure a disease without having to calculate how wicked a man may be before he stops being eligible to take medicine."

"But Doctor," I answered: "what would you say if the first use this scoundrel made of his new-found good health —restored, thanks to your medicine—was to murder your dearest friend? Tell me, now, in all sincerity: Wouldn't you be sorry you had cured him? Wouldn't your conscience cry out

---

* Cartouche was a celebrated highwayman and Nivet was another famous cutthroat of the eighteenth century.

† The reference is to a long and embittered quarrel among French Catholics, dating from the mid-seventeenth century; the dispute centered in a difference over the doctrine of free will, on which the followers of Jansen were eventually declared unorthodox by the Pope. The Jesuits were the principal supporters of the victorious side, taking their arguments from the writings of the sixteenth-century theologian Louis Molina.

reproachfully: 'Why, oh why, did I save him? Why didn't I let him die!' Wouldn't that be enough to make the rest of your days a burden to you?"

DR. BISSEI. Well, of course, I should be prostrate with grief, but I should feel no sense of guilt.

MYSELF. But what sense of guilt could you have—I don't say, for taking his life, for there isn't any question of that—but at letting a mad dog perish? Mark my words, Doctor: I am less timid than you are, and I wouldn't allow specious reasoning to hold me back. Suppose I am a doctor. When I see my patient, I recognize him for a notorious rogue, and this is what I would say to him: "Hurry up and die, you swine. That's the best thing that can happen to you, considering both your own interests and those of other people. I know exactly what to do to relieve the pain that troubles you there in your side, but I am going to be damned careful not to do it because I don't bear enough of a grudge against my fellow citizens to send you out again, hale and hearty, into their midst. If I did that, I should only be letting myself in for the lifelong torment of feeling partly responsible for all the new crimes you would surely commit. I refuse to be your accomplice. The law would punish anyone who hid you in his house—is it credible that the man who saved your life would be innocent of wrongdoing? He couldn't possibly be guiltless! If I have any regret at all, it is only that in letting you die of your illness I shall be sparing you the final agonies on the scaffold which you so richly deserve. I am not going to take the trouble to bring you back to life when I am bound by natural justice, by concern for the good of society and for the welfare of my fellow citizens, to turn you over to the hangman. So go ahead and die. Let no one say that my skill or conscientiousness is to blame for the survival of even one monster such as you are!"

DR. BISSEI. Well, well! Good night, Papa. And mind you—not so much coffee after supper, do you hear?

MY FATHER. But Doctor—coffee tastes so good to me!

DR. BISSEI. All right, drink it, then, but see that you take a great deal of sugar in it.

MY SISTER. Please, Doctor, all that sugar will make us break out in a sweat.

DR. BISSEI. Poppycock! Well, good-by, Philosopher.

MYSELF. Wait just a moment, Doctor. Galen, who lived under the Emperor Marcus Aurelius, and who was surely a very able man, even if he did believe in dreams, charms and witchcraft, had this to say about his method for saving the lives of newborn babies: "I intend these precepts only for the Greeks, the Romans and those who follow in their footsteps to advance human knowledge. As for the Germans and other barbarians, they are no more worthy to know such things than bears, lions, wild boars and the rest of the beasts of prey."

DR. BISSEI. Yes, I know all that. You are both wrong—Galen for having taught such a foolish thing, and you for citing him as an authority. You yourself would never have been born—and your praise or blame of Galen would never have been spoken—if Nature had not had better methods than his for ensuring the survival of the Germans' babies.

MYSELF. Furthermore, during the most recent outbreak of plague in Marseille——

DR. BISSEL. Make it short; I'm in a hurry.

MYSELF. Well, there were hordes of brigands who went swarming through the city, looting houses, killing, and taking advantage of the general disorder to get money by all sorts of foul means. One of these bandits fell victim to the plague and was recognized by a gravedigger who had been ordered by the police to carry away the dead. As he and his helpers were going from house to house, throwing the corpses out into the street, the gravedigger saw the thug and said: "Oho, you scum! So you're here, are you?" Whereupon he laid hold of the sick man's feet and dragged him toward a window. The bandit began to shriek, "But I'm not dead, I'm not dead!" To which the gravedigger made reply: "You're dead enough!"—pitching him at the same instant out of a fourth-story window. Doctor, I tell you frankly—in my eyes that gravedigger, who so cavalierly polished off a plague-ridden rascal, is less guilty of wrongdoing than a skillful physician like you who would have saved his life. That's all I have to say on the subject.

THE DOCTOR. My good Philosopher—I admire your spirit and your enthusiasm more than words can say, but I'm afraid I can't subscribe to your doctrine of morality; it doesn't suit me, and I'll wager it doesn't please the abbé any better than it does me.

THE ABBÉ. You'd surely win that bet.

I was on the point of having a go at the abbé; but my father turned to me with a smile and said: "You're arguing on the side that's opposite from the one you really believe in."

MYSELF. How so, Father?

MY FATHER. You want that infamous steward of M. de La Mésangère to die, don't you? Well, then, just let the doctor go on about his business. . . . Did you mutter something just now?

MYSELF. I was only saying that Bissei will probably never get to deserve the inscription which the Romans placed above the door of the physician who attended Pope Adrian VI in his last illness: *To the Liberator of the Nation.*

MY SISTER. And if he had been personal physician to Cardinal Mazarin, he would not, like Guénault, have caused the wagon drivers to say after the Chief Minister's death, "Let the doctor go by, fellows; he's the man who did us the favor of killing the Cardinal."

My father smiled and said, "Now where was I in the story I was telling?"

MY SISTER. You'd got as far as where you went to see Father Bouin.

MY FATHER. Well, I told him all the facts in the case. Then Father Bouin said to me: "Nothing, Sir, could be more praiseworthy than the compassionate feelings that you have toward these unlucky heirs. By all means suppress the will and relieve their poverty—I gladly agree, but only on condition that you make up to the sole rightful heir the exact sum you will have deprived him of, no more and no less." But wait a moment— I feel as though someone had put a big cake of ice between my shoulder blades; the doctor must have left the front door ajar. Sister, will you please go and close it?

MY SISTER. I'm on my way, but I hope you won't go on with the story until I get back.

MY FATHER. No, certainly not.

After she had been gone a few moments longer than necessary, my sister came back into the room a little out of sorts and said, "It was that silly fellow who tacked up two notices on his door, one of them reading: *House for sale, 20,000 francs, or for rent at 1,200 francs a year,* and the other: *20,000 francs to lend for one year at 6 per cent.*

MYSELF. Perhaps, Sister, the man isn't so silly as you think. You say you saw two different notices, but what if the two are really only one, and the second is only another version of the first? But let's pass over that and get back to Father Bouin.

MY FATHER. Well, Father Bouin went on to say, "Who, if you please, has given you the power to decide whether a legal document shall be binding or not? Who has authorized you to interpret dead men's intentions?"

"But Father Bouin, what about the old wreck of a chest?"

"What right have you to decide whether the will was deliberately thrown away or carelessly mislaid? Haven't you ever thrown away an important paper by mistake, only to find it later at the bottom of a wastebasket?"

"But Father Bouin, what about the date of the will, and what about the manifest injustice of its provisions?"

"You have no authority to pass upon the justice or injustice of this document or to decide that the sole legatee is not entitled to his inheritance—the curé's gift to him may perfectly well be interpreted as an act of restitution or as any other kind of legitimate payment you may like to imagine."

"But Father Bouin, what about the poor relations, who are close kin to the deceased, while the rich heir is only a very distant cousin?"

"Has anyone given you the responsibility of measuring the extent of the dead man's obligations to his nearest relatives? Besides, you know nothing about them except that they are poor."

"But Father Bouin, what about the stack of old letters from the rich heir which the late curé never even took the trouble to open?"

This (my father remarked in an aside) is a detail I had forgotten to mention. I did, however, find in the chest of old papers twenty or thirty, perhaps even more, letters from the Frémins, all of them still sealed.

"None of those details," said Father Bouin, "has the slightest

significance—the chest, the date, the letters—all are totally
irrelevant, and so is Father Bouin's opinion, and so are all
your 'ifs' and 'buts.' Nobody has a right to meddle with the
law by trying to read a dead person's mind or by disposing of
someone else's property. If Providence wants to punish the
next-of-kin, the legatee, or the deceased curé—how can we
know which it may be?—and to that end has preserved this will
as if by accident, then the will must be allowed to take effect."

After getting so clear and precise a decision from the most
enlightened member of our clergy, I sat for a moment stupefied,
trembling as I thought to myself what would have become
of me—and of you, dear children—if I had happened to burn
that will as I had been strongly tempted to do at least a dozen
times, and if I had subsequently been racked with doubts and
had gone only then to consult Father Bouin. I would have
made the amount good—oh yes, I would have had to cough it
up, all right, as sure as sure can be—and you would have been
ruined!

MY SISTER. But Papa, after that you had to go back to the
curé's house and tell all those beggars that not a single morsel
of what was there belonged to them, and that there was
nothing for them to do but go back where they had come from
no richer than before. How did you ever nerve yourself up to
do it—a tender-hearted soul like you!

MY FATHER. I swear, I don't know to this day how I managed
to find the courage. My first thought was of resigning my
power of attorney, turning it over to a lawyer who would
take my place. But then I thought that a lawyer would probably treat those poor people pretty harshly, sticking close to
the strict letter of the law, and I didn't want them to be taken
hold of by the shoulders and thrown bodily out of doors—I
realized that by softening the blow, I might perhaps lighten
their misfortunes a little.

So I went back that same day to Thivet. My sudden departure, together with the precautions I had taken before
setting out, had created a good deal of uneasiness in the
house, and when I came in again wearing a long face they
were still more upset. I gritted my teeth, though, and tried
my best not to let them see too much of my feelings.

MYSELF. Knowing your powers of dissimulation, I daresay they could read your face like an open book.

MY FATHER. First, I locked up everything that had any considerable value. Then I called into the house a number of local people, thinking that it would be well to have a few strong arms to help me if matters should come to such a pass. Then I unlocked the cellar and the storeroom and turned the contents over to the poor wretches whom I advised to eat and drink their fill and then to divide up all the wine, grain and other edibles that remained.

THE ABBÉ. But Father——

MY FATHER. Yes, yes, I know: they had no more claim to those things than to the rest of the estate.

MYSELF. Keep quiet, Abbé, and stop interrupting.

MY FATHER. Then, pale as death and shaking from head to foot, I opened my mouth to speak, but not a word could I muster. I sat down, stood up; I tried to begin a sentence, but wasn't able to finish it. At last I burst into tears, which frightened the whole crowd and started them shouting on all sides: "Hurry up, Sir! What's the matter?"

"What's the matter?" I repeated; "the matter is that I've found a will—a will that disinherits every one of you!" These few words cost me such an effort that I felt I was about to fall in a faint.

MY SISTER. I should say you must have been.

MY FATHER. What a scene, children, what a scene! I shall never forget what followed, and I shudder as I recall it. It seems to me that I shall hear their cries of pain, their shouts of anger, their howls of rage, the curses they bellowed out. (Here my father put his hands over his eyes and then over his ears.) Those women (he went on), I can almost see them now —some rolling over and over all around the room, pulling out great fistfuls of their own hair, tearing at their faces and breasts with their nails. Some foaming at the mouth, held their babies by the heels and were all ready to dash their brains out on the stone floor if we hadn't stopped them. The men laid hold of the chairs, tipped over the tables, and smashed everything that came to hand; some of them started to set fire to the house, while others got down on all fours and scratched at the floor with their fingernails as though they were trying to dig up the old priest in order to tear his corpse to pieces. Above this bedlam I could hear the children's shrieks, for they were as much overcome by despair as their elders, even though they didn't quite know what it was all about, clinging to their mothers' dresses only to be savagely thrust aside. I don't know when in all my life I have had such a painful experience.

I had written, however, to the heir in Paris, informing him of just how matters stood and urging him to come as soon as he possibly could. This was the only way to be sure of preventing some tragic accident which, left to my own devices, I might not have been able to ward off.

Meanwhile I had some success in calming the poor relations by telling them of my hope—which I really thought might work out—of persuading the heir to renounce his rights under the will, or at least of talking him into a generous settlement with the old priest's next-of-kin. Then I sent the latter to stay with local families, scattering them among the cottages in the farthest outskirts of the village.

Well, Frémin came down posthaste from Paris, but I had only to take one good look to see that he had a hard, cruel face which held no promise of any good outcome for my friends.

MYSELF. Great, black, tufted eyebrows; small, hooded eyes; a big mouth set somewhat at an angle; and a rather sallow skin all pitted by smallpox?

MY FATHER. That's him to the life. It had taken him only thirty hours to travel more than 180 miles. I began by introducing him to the poor devils whose cause I had to plead. They all stood silently before him; the women were weeping quietly; the men, bareheaded, leaned on their sticks and held their caps in their hands. Frémin just sat there in his armchair, his eyes closed and his head bent forward so that his chin touched his chest, not even looking at them.

I spoke in their behalf as eloquently as I knew how—and it will always be a mystery to me how anyone can think what to say on such an occasion. I made it as plain to him as the nose on his face that his claim to the estate was of very uncertain validity; I pleaded with him to consider how wealthy he was already, and how wretched were the poor beggars who stood before him. I think I may even have thrown myself at his feet—but I couldn't pry him loose from so much as a single sou.

He replied that he saw no reason to go into the various circumstances I had mentioned; there was a will; he didn't care a straw about its history; and he found my conduct more to be admired than my oration. In an outburst of indignation I threw the keys in his face, but he merely picked them up very calmly and went about taking possession of every last item of property.

I came home so troubled, so miserable, and so different from my usual self that your mother, who was still living at that time, thought when she saw me that I had met with some terrible misfortune. . . . Ah, children, that fellow Frémin must have been made of stone!

We sat silent for a while after my father had finished telling his story, each of us meditating after his own fashion upon the singular adventure he had described. Soon more visitors put in an appearance: a clergyman whose name I have forgotten— he was prior of a wealthy abbey, a corpulent fellow more at his ease in discussing good wine than in debating questions of morality, and a man who had spent more time reading his *How to Shine in Polite Society* than the *Grenoble Lectures.** There was also a judge, who served also as notary and as chief of police, a man named Dubois. A little later there appeared a master craftsman who wanted a few words with my father. He was invited in, along with a retired civil engineer who had also once been a teacher of mathematics, a study which he now cultivated as his hobby; he was a next-door neighbor to the craftsman, who was a hatmaker.

The last led off by giving my father to understand that the company was a little too numerous for what he had to say. Whereupon the others stood up, said good night, and went out,

* Respectively, a manual of etiquette and a collection of discourses on ethics and morality.

leaving only the prior, the judge, the geometrician and myself
—for the hatmaker had held me by the sleeve when I started to
go out with the others.

"M. Diderot," said he to my father, after he had looked all
around the room to make sure he could not be overheard, "I've
come to you because you have a great reputation for honesty
and wisdom, and I am not sorry to find here these gentlemen,
all of whom I know even if they don't all know me: a priest, a
lawyer, a scientist, a philosopher, and a man of perfect integrity—what an assembly! It would be strange indeed if I
failed to obtain the advice I need among men of such varied
callings, all of them equally just and enlightened."

Then the hatmaker went on: "First, I must ask you to
promise that you will hold in confidence everything I am
about to tell you, no matter what I finally decide to do about
my problem."

We promised, and he continued.

"Although I have been married more than once, I have no
children by former marriages. Nor did I have any by my last
wife, whom I lost about a fortnight ago. Since her death I
have been more dead than alive; I have been unable to eat,
drink, sleep, or work. I get up, get dressed, go outdoors and
prowl through the whole town, tormented by the most horrible
anxiety. During all the eighteen years of my wife's illness I
waited on her hand and foot, doing everything in my power to
give her the special little attentions that her unhappy condition made so necessary. The outlays I have made on her
account have more than eaten up our modest income from
our investments together with the amount I have earned by
my trade, and have left me under a heavy burden of debt. Now,
at her death, I have worn myself out by taking care of her, and
have nothing to show for the best years of my life—in a nut-
shell, I shall be no farther ahead than when I first set up
shop, if I fulfill the strict letter of the law and pay to my late
wife's distant cousins the share of her dowry that should
revert to them at her death. She brought with her a splendid
trousseau, for her father and mother were extremely fond of
their daughter and did all they could—indeed, more than

they could really afford—to give her a proper dowry. There were fine, heavy linens, plenty of them, which are still as good as new, for my poor wife never had any opportunity to use them; in addition, there were twenty thousand francs in cash, the proceeds of a note repaid by M. Michelin, the deputy procurer-general. My wife's eyes had hardly been closed five minutes before I hid the linens and the money in a place where no one else can find them.

"Now, gentlemen, you know all the details of my problem right up to date. Did I do right or wrong? My conscience bothers me: it seems to be telling me: You're a thief, you're a thief—give it back, give it back! What do you think, gentlemen? Remember that my wife, having now departed this life, was the recipient of all my earnings for twenty years, that I am soon going to be too old to work for my living, that I have large debts, and that if I make restitution to my in-laws, it will be the poorhouse for me, if not tomorrow, then the day after. So tell me, gentlemen, what conclusions you have reached. Must I make restitution and go to the poorhouse?"

"The spiritual power takes precedence over the temporal," said my father, bowing toward the priest, "so, Prior, you have the floor."

"My son," said the prior to the hatmaker, "I have no patience with people who have too many scruples: they only addle their brains and never to any useful purpose. Maybe you ought not to have taken that money, but since you have already taken it, my advice is to keep it."

MY FATHER. But hold on, Prior, surely you aren't going to let it go at that?

THE PRIOR. Upon my word, that's the best advice I can give.

MY FATHER. Well, it's not very good advice. Now it's your turn, Judge.

THE JUDGE. My friend, you are in an embarrassing predicament. Some people might perhaps advise you to make over the money to your deceased wife's relations, so that when you die it will not pass to your own heirs and be lost to them, but with the proviso that you are to enjoy, as long as you live, the income from it. But the law is perfectly clear, and it gives you no right whatsoever to the money, neither to the income from it nor to the capital sum itself. Take my advice: it would be better to behave like an honest man and abide by the law, even if you have to go to the poorhouse.

MYSELF. So that's the law, is it? A fine law *that* is!

MY FATHER. Now your opinion, Mathematician. How would you solve the problem?

THE GEOMETRICIAN. My friend, didn't you say you had taken about twenty thousand francs?

THE HATMAKER. Yes, sir.

THE GEOMETRICIAN. And how much has your wife's illness cost you, approximately?

THE HATMAKER. Just about the same amount.

THE GEOMETRICIAN. Very well, then: from twenty thousand francs subtract twenty thousand francs—remainder: zero.

MY FATHER (to me). And what does our philosopher say?

MYSELF. Philosophy is silent when the law is absurd.

My father sensed that it would not do to get me stirred up, so he turned and spoke at once to the hatmaker: "Master Such-a-one," he said, "you have already admitted to us that no sooner had you stolen the inheritance of your wife's relations than you lost your peace of mind. So what good is all that money to you, seeing that it has robbed you of the most precious thing in the world? Get rid of it quickly, so you can eat, drink, sleep, work, and be at peace with yourself—in your own home if you can hold onto it, or somewhere else if worse comes to worst."

The hatmaker answered abruptly, "No, Sir, I'm going to go and live in Geneva."

"All right, but do you think you can leave your guilty conscience here behind you?"

"I don't know, but I'm going to Geneva anyway."

"Go where you please—you'll find your conscience waiting for you when you get there."

At this the hatmaker took his leave, and his odd reply became the topic of our conversation. We were in agreement that perhaps all human feelings, all pangs of conscience—even the knowledge of one's criminal guilt—are more or less weakened by a long lapse of time or by great distances. A murderer who has fled to the shores of China is too far away to see the bleeding corpse he left on the banks of the Seine. The sense of guilt arises, perhaps, more from our fear of others than from our horror at what we have done; less from the shame of the deed itself than from the blame and punishment we would have to suffer if the deed should happen to be found out. What criminal in hiding feels so safe in his dark corner that he has ceased to fear lest some indiscretion, some careless word, or some unforeseen accident betray him? How can he be sure that he will not give himself away while talking in his sleep or in the delirium of a fever? If someone near the scene of his crime should overhear him under those circumstances, he would be undone. But in China those around him would not understand what he was saying. "My children, the days of the wicked are full of alarms. Peace of mind belongs only to the upright man, for he alone shall live and die in tranquillity."

Having exhausted this text, we bade our visitors good night. When they had gone, my brother and sister came back in, and we picked up our earlier conversation where it had been broken off. My father exclaimed, "God be praised! Here we are by ourselves at last. I enjoy having company, but I like it still better to be alone with you children." Then, turning to me, he went on: "Why didn't you want to give the hatmaker your opinion?"

"Why, because you didn't let me."

"And wasn't my advice right?"

"No, because there is no such thing as giving good advice to a fool. What the devil! Isn't that man his wife's closest relation? As for the property he has withheld, wasn't it given to him as part of his wife's dowry? Doesn't it belong to him by the most legitimate title one can think of? What claim can those distant cousins have to it?"

MY FATHER. You're paying attention only to the letter of the law, and you should be guided by its intention.

MYSELF. Like you, Father, I see how few rights women have, treated as they are with contempt by their husbands, who persecute them whatever they do, and I see how unsafe women would be if husbands came automatically into possession of their wives' marriage portions at the latters' death. But how does all that reasoning apply to an honest man who has always been scrupulous in doing his duty toward his wife? Isn't it bad enough for him to lose her? Does the law have to come along and snatch away from him all her worldly goods?

MY FATHER. But if you admit that the motive behind the law is good, then it seems to me you ought to abide by it.

MY SISTER. If there were no law, there would be no such thing as stealing.

MYSELF. No, Sister, there you're mistaken.

MY BROTHER. She's right. Without the law, everything would belong to everybody, and hence there would be no more rights of property.

MYSELF. No, Brother, you're wrong too.

MY BROTHER. Well, then, what does give foundation to property rights?

MYSELF. In origin it was the right of possessing something on which one's labor had been expended. Nature's laws have been good ones since the beginning of the world, and any use of force to compel their observance is legitimate. While this use of force may be unlimited against those who behave badly, it should never be used at all against those who are good. Assuming that I am a good man, here is what ought to happen in a case like the one we're discussing, and in any number of others I could describe to you: I summon the law before the tribunal of my own conscience, my reason and my heart—that is, before the court of natural justice; I put questions to it; then I decide either to submit to it or declare it null and void.

MY FATHER. Just go ahead and preach your doctrine from the housetops—I promise you it will convert a great many people, and then you'll be able to see the splendid results that will follow.

MYSELF. Don't worry, I'm not going to preach it at all. There are some truths that were never meant for fools; but that's no reason not to keep them by me for my own use.

MY FATHER. You mean, for use of a sublimely wise man like yourself?

MYSELF. Exactly.

MY FATHER. Well, then, according to what you've just been saying, I presume you would likewise disapprove of the course I took in the affair of the old priest at Thivet. But what's your opinion, Abbé?

THE ABBÉ. Why, I think, Father, that you acted very prudently in seeking Father Bouin's advice and also in following his recommendations. If you had yielded to your first impulse, we should all have been ruined, and no question about it.

MY FATHER. And you, Great Philosopher, aren't you of the same opinion?

MYSELF. No.

MY FATHER. Well, that's a concise answer. But let's hear your reasons.

MYSELF. You really insist?

MY FATHER. Naturally.

MYSELF. You want me to be perfectly frank?

MY FATHER. By all means.

MYSELF. Then I am decidedly not of your opinion (I replied with some warmth). I think, personally, that if you ever did anything wrong in your whole life, that was the time. I think, too, that while you felt you would have been obliged to make restitution to the heir named in the will in the event you had torn it up, you were under an even stronger obligation to indemnify the next-of-kin for having failed to do so.

MY FATHER. I must admit that I have never felt entirely easy in my own mind about the way I finally dealt with the problem; but Father Bouin——

MYSELF. With all his reputation for knowledge and piety, your Father Bouin was nothing but a poor logic-chopper, a narrow-minded bigot.

MY SISTER (half under her breath). And have you really got your heart set on sending us all to the poorhouse?

MY FATHER. Hush, hush! Never mind Father Bouin. Just tell us your train of thought without insulting anybody.

MYSELF. My train of thought? It's very simple, and it goes like this: either the old priest intended to throw away the will, which he had made at a time when his heart was hardened against his poor relations—all the facts tend to bear out this hypothesis—and you have defeated his attempt to make amends; or else he intended this atrocious will to take effect, and you have made yourself an accomplice to his unjust act.

MY FATHER. His unjust act? It's easy to call it unjust, but who's to decide?

MYSELF. Yes, yes, his unjust act. Everything Father Bouin told you to the contrary was empty quibbling, poor guess-work—"perhapses" and "maybes" without any real weight—that loses any vestige of plausibility it might have *in abstracto* when confronted with the facts: I mean the circumstances under which you found this abominable piece of paper, rescued it from the rubbish heap, produced it as a true will and so re-established its validity. Think of it—a box full of waste-paper, buried in it an old scrap of parchment discredited by its date, by its manifest injustice, by its presence in a pile of trash, by the death of the executors, by the old priest's disdain for Frémin's letters, and by the latter's great wealth as well as by the poverty of the true heirs, the next-of-kin!

Against all that evidence, what can be shown on the other side? You presume that the curé wanted to make restitution for some unknown reason! Do you imagine that the poor devil of a priest, who had not a sou to his name when he came to his parish, and who spent eighty years of his life heaping up a hundred thousand francs by piling one on top of another, may at one time or another have stolen a hundred thousand francs from the Frémins, under whose roof he never lived for so much as one day, and whom he may well have known only by name? And even if he had stolen it, what an undeserved piece of bad luck for Frémin! . . . In your place I should have burned that evil document. You were under an obligation to burn it, I tell you. You were under an obligation to heed the promptings of your own kind heart, which has ever since been protesting against what you finally did. Your heart was a much wiser guide than that idiot Bouin, whose decision only proves that religious doctrines have a fearful power over even the most acute minds, that unjust laws can produce disastrous results, and that false principles are destructive of both common sense and natural equity. If you had been at the curé's side when he wrote that accursed will, wouldn't you have snatched it and torn it to pieces? Why on earth did you preserve it when fate put it into your hands?

MY FATHER. And what if the curé had made you his sole heir?

MYSELF. Then the wretched will would have been canceled all the more easily.

MY FATHER. I suppose so. But isn't it one thing to decline a gift intended for oneself, and quite another thing to decline, without that person's consent, a gift meant for someone else?

MYSELF. There's no difference. In either event the gift is just or unjust, praiseworthy or reprehensible.

MY FATHER. But when the law categorically requires that all a man's papers—without exception—be read and inventoried after his death, there must be some good reason behind it. What do you suppose it is?

MYSELF. If I were to be sarcastic I would say: To eat up the substance of the estate by multiplying what the lawyers call "defects in the will." But bear in mind that you were not a member of the legal guild. You were exempt from all obligation to follow the exact judicial procedure—the only duty you had to perform was that of serving the interests of generosity and natural equity.

My sister had been listening quietly, but at this she reached over and pressed my hand as a sign of approval. The abbé put his hands over his ears. My father said, "You managed to get in a few more sly digs on the subject of Father Bouin. But I hope you'll agree, at least, that my religion can give me absolution for any mistake I may have made."

MYSELF. Yes, unfortunately for your religion, I'm afraid you'll get absolution.

MY FATHER. Tell me, do you think the will, which you would have taken it upon yourself to burn, would have stood up in a court of law?

MYSELF. Possibly. But so much the worse for the law.

MY FATHER. Do you believe the judges would have paid no heed to all those facts about the discovery of the document on which you have held forth so eloquently?

MYSELF. I have no idea, but I should have wanted to get them off my chest at the very least. So, in your place, I should have spent fifty louis to hire a good lawyer—it would have been an excellent form of charity—and then I should have challenged the will in court on behalf of the poor relations.

MY FATHER. Oh well, as for that, if only you had been there to give me the suggestion you've just made, the chances are that I'd have taken your advice—even though fifty louis seems like a lot of money when a man is just getting his family and his business started.

THE ABBÉ. As for me, I'd rather have seen the money given as alms to the poor relations than wasted on lawyers' fees.

MYSELF. And are you convinced, Brother, that our case would have been lost?

MY BROTHER. I'm sure of it. The judges, to their credit, stick close to the letter of the law, like our father and Father Bouin. In a case like this they would close their eyes to these secondary considerations, just as Father Bouin and our father did, for fear of the bad precedents that would be established—and they would be right. Often they must even decide contrary to the dictates of their own consciences, and, like our father and Father Bouin, sacrifice the interests of unfortunate or innocent persons when these can be protected only by giving free rein to a hundred scoundrels—and the judges are right. They dread with good reason, as did our father and Father Bouin, to hand down a decision that might be perfectly just in some particular case but dangerous in a thousand others because of the crimes or frauds to which it would open the door. And in the case of this will we have been discussing——

MY FATHER (to me). Your reasons, in themselves, may be all very well, but they're not suitable to be set up as public maxims. I could no doubt have found a not-too-scrupulous lawyer who would have whispered in my ear: "Burn the will," but who would not have been willing to put that advice in writing.

MYSELF. By which I understand: This matter was not a fit one to come before a court of law. And, by God, if I'd been there in your place, it never would have.

MY FATHER. You would have valued your own reason more highly than that of the general public; that is, you'd have let one man's decision override the law.

MYSELF. Precisely. Doesn't man, as man, take precedence over man in his legal capacity? Isn't the natural wisdom of humanity many times more sacred than that of some lawgiver? We call ourselves civilized, yet often we behave worse than savages. Apparently we have to go monotonously on, century after century, repeating the same errors and the same excesses, before we can achieve even a faint glimmering of sound judgment. Pure instinct, unhindered, would have led us straight to our goal. But no! We have so thoroughly lost our sense of direction that——

MY FATHER. Yes, yes, my son—I agree with you that reason is a good pillow, but I have found that my head rests more peacefully on that of religion and the laws. And don't give me your rebuttal of that now because I don't want to lie awake half the night. I hope you're not going to get out of sorts over this, but I wish you'd tell me something if I had burned the will, would you have held out against my indemnifying the injured legatee?

MYSELF. No, Father. Your peace of mind is worth much more to me than all the money in the world.

MY FATHER. That's an answer I can't find fault with, and for a very good reason.

MYSELF. And will you tell us the reason?

MY FATHER. With pleasure. You may recall that your uncle, Canon Vigneron, was a very stiff-necked fellow and never got on well with his colleagues, the other canons of the cathedral chapter, chiefly because his every word and deed could be taken as a direct or indirect criticism of their ways. You, my son, were in line to be his successor. But when he lay dying the family thought it would be wiser to send his resignation, made in your favor, directly to Rome for confirmation than to let it go to the local chapter and run the risk of its being rejected. So away went the letter in the mail. Your uncle died an hour or two before the arrival of the coach that was expected to bring us our reply, and so the canonicate and its yearly stipend of 1,800 francs was lost. Your mother, your aunts, their relatives, and all our close friends were in favor of withholding the announcement of the canon's death. But I overruled their idea and had the church bells rung immediately.

MYSELF. You did the right thing.

MY FATHER. If I had listened to those estimable ladies and had had pangs of remorse later on, I'm sure you wouldn't have hesitated to give up your canonicate in order to put my conscience at rest.

MYSELF. Even apart from your conscience, I should have preferred to be either a good philosopher or nothing at all to being a bad canon.

The fat prior came in again, just in time to overhear my last remark, and said, "A bad canon! I'd like to know how it's possible to be either a good or a bad canon or a good or a bad prior—both are titles that make so few demands on the holder of them." My father shrugged and excused himself, saying that he had to say his prayers. The prior observed, "I'm afraid I shocked the old man a little."

MY BROTHER. Yes, I think so.

Then, pulling a book out of his pocket, he added, "I must read you a few pages out of this description of Sicily by a certain Father Labat."

MYSELF. I'm already familiar with the book. You've come to the story about the cobbler of Messina.

MY BROTHER. That's right.

THE PRIOR. Well, what about him?

MY BROTHER. The author relates that the cobbler in question was by nature virtuous and devoted to law and order. He was most unhappy in a country where the laws were not only lacking in rigor, but were not even enforced. Each day some revolting crime was committed. Known murderers walked the streets with their noses insolently in the air, showing their contempt for public opinion. Not a few parents were plunged into despair when their daughters were seduced and then thrust down from dishonor to misery, victims of the seducers' heartlessness. Licensed monopolies mulcted the industrious citizen of his substance and that of his children. The oppressed inhabitants were driven to weep bitter tears by the gouging and extortion of all kinds that went on. The guilty always avoided punishment, thanks to their connections, to their wealth, or to their success in slipping through the loopholes in the law. The honest cobbler saw all this, and he was sick at heart. As he sat at his bench he used to turn over incessantly in his mind the various measures that might be taken to restore law and order.

THE PRIOR. But what could a poor devil like him do—all by himself?

MY BROTHER. You're on the point of finding out. One day he established a private court of justice in his shop.

THE PRIOR. What do you mean by that?

MYSELF. The prior wants you to get to the end of your story as expeditiously as he gets to the end of his prayers.

THE PRIOR. And what's wrong with that? According to the best rules of oratory a story should be brief, and the Bible tells us to make our prayers short.

MY BROTHER. Well, whenever the cobbler heard of some atrocious crime, he instituted secret, but very strict, judicial proceedings against the criminal before this private court of his. Once he had performed his double function as prosecutor and judge, and had passed sentence, he went out with an arquebus under his cloak. Then, when he came upon the criminal by daylight in some secluded spot or when he encountered one of them prowling about the streets at night, he would raise his gun and calmly put five or six bullets into the rogue's carcass.

THE PRIOR. I'm very much afraid the story is going to end with this excellent fellow being drawn and quartered alive, and I am going to be very sorry for him.

MY BROTHER. After one of these "executions," he would let

the corpse lie where it had fallen, taking care not to go near it, and would stroll calmly back to his shop feeling as pleased with himself as though he had just killed a mad dog.

THE PRIOR. And did he get to kill a lot of mad dogs?

MY BROTHER. He had already polished off more than fifty, all of them important people, when the viceroy offered a reward of two thousand crowns to anyone who would inform against him, and he also swore before the high altar to pardon the guilty man if he gave himself up of his own accord.

THE PRIOR. Only an utter fool would have done that, though.

MY BROTHER. The cobbler, fearing that suspicion or punishment might fall on some innocent person——

THE PRIOR. —went and gave himself up to the viceroy!

MY BROTHER. Yes, and this is what he said to him: "I have been doing your job for you. I have tried, sentenced, and put to death the rascals you should have punished long ago. Here are the court records that show how their guilt was conclusively proven. If you read them you will see how faithfully I have followed correct judicial procedure in every detail. When I started out, I was sorely tempted to put you on trial first of all, but I decided instead to respect in your person the august sovereign whose representative you are. My life is in your hands—do what you will with me."

THE PRIOR. He didn't live to grow much older, of that you may be sure.

MY BROTHER. I don't know. But I am sure that he was no better than an assassin, despite all his fine zeal to see justice done.

THE PRIOR. An assassin! That's a very harsh name to call such a man. What would you call him if he had gone about slaughtering honest, respectable people?

MYSELF. Brother, how you rave!

MY SISTER. It would be nice if you two——

MY BROTHER (to me). All right, then, let's suppose you're the king of Naples and this case is referred to you for decision—what would you do?

MYSELF. Abbé, you're setting a trap for me, but I don't mind letting myself be caught in it. I would condemn the viceroy to death in place of the cobbler and I would appoint the cobbler my new viceroy.

MY SISTER. Hear, hear, Brother!

My father came in again, wearing the serene expression that he always had after saying his prayers. We told him the story about the cobbler, and his judgment was the same as the abbé's. My sister's comment was, "Well, you have put to death—if not the only just man—at least the only courageous citizen of Messina, and I think it's a great pity."

Some food was brought in by the servant, and my father and brother argued with me for a while longer; then we made a few jokes about the prior's advice to the hatmaker and we twitted him a good deal about his low opinion of priors and canons. Finally we got around to tell him my father's problem in connection with the will; but instead of giving us his solution straight off he told us of an incident he had been a party to:

THE PRIOR. Do you recall the spectacular bankruptcy of old Bourmont, the moneylender?

MY FATHER. Do I recall it! He owed me a tidy little sum.

THE PRIOR. Good.

MY FATHER. Why do you say "good"?

THE PRIOR. Because if I acted wrongly I shall be able to get some of the load off my conscience by telling you about my part in the affair. You see, I was appointed to be chief administrator on behalf of all his creditors. Now, among Bourmont's assets there was a promissory note for one hundred crowns signed by one of his neighbors, a poor grain merchant. If each one of the many creditors had gotten his proportionate share of this note's face value, none of them would have received more than twelve sous. On the other hand, the grain merchant would have been ruined if he had suddenly to make good on his note. I took it for granted——

MY FATHER. —that none of the creditors would have refused to give twelve sous to the poor devil. So you tore up the note and gave him a charitable gift out of my pocket.

THE PRIOR. That's the truth. Are you angry?

MY FATHER. No.

THE PRIOR. Then be magnanimous enough to believe that the others would have been no more displeased than you are, and there's nothing more to be said.

MY FATHER. But Prior, if you tear up one promissory note, acting on your own private authority, why not tear up two, three, four, or as many notes as there may be poor beggars in need of a handout at someone else's expense. Your conception of giving charity could lead, Prior, to Heaven knows what! But there are the demands of justice, justice——

THE PRIOR. Which, as someone has said, is sometimes the greatest injustice of all.

At that moment a young woman who lived on the second floor came downstairs and joined us. She was the personification of all that is gay and heedless. My father asked her what news she had had of her husband; the latter was a wastrel who had set an example of loose behavior for his wife to follow, and I believe she had done so, at least to some degree. To escape from his creditors this gentleman had shipped out to Martinique. Mme. d'Isigny—for this was our lodger's name —replied to my father's question, "M. d'Isigny? Thank God, I haven't heard a single word from him. Perhaps he's at the bottom of the sea by now."

THE PRIOR. At the bottom of the sea? Then I congratulate you.

MME. D'ISIGNY. What is it to you, Prior?

THE PRIOR. Nothing. But is it nothing to you?

MME. D'ISIGNY. Why should it make any difference to me?

THE PRIOR. But people say——

MME. D'ISIGNY. And what do they say?

THE PRIOR. Well, if you insist, they say that he got hold of some letters you had written.

MME. D'ISIGNY. What of it? You should see the fine collection of *his* letters that *I* have. . . .

Then there ensued a debate, as comical as anything could be, between the prior and Mme. d'Isigny over the privileges to which each of the two sexes is entitled. Mme. d'Isigny finally called on me to come to her defense, and I went on to prove to the prior that whenever a husband or wife was the first to violate the marriage vow, he or she thereby relieved the other partner of all obligation to respect it. But at this juncture, my father asked for his nightcap, broke off the conversation, and sent us all to bed. When it came my turn to kiss him good night, I whispered in his ear as I embraced him: "Father, the point is that when you come right down to it, there are no laws for a wise man. . . ."

"Don't talk so loud. . . ."

"Every law has its exceptions, and it takes wisdom to decide which cases come under the rule and which are to be dealt with as exceptions."

"I wouldn't be too sorry," he replied, "if there were one or two fellows like you in town; but if everybody thought as you do, I'd move somewhere else!"

6

THE ENCYCLOPEDIA

(First published in 1755.)

ENCYCLOPEDIA, noun, feminine gender. *(Philosophy.)* This word signifies *unity of knowledge;* it is made up of the Greek prefix EN, *in,* and the nouns KYKLOS, *circle,* and PAIDEIA, *instruction, science, knowledge.* In truth, the aim of an *encyclopedia* is to collect all the knowledge that now lies scattered over the face of the earth, to make known its general structure to the men among whom we live, and to transmit it to those who will come after us, in order that the labors of past ages may be useful to the ages to come, that our grandsons, as they become better educated, may at the same time become more virtuous and more happy, and that we may not die without having deserved well of the human race.

It would have been difficult to set for oneself a more enormous task than this of dealing with everything that relates to man's curiosity, his duties, his needs and his pleasures. Accordingly, some people, accustomed as they are to judging the feasibility of an enterprise by the poverty of their own resources, have asserted that we would never finish our task. (See the latest edition of the [Jesuits'] *Dictionnaire de Trévoux,* at the word *encyclopédie.*) Our only answer to them will be the following passage from the writings of Chancellor Bacon, which seems to be addressed especially to them: "Those works are possible, which may be accomplished by some person, though not by every one; which may be done by many,

277

though not by one; which may be completed in the succession of ages, though not within the hour-glass of one man's life; and which may be reached by public effort, though not by private endeavor." (*The Advancement of Learning*, Book II, Chapter I)

When one comes to reflect upon the vast subject matter of an encyclopedia, the one thing that can be perceived distinctly is that it cannot be the work of a single man. For how could one man, in the short space of his lifetime, hope to know and describe the universal system of nature and of art, seeing that the numerous and erudite society of academicians of *La Crusca** has taken forty years to compose its dictionary, and that the members of our French Academy worked sixty years on their *Dictionary* before publishing its first edition? Yet what is a linguistic dictionary, what is a compilation of the words of a language, assuming that it is executed as perfectly as possible? It is a very exact résumé of the articles to be included in a systematic encyclopedic dictionary.

But a single man, it may be said, can master all existing knowledge and can make such use as he desires of all the riches that other men have piled up. I cannot agree with this assumption. I am unable to believe that it is within the power of a single man to know all that can be known; to make use of all the knowledge that exists; to see all that is to be seen; to understand all that is comprehensible. Even if a systematic dictionary of the sciences and of the arts were to be nothing but a methodical collection of elementary principles, I should still want to know who is capable of discerning what is fundamental, and I should still ask who is the proper person to compose the elementary explanations; whether the description of the fundamental principles of a science or art should be a pupil's first attempt or the mature work of a master.

But to demonstrate, with the utmost degree of clarity, how difficult it is for one man ever to bring to completion a syste-

---

* The *Accademia della Crusca* was a society of scholars, mostly Italians, who were interested in the study of natural science as well as literature, religion and philosophy.

matic dictionary of all knowledge, it is enough to emphasize only the difficulties that arise during the composition of a simple dictionary of words.

A general dictionary of words is a work in which one aims at establishing the meaning of the terms of a language, defining those which can be defined by giving a brief, accurate, clear, and precise enumeration of the qualities or ideas that are attached to them. The only good definitions are those which bring together the essential attributes of the thing to which the word refers. But does everyone have the talents required for knowing and explaining those attributes? Is the art of making good definitions so very common? Are we not all more or less in the same situation as children, who use, with extremely nice precision, an infinite number of words in place of which it would be absolutely impossible for them to substitute the true sets of qualities or ideas which the words stand for? How many unforeseen difficulties arise from this fact when we have occasion to establish the meaning of the most common expressions! We are continually discovering that the ones we least understand are also the ones that we use most often. What is the cause of this strange phenomenon? It is that we are continually called upon to declare that a thing is *thus-and-so*, but almost never are we obliged to determine what it is *to be thus-and-so*. Our judgments most frequently refer to particular cases, and long habituation to the language and to social life suffices to guide us aright. We do nothing but repeat what we have heard all our lives. It is not at all the same thing when we seek to frame general theories that will embrace, without exception, a given number of particular cases. Nothing but the most profound meditations coupled with the most astonishing breadth of knowledge can lead us surely. I will clarify these principles by giving an example. We say—and no one ever makes a mistake on this point—of an infinite number of articles of all kinds that *they are luxuries;* but what is this *luxury* that we so infallibly attribute to so many things? This is the question which no one can satisfactorily answer with any degree of accuracy until after a discussion among all those

who show the most discrimination in their use of the term
luxury—a discussion which has never taken place and which
is perhaps beyond the capacities of the persons concerned.

All terms must be defined, excepting only the radicals,
that is to say, those which refer to simple sensations or to the
most abstract general ideas. If any have been left out, the
dictionary is incomplete. . . . And who will furnish an exact
definition of the word *congruent* unless it be a geometrician?
of the word *conjugation* unless it be a grammarian? of the
word *azimuth* unless it be an astronomer? of the word *epic* unless it be a man of letters? of the word *exchange* unless it be a
merchant? of the word *vice* unless it be a moralist? of the word
hypostasis unless it be a theologian? of the word *metaphysics*
unless it be a philosopher? of the word *gouge*, unless it be a
man well-versed in the manual arts? Whence I conclude that if
the French Academy did not unite in its assemblies all the
various kinds of human knowledge and the most diverse
talents, it would be impossible for it not to overlook a large
number of expressions which one would search for in vain in
its *Dictionary;* or for it not to allow false, incomplete, absurd,
or even ridiculous definitions to creep in.

I am fully aware that these views are not shared by those
who lecture to us about everything and who nevertheless
know nothing; who are not members of our academies and
who never will be because they are not worthy to be members;
yet who take it upon themselves to decide who should fill
vacant places; who, while they presume to set limits to the
subjects which the French Academy should consider, are
almost indignant to see men like Mairan, Maupertuis, or
D'Alembert enter that company; and who do not know that
the first time one of these men spoke in the Academy it was
to rectify the definition of the word *noon.* One would think,
to hear them talk, that they would like to restrict linguistic
science and the *Dictionary* of the Academy to those few words
which are familiar to them. And, indeed, if they looked a
little more closely, they would find a large number of terms
even among these—such as tree, animal, plant, flower, vice,
virtue, truth, force, laws—for a rigorous definition of which

they would have to call the philosopher, the jurist, the historian, or the naturalist to their assistance. In sum, they would need the help of men who know the real or abstract qualities that make a thing what it is and give it its individual or specific character, depending upon whether the thing is unique or one of a class.

We shall have to conclude, then, that a good dictionary can never be brought to completion without the co-operation of a large number of men endowed with special talents, because definitions of words are in no way different from definitions of things, and because a thing cannot be well defined or described except by those who have made a long study of it. But if this is admitted, how much more would be required for the execution of a work which, far from being limited to the definition of words, aims at describing in detail all that pertains to things!

A systematic universal dictionary of the arts and sciences cannot, therefore, be the work of one man alone. I will go further and say that I do not believe it can be done by any of the learned or literary societies that now exist, taken singly or together.

The French Academy could furnish an encyclopedia only with what pertains to language and its usage; the Academy of Inscriptions and Belles-Lettres, only knowledge relating to ancient and modern profane history, to chronology, to geography, and to literature; the Sorbonne, only theology, sacred history, and superstitions; the Academy of Sciences, only mathematics, natural history, physics, chemistry, medicine, anatomy, and the like; the Academy of Surgery, only the art of the surgeon; that of Painting, only painting, sculpture, engraving, drawing, architecture, and related topics; the University, only that which we understand by the humanities, scholastic philosophy, jurisprudence, printing, and the like.

Run through the other societies that I may have omitted and you will find that each is occupied with a single field of knowledge—a field that is doubtless within the purview of an encyclopedia—but that each neglects an infinite number of other subjects that must be included. You will not find any single society that can provide you with that fund of general

knowledge which you want. Better yet, lay them all under tribute, and you will discover how many things are still lacking;
you will be obliged to have recourse to a large number of men
of different sorts and conditions—men of genius to whom the
gates of the academies are closed by reason of their low rank
in their social scale. There are too many members of these
learned companies if one's need is simply for human knowledge; there are not enough in all these societies if one is in
search of a general science of man.

Without doubt it would be very useful to have all that one
could obtain from each particular learned society; and the sum
of what they could all provide would advance a universal dictionary a long way toward completion. There is, indeed, a task
which, if undertaken, would render the academicians' labors
even more directly subservient to the purpose of such a dictionary, and which the academies ought to be asked to do.
I can conceive of two ways of cultivating the sciences: one
is to increase the general fund of knowledge by making discoveries, and it is by this method that one comes to deserve
the name of *inventor;* the other is to bring past discoveries
together and reduce them to an ordered scheme so that more
men may be enlightened and that each may contribute within
the limits of his capacity to the intellectual progress of his
age; we use the term *writers of texts* to apply to those who
succeed in this second kind of enterprise, which is by no means
an easy one. I am convinced that if the learned societies that
exist throughout Europe would bestir themselves to collect all
ancient and modern knowledge with a view to linking it all
together by publishing complete and systematic treatises on
all subjects, it would be an excellent thing—at least the disappointing results thus far obtained in this direction lend
support to such a judgment. Compare the twenty-four quarto
volumes compiled by the Academy of Sciences, permeated as
these are by the outlook that dominates our most famous
academies, with eight or ten volumes to be prepared as I
have suggested, and see if it would not be easy to choose between the two sets. The latter would contain a vast amount
of excellent information now dispersed in a large number of

works, locked up where it can have no useful effect, like scattered coals which can never make a fire. And of these ten volumes you could scarcely put together one or two out of the most voluminous academic collection now in existence. One need only glance at the *Mémoires* of the Academy of Inscriptions and calculate how many pages one would borrow for a scientific treatise on history. What shall I say of the *Philosophical Transactions* or of the *Actes des curieux de la nature?* It is for this reason that all these enormous collections are beginning to lose their prestige, and there is no doubt that the first compiler of abridgments who happens to have some skill and good taste will drive them completely off the booksellers' shelves. This is bound to be their ultimate fate.

Having thought very seriously about the matter, I believe that the special task of an academician should be the advancement of the branch of learning to which he is attached. He should strive for immortality by writing books that would have nothing to do with the academy and would not form part of its collections, but would be published under his own name. The academy, for its part, should take as its task the assembling of all that is published on each subject. It should digest this information, clarify it, condense it, arrange it in an orderly way, and publish it in the form of treatises in which no topic would occupy more space than it deserves nor assume any importance except that which cannot be denied it. How many of the memoirs that now burden our collections would furnish not one single line to treatises of this kind!

An encyclopedia ought to make good the failure to execute such a project hitherto, and should encompass not only the fields already covered by the academies, but each and every branch of human knowledge. This is a work that cannot be completed except by a society of men of letters and skilled workmen, each working separately on his own part, but all bound together solely by their zeal for the best interests of the human race and a feeling of mutual good will.

I say, *a society of men of letters and of skilled workmen,* for it is necessary to assemble all sorts of abilities. I wish the members of this society to work separately because there is no

existing society from which one could obtain all the knowledge one needs, and because if one wanted the work to be
perpetually in the making, but never finished, the best way to
secure that result would be to form a permanent society. For
every society has its meetings; there are intervals between meetings; each meeting lasts for only a few hours; part of this time
is wasted in disputes; and so the simplest problems consume
entire months. . . .

I add: *men bound together by zeal for the best interests of
the human race and by a feeling of mutual good will,* because
these motives are the most worthy that can animate the souls
of upright people and they are also the most lasting. One has
an inward sense of self-approval for all that one does; one becomes enthusiastic, and one undertakes, out of regard for
one's friends and colleagues, many a task that one would not
attempt for any other consideration. I can certainly testify
from my own experience that the success of such attempts is
all the more assured. The *Encyclopedia* has brought together
its materials in a very short time. It is no sordid self-interest
that has assembled and spurred on the authors; rather they
have seen their efforts seconded by the majority of the men
of letters from whom they expected assistance, and the only
annoyance they have suffered in the course of their work has
been caused by persons who had not the talent necessary to
contribute one single good page.

If the government were to meddle with a work of this sort
it would never be finished. All that the authorities ought to do
is encourage its completion. A monarch may, by a single word,
cause a palace to rise up out of the grass; but a society of men
of letters is not the same thing as a gang of laborers. An encyclopedia cannot be produced on order. It is a task that needs
rather to be pursued with perseverance than to be begun with
ardor. An enterprise of this sort may on occasion be proposed
in the course of a conversation at Court; but the interest which
it arouses in such circles is never great enough to prevent its
being forgotten amidst the tumult and confusion of an infinite
number of more or less pressing affairs. Literary projects which
great noblemen conceive are like the leaves that appear in

the spring, grow dry in the autumn and fall in a heap in the depths of the forest, where the sustenance they give to a few sterile plants is all the effect they can be seen to produce. Out of a large number of instances in all the fields of literature that are known to me I will cite but a single one. A series of experiments on the hardness of various kinds of woods had been planned. The bark was to be removed and the standing trees were to be left to die. So the bark was stripped off, the trees died, and were apparently cut down; that is, everything was done except to make the experiments on the hardness of wood. And, indeed, how could they possibly have been made? Six years were to have elapsed between the giving of the initial orders and the final operations. If the man to whom the sovereign entrusted the work happened to die or to fall from favor, all work had to be suspended. Nor would it ever be resumed, for a new minister does not as a rule adopt the projects of his predecessor, although to do so would render him deserving of a kind of glory that would be, if not greater, at least more rare, than that of having conceived them. Private individuals are eager to harvest the fruits of what they have sown; the government has none of this economic zeal. I do not know what reprehensible motive it is that leads people to deal less honestly with a prince than with his subjects. One assumes the lightest of obligations and then expects the most handsome rewards. Uncertainty as to whether the project will ever have any useful results fills the workmen with inconceivable indolence. To lend to all these disadvantages the greatest possible force, projects ordered by sovereigns are never conceived in terms of pure utility, but always in terms of dignity of the sponsor; that is to say, the scale is as large as possible; obstacles are continually arising; men, special abilities, and time are needed in proportion to surmount them; and before the end is in sight, there is sure to intervene a change of ministers. . . . If the average life expectancy of an ordinary man is less than twenty years, that of a minister is less than ten. And not only are interruptions more frequent when it is a question of some literary project; they are also more damaging when the government is the sponsor than when the publishing enterprise is conducted by private individuals. In the event of shipwreck, the individual at least gathers up the debris of his undertaking and carefully preserves the materials that may be of service to him in a happier time; he hastens to salvage something from his investment. But the spirit of monarchy scorns this sort of prudence; men die, and the fruit of their toil disappears so completely that no one can discover what became of it.

The most important consideration, however, and one that lends added weight to the previous ones, is that an encyclopedia, like a dictionary, must be begun, carried forward and completed within a certain period of time. But sordid self-interest exerts itself to prolong any work that a king has commissioned. If one should devote to a universal and systematic dictionary all the long years that the vast scope of its subject matter seems to require, it would come about, thanks to the revolutionary changes which are scarcely less rapid in the arts and sciences than in language, that this dictionary would be a hundred years out of date, just as a dictionary of language which was composed slowly could end only by being a list of words used in the previous century. . . .

Revolutionary changes may be less abrupt and less obvious in the sciences and liberal arts than in the mechanical arts, but change has nonetheless occurred. One need only open the dictionaries of the last century. One will not find under the word "abberation" the slightest hint of what our astronomers understand by this term; on "electricity," that extremely promising phenomenon, there will be found but a few lines which contain nothing but false notions and ancient prejudices. How many terms are there relating to mineralogy or natural history of which the same could be said! If our own dictionary had been undertaken a little earlier, we should have been obliged to repeat all the errors of past ages on the diseases of grain and on the grain trade because the discoveries of M. Tillet and the methods of M. Herbert are very recent.

When one discusses the phenomena of nature, what more can one do than summarize as scrupulously as possible all their properties as they are known at the time of writing? But observation and experimental science unceasingly multiply both phenomena and data, and rational philosophy, by comparing and combining them, continually extends or narrows the range of our knowledge and consequently causes the meanings of accepted words to undergo change, renders their former definitions inaccurate, false, or incomplete, and even compels the introduction of new words.

But the circumstance that will give a superannuated appearance to the work and bring it the public's scorn will be above all the revolution that will occur in the minds of men and in the national character. Today, when philosophy is advancing with gigantic strides, when it is bringing under its sway all the matters that are its proper concern, when its tone is the dominant one, and when we are beginning to shake off the yoke of authority and tradition in order to hold fast to the laws of reason, there is scarcely a single elementary or dogmatic book which satisfies us entirely. We find that these works are put together out of the productions of a few men and are not founded upon the truths of nature. We dare to raise doubts about the infallibility of Aristotle and Plato, and the time has come when the works that still enjoy the highest reputation will begin to lose some of their great prestige or even fall into complete oblivion. Certain literary forms—for want of the vital realities and actual custom that once served them as models will no longer possess an unchanging or even a reasonable poetic meaning and will be abandoned; while others that remain, and whose intrinsic value sustains them will take on an entirely new meaning. Such are the consequences of the progress of reason, an advance that will overthrow so many old idols and perhaps restore to their pedestals some statues that have been cast down. The latter will be those of the rare geniuses who were ahead of their own times. We have had, if one may thus express it, our contemporaries in the age of Louis XIV.

Time, which has somewhat modified our tastes in the matter of critical controversy, has made a portion of Bayle's dictionary seem insipid. There is no other author who has lost so much merit in some respects and gained so much in others. But if such has been the fate of Bayle, how much worse would have been the fortune of an encyclopedia executed in his generation! With the exception of Perrault, and of several others whose merits that versifier Boileau was unable to appreciate (I mean La Mothe, Terasson, Boindin and Fontenelle, with whom reason and the philosophical spirit—the spirit of doubt—made such great progress), there was in that age perhaps not a single man who could write a page that people would condescend to read nowadays. For let there be no mistake, there is a world of difference between those who by force of genius give birth to works that secure the plaudits of a single nation (which has its momentary greatness, its taste, its ideas, and its prejudices), and those who trace out the fundamental principles of creative art as these arise from real, mature knowledge of the human spirit, of the nature of things, and of right reason, which are the same in all ages. The genius acknowledges no rules; yet he never strays far from them when his efforts succeed. Philosophy knows only rules that are grounded in the nature of things, and this nature is eternal and immutable. Let the last century furnish examples of genius; it is for our own age to prescribe the rules. . . .

In a systematic, universal dictionary, as in any work intended for the general education of mankind, you must begin by contemplating your subject in its most general aspects; you must know the state of mind of your nation, foresee the direction of its future development, hasten to anticipate its progress so that the march of events will not leave your book behind but will rather overtake it along the road; you must be prepared to work solely for the good of future generations because the moment of your own existence quickly passes away, and a great enterprise is not likely to be finished before the present generation ceases to exist. But if you would have your work remain fresh and useful for a long time to come—by virtue of its being far in advance of the national spirit, which marches steadily forward—you must shorten your labors by multiplying the number of your helpers, an expedient that is not, indeed, without its disadvantages, as I shall try to make plain hereafter.

Nevertheless, knowledge is not infinite, and cannot be universally diffused beyond a certain point. To be sure, no one knows just where this limit may be. Still less does anyone know to what heights the human race might have attained nor of what it might be capable, if it were in no way hampered in its progress. Revolutions are necessary; there have always been revolutions, and there always will be; the maximum interval between one revolution and another is a fixed quantity, and this is the only limit to what we can attain by our labors. For there is in every science a point beyond which it is virtually impossible to go. Whenever this point is reached, there will be created landmarks which will remain almost forever to astonish all mankind.

But if humanity is subject to certain limitations which set bounds to its strivings, how much narrower are the limits that circumscribe the efforts of individuals! The individual has but a certain quantity of energy both physical and intellectual. He enjoys but a short span of existence, he is constrained to alternate labor with repose; he has both instincts and bodily needs to satisfy, and he is prey to an infinite number of distractions. Whenever the negative elements in this equation add up to the smallest possible sum, or the positive elements add up to the largest possible sum, a man working alone in some branch of human knowledge will be able to carry it forward as far as it is capable of being carried by the efforts of one man. Add to the labors of this extraordinary individual those of another like him, and of still others, until you have filled up the whole interval of time between one scientific revolution and the revolution most remote from it in time, and you will be able to form some notion of the greatest perfection attainable by the whole human race—especially if you take for granted a certain number of accidental circumstances favorable to its labors, or which might have diminished its success had they been adverse.

But the general mass of men are not so made that they can either promote or understand this forward march of the human spirit. The highest level of enlightenment that this mass can achieve is strictly limited; hence it follows that there will always be literary achievements which will be above the capacities of the generality of men; there will be others which by degrees will fall short of that level; and there will be still others which will share both these fates.

No matter to what state of perfection an encyclopedia may be brought, it is clear from the very nature of such a work that it will necessarily be found among this third class of books. There are many things that are in daily use among the common people, things from which they draw their livelihood, and they are incessantly busy gaining a practical knowledge of these things. As many treatises as you like may be written about these matters and still there will always come a time when the practical man will know more about them than the writer of the book. There are other subjects about which the ordinary man will remain almost totally ignorant because the daily accretions to his fund of knowledge are too feeble and too slow ever to form any considerable sum of enlightenment, even if you suppose them to be uninterrupted.

Hence both the man of the people and the learned man will always have equally good reasons for desiring an encyclopedia and for seeking to learn from it.

The most glorious moment for a work of this sort would be that which might come immediately in the wake of some catastrophe so great as to suspend the progress of science, interrupt the labors of craftsmen, and plunge a portion of our hemisphere into darkness once again. What gratitude would not be lavished by the generation that came after this time of troubles upon those men who had discerned the approach of disaster from afar, who had taken measures to ward off its worst ravages by collecting in a safe place the knowledge of all past ages! In such a contingency—I may say it without being immodest because our *Encyclopedia* will perhaps never attain the perfection that would make it deserving of such honor—in such a contingency, men would speak, in the same breath in which they named this great work, of the monarch in whose reign it was undertaken, of the minister to whom it was dedicated, of the eminent men who promoted its execution, of the authors who devoted themselves to it, and of all the men of letters who lent their aid. The same voice that recalled these services would not fail to speak also of the sufferings that the authors were obliged to undergo, of the indignities that were heaped upon them; and the monument raised to their fame would have several faces where one would see in turn the honors accorded to their memory and the signs of posterity's reprobation for the names of their enemies. . . .

Both the real universe and the world of ideas have an infinite number of aspects by which they may be made comprehensible, and the number of possible "systems of human knowledge" is as large as the number of these points of view. The only system that would be free from all arbitrariness is, as I have said in our "Prospectus," the one that must have existed from all eternity in the mind of God. Hence the plan according to which one would begin with this eternal Being and then descend from Him to all the lesser beings that have emanated from His bosom in the course of time. This plan would resemble the astronomical hypothesis in which the scientist transports himself in imagination to the center of the sun so as to be able to calculate there the behavior of the heavenly bodies that surround him. It is a scheme that has both simplicity and grandeur, but one may discern in it a defect that would be serious in a work composed by men of science and addressed to all men in all ages to come. This is the fault of being too closely tied to our prevailing theology—a sublime science and one that is undoubtedly useful by reason of the knowledge that the Christian receives from it, but even more useful by reason of the sacrifices it demands and the rewards it promises.

As for a general system from which all that is arbitrary would be excluded—something we mortals can never hope to possess—it might not, perhaps, be so great an advantage to possess it. For what would be the difference between reading a book in which all the hidden springs of the universe were laid bare, and direct study of the universe itself? Virtually none: we shall never be capable of understanding more than a certain portion of this great book. To the extent that our impatience and our curiosity—which overmaster us and so often break up the course of our observations—disturb the orderly conduct of our reading, to that extent is our knowledge liable to become disjointed, as it now is. Losing the chain of inductive logic, and ceasing to perceive the connections between one step and those before and after, we would speedily come upon the same lacks and the same uncertainties. We are now busy trying to fill up the voids by means of the study of nature; we would still be busy trying to fill them up if we possessed and could meditate upon that huge book of which I have spoken; but the book would seem no more perfect to our eyes than would the universe itself, and the book would therefore be no less exposed to our presumptuous doubts and objections.

Since an absolutely perfect general plan would in no way supply the deficiencies arising from the weakness of our understanding, let us instead take hold of those things that are bound up with our human condition, being content to make our way upward from them toward some more general notions. The more elevated the point of view from which we approach our subject, the more territory it will reveal to us, the grander and more instructive will be the prospect we shall survey. It follows that the order must be simple, for there is rarely any grandeur without simplicity; it must be clear and easy to grasp, not a tortuous maze in which one goes astray and never sees anything beyond the point where one stands. No, it must rather be a vast, broad avenue extending far into the distance, intersected by other highways laid out with equal care, each leading by the easiest and shortest path to a remote but single goal.

Another consideration must be kept in view. I mean that if one banishes from the face of the earth the thinking and contemplating entity, man, then the sublime and moving spectacle of nature will be but a sad and silent scene; the universe will be hushed; darkness and silence will regain their sway. All will be changed into a vast solitude where unobserved phenomena take their course unseen and unheard. It is only the presence of men that makes the existence of other beings significant. What better plan, then, in writing the history of these beings, than to subordinate oneself to this consideration? Why should we not introduce man into our *Encyclopedia*, giving him the same place that he occupies in the universe? Why should we not make him the center of all that is? Is there, in all infinite space, any point of origin from which we could more advantageously draw the extended lines which we plan to produce to all the other points? With man at the center, how lively and pleasing will be the ensuing relations between man and other beings, between other beings and man!

For this reason we have decided to seek in man's principal faculties the main divisions within which our work will fall. Another method might be equally satisfactory, provided it did not put a cold, insensitive, silent being in the place of man. For man is the unique starting point, and the end to which everything must finally be related if one wishes to please, to instruct, to move to sympathy, even in the most arid matters and in the driest details. Take away my own existence and that of my fellow men and what does the rest of nature signify?

Although I believe that there is a point beyond which it is dangerous to add further material, I also think that one should not stop until one is very sure that this point has been reached. All the arts and sciences have their metaphysical principles, and this part is always abstract, elevated and difficult. None the less this part must be the main concern of a philosophical dictionary; and one must admit, too, that no matter how much remains to be done in this field, there will still be phenomena that cannot be explained. . . . It happens inevitably that the man of letters, the savant, and the craftsman sometimes walk in darkness. If they make some small amount of progress it is due to pure chance; they reach their goal like a lost traveler who has followed the right path without knowing it. Thus it is of the highest importance to give a clear explanation of the metaphysical basis of phenomena, or of their first, most general principles.

By this means the rest will be made more luminous and more certain in the reader's mind. Then all those alleged mysteries, for which some sciences are so much blamed—and

which other scientists so often dwell upon in order to excuse
their own obscurities—will vanish in the course of a sound
metaphysical discussion like the phantoms of the night at the
approach of day. The arts, their path well-lighted from the
very first step, will advance rapidly and safely, and always by
the shortest way. One must therefore make the most serious
attempt to explain the reasons that lie at the roots of things,
when these exist. One must assign causes when they are known,
indicate effects when these are certain, resolve difficulties by
the direct application of fundamental principles, demonstrate
truths, expose errors, skillfully discredit prejudices, teach men
to doubt and to wait, dissipate ignorance and put a just value
on the different kinds of human knowledge, distinguish the
true from the false, the true from the probable, the probable
from the miraculous and the incredible, the common event
from the extraordinary, the certain fact from the doubtful
one, and the latter from those that are absurd and contrary
to the laws of nature, understand the general course of natural
events and take each thing only for what it is, and—consequently—inspire in men a taste for science, an abhorrence of
lies, a hatred of vice and a love of virtue; for whatever does
not have happiness and virtue as its final goal is worth
nothing.

A thing that I consider intolerable is that one should lean
upon some ancient writer's authority in questions that require
only the use of reason. In what way is the truth changed by
an attempt to bolster it with the name of some man who is in
no wise infallible? Above all, let us have no quoting of poetry,
for this is sure to seem feeble and poor in the midst of a philosophical discussion: let us rather consign these fragile orna-
ments to the articles dealing with literature. In that context
I approve of them, on condition that they are tastefully used,
or made to serve as examples to illustrate forcefully the point
being made—either some defect that one wishes to correct or
some especially felicitous bit that is singled out for praise.

In scientific writings it is the logical connection of ideas or of
phenomena that directs our progress step by step as we advance; the subject is developed either by becoming more gen-

eral or by descending to particulars depending upon our choice of method. The same will hold true of the general form of the articles in the *Encyclopedia*, but with the difference that in our dictionary we shall, thanks to the co-ordination of articles, enjoy advantages which one can scarcely hope to find in a scientific treatise, save at the expense of some sacrifice in quality. The use of *cross references*, the most important part of our encyclopedic scheme, will provide us with these opportunities.

I have in mind two sorts of cross reference—one concerned with words and the other with things. Cross references to things clarify the subject; they indicate its close connections with other subjects that touch it directly as well as its more remote connections with still other matters that might otherwise be thought irrelevant; and they suggest common elements and analogous principles. They also put added stress on elements of internal consistency within groups of facts, they elaborate upon the connections that each special branch of knowledge has with its parent tree, and they give to the whole *Encyclopedia* that unity so favorable to the establishment of truth and to its propagation. Moreover, whenever the occasion demands, they will also lend themselves to a contrasting purpose—they will confront one theory with a contrary one, they will show how some principles conflict with others, they will attack, undermine and secretly overthrow certain ridiculous opinions which no one would dare to oppose openly. When the author is impartial, they will always have the double function of confirming and of confuting, of disturbing and of reconciling.

There should be great scope for ingenuity and an infinite advantage for the authors in this latter sort of cross reference. From them the work as a whole should acquire an inner force and a secret efficacy, the silent results of which will necessarily be felt with the passage of time. Each time, for instance, that a national prejudice seems to merit respect, it will be necessary, in the article specially devoted to it, to discuss it respectfully and to surround it with all its panoply of probability and attractiveness; but by giving cross references to articles where solid principles serve as the foundation for diametrically opposed truths, we shall be able to throw down the whole edifice of mud and scatter the idle heap of dust. This method of putting men on the right path works very promptly upon good minds, and it operates unfailingly, without the least undesirable effect, secretly and unobtrusively, upon all minds. This is the way to lead people, by a series of tacit deductions, to the most daring conclusions. If these cross references, which now confirm and now refute, are carried out artistically according to a plan carefully conceived in advance, they will give the *Encyclopedia* what every good dictionary ought to have—the power to change men's common way of thinking.

Finally, there is a kind of cross reference—it can refer either to words or to things—which I should like to call satirical or epigrammatic. Such, for example, is the one to be found in one of our articles where, at the end of a pompous eulogy, one reads: "See CAPUCHON." The comic word, "capuchon" [monk's hood], together with what the reader will find under the heading "CAPUCHON," can easily lead him to suspect that the pompous eulogy was meant ironically, and that it is wise to read the article with the utmost precaution and with attention to the careful weighing of every word.

I should not like altogether to do without this kind of reference; it is often very useful. One can aim it secretly against certain ridiculous customs in the same way that the philosophical reference is directed against certain prejudices. It frequently affords a delicate and amusing way to pay back an insult without even seeming to put oneself on the defensive, and it offers an excellent means of snatching off the masks from the faces of certain grave personages.

We have had occasion to learn in the course of our editorial labors that our *Encyclopedia* is a work that could only be attempted in a philosophical century; that this age has indeed dawned; and that posterity, while raising to immortality the names of those who will bring man's knowledge to perfection in the future, will perhaps not disdain to remember our own

names. We have felt ourselves spurred on by the ever so agreeable and consoling idea that men may speak to one another
about us, too, when we shall have ceased to exist; we have been
encouraged by hearing from the mouths of a few of our contemporaries a certain seductive murmur that gives us some hint
of what may be said of us by those happy and enlightened
men in whose interests we have sacrificed ourselves, whom we
esteem and whom we love, even though they have not yet been
born. We have sensed within ourselves a growing spirit of
emulation which has moved us to sacrifice the better part of
ourselves and which has ravished away into the void the few
hours of our lives of which we are genuinely proud. Indeed,
man reveals himself to his contemporaries and is seen by them
for what he is: an odd mixture of sublime talents and shameful weakness. But our failings follow our mortal remains into
the tomb and disappear with them forever; the same earth
covers them both, and there remains only the eternally lasting
evidence of our talents enshrined in the monuments we raise
to ourselves, or in the memorials that we owe to public gratitude and respect—honors which a proper awareness of our
own deserts enables us to enjoy in anticipation, an enjoyment
that is as pure, as great, and as substantial as any other
pleasure, and in which there is nothing imaginary except, perhaps, the title deeds on which we base our pretensions. Our
own claims are consigned to posterity in the pages of this
work, and in the future they will be judged.

I have said that it could only belong to a philosophical age
to attempt an *Encyclopedia;* and I say so because a work such
as this demands more intellectual courage than is commonly
to be found in ages of pusillanimous taste. All things must be
examined, all must be winnowed and sifted without exception
and without sparing anyone's sensibilities. One must dare to
see, as we are beginning to do, that the history of literary forms
is much the same as that of the first codification of law or the
earliest foundation of cities—all owe their origin to some
accident, to some odd circumstance, sometimes to a flight of
human genius; and those who come after the first inventors

are for the most part no more than their slaves. Achievements that ought to have been regarded only as first steps came blindly to be taken for the highest possible degree of development, and so, instead of advancing a branch of art toward perfection, these first triumphs only served to retard its growth by reducing all other artists to the condition of servile imitators. As soon as a name was given to some composition of a particular kind everyone was obliged to model all his productions rigorously after that model, which was perhaps only a sketch. If, from time to time, there appeared men of bold and original genius who, weary under the prevailing yoke, dared to shake it off, to strike out in a new direction away from the beaten path, and to give birth to some work of art to which the conventional labels and the prescribed rules were not exactly applicable, they fell into oblivion and remained for a long time forgotten.

Now, in our own age, we must trample mercilessly upon all these ancient puerilities, overturn the barriers that reason never erected, give back to the arts and sciences the liberty that is so precious to them. . . . The world has long awaited a reasoning age, an age when the rules would be sought no longer in the classical authors but in nature, when men would come to sense the false and the true that are mingled in so many of the arbitrary philosophies of art, whatever field one works in. (I take the term *philosophy of art* in its most general meaning, that of a system of accepted rules to which it is claimed that one must conform in order to succeed.)

But the world has waited so long for this age to dawn that I have often thought how fortunate a nation would be if it never produced a man of exceptional ability under whose aegis an art still in its infancy makes its first too-rapid and too-ambitious steps forward, thereby interrupting its natural, imperceptible rhythm of development. The works of such a man must necessarily be a monstrous composite for the reason that genius and good taste are two different things. Nature bestows the first in an instant; the second is the product of centuries. These monsters come to be models for a whole nation; they determine standards of taste for a whole people. Men of talent who come later find that a preference in favor of the earlier genius has taken so firm a hold that they dare not affront it. The idea of what is beautiful will then grow dim, just as the idea of what is good would grow dim among savages who fell into an attitude of excessive veneration for some chieftain of dubious character who might have earned their gratitude by his pre-eminent services or by his fortunate vices. In morality, only God should serve men as a model, and in the arts, only nature. When the arts and sciences advance by imperceptible degrees, one man will not differ enough from another man to inspire the latter with awe, to lay the foundations of a new style or to form the national taste. Consequently, nature and reason are safeguarded in all their rights. Should these have been lost, they are on the point of being recovered; we shall go on to show how important it is to be able to recognize and to seize upon such a moment.

As long as the centuries continue to unfold, the number of books will grow continually, and one can predict that a time will come when it will be almost as difficult to learn anything from books as from the direct study of the whole universe. It will be almost as convenient to search for some bit of truth concealed in nature as it will be to find it hidden away in an immense multitude of bound volumes. When that time comes, a project, until then neglected because the need for it was not felt, will have to be undertaken.

If you will reflect upon the state of literary production in those ages before the introduction of printing, you will form a mental picture of a small number of gifted men who are occupied with composing manuscripts, and a very numerous body of workmen who are busy transcribing them. If you look ahead to a future age, and consider the state of literature after the printing press, which never rests, has filled huge buildings with books, you will find again a twofold division of labor. Some will not do very much reading, but will instead devote themselves to investigations which will be new, or which they will believe to be new (for if we are even now ignorant of a part of what is contained in so many volumes published in all sorts of languages, they will know still less of

what is contained in those same books, augmented as they will
be by a hundred—a thousand—times as many more). The
others, day laborers incapable of producing anything of their
own, will be busy night and day leafing through these books,
taking out of them the fragments they consider worthy of being collected and preserved. Has not this prediction already
begun to be fulfilled? And are not several of our literary men
already engaged in reducing all big books to little ones, among
which there are still to be found many that are superfluous?
Let us assume that their extracts have been competently made,
and that these have been arranged in alphabetical order and
published in an orderly series of volumes by men of intelligence—you have an *encyclopedia!*

Thus we have now undertaken, in the interests of learning
and for the sake of the human race, a task to which our grandsons would have had to devote themselves; but we have done
so under more favorable circumstances, before a superabundance of books should have accumulated to make its execution
extremely laborious.

Because it is at least as important to make men better as it is
to make them less ignorant, I should not be at all displeased
if someone were to make a collection of all the most striking
instances of virtuous behavior. These would have to be carefully verified, and then they could be arranged under various
headings which they would illuminate and make vivid. Why
should we be so concerned to preserve the history of men's
thoughts to the neglect of the history of their good deeds? Is
not the latter history the more useful? Is it not the latter that
does the most honor to the human race? I have no wish to see
evil deeds preserved; it would be better if they had never taken
place. Men have no need of bad examples, nor has human
nature any need of being further cried down. It should not be
necessary to make any mention of discreditable actions except
when these have been followed—not by the loss of the evil-
doer's life and worldly goods, which is all too often the sad
consequence of virtuous behavior—but by a more fitting punishment of the wicked man: I want him to be wretched and
despised as he contemplates the splendid rewards he has gained
by his crimes. . . .

One must, of course, be especially careful to avoid adulation. But as for praise that is deserved, it would be highly unjust to give it only to the cold and inert ashes of those who can no longer hear it. And should the principle of equity, which requires the bestowing of praise, give way to the modesty of those who do not wish to receive it? Praise is an encouragement to virtue; it is a public contract that you cause the virtuous man to enter into. If all a man's good deeds were inscribed on a marble column, would he lose sight, even for a moment, of this imposing monument? Would not this be one of the strongest supports that one could lend to human weakness? In doing wrong this man would be obliged to shatter his own statue with his own hands. The praise of one honest man is the sweetest and most worthy reward that another good man can hope for; after the assent of one's own conscience the approval of an upright man is the most flattering. Oh, Rousseau, my dear and worthy friend! I have never been able to refuse the praise you have given me, and I feel that it has increased my devotion to truth as well as my love of virtue. . . .

Whoever assumes responsibility for writing the part of a future encyclopedia devoted to the mechanical arts will never be able to perform his task to his own satisfaction or to that of others unless he has made a profound study of natural history (especially of mineralogy), unless he is expert in things mechanical, unless he is well-versed in theoretical as well as experimental physics, and unless he has made an extensive study of chemistry.

As a naturalist he will recognize at a glance the materials employed by craftsmen and artisans, materials which they generally claim are endowed with all sorts of mysterious properties.

As a chemist he will be fully conversant with the properties of these materials, and the reasons for a multitude of operations will be known to him. He will smell out secret recipes, and the workmen will not be able to pull the wool over his eyes, for he will perceive in an instant the absurdity of their lies. He will grasp the whole nature of a process, no motion of the hand will escape him, for he will easily distinguish a meaningless flourish from an essential precaution. Everything he writes on the raw materials used in industry will be clear, authoritative, and instructive. Suggestions as to the means of perfecting the materials now in use, the possibility of recovering lost processes, and the ways of discovering new ones will present themselves abundantly to his mind.

Physics will make him master of an infinite number of phenomena which continue to be a source of lifelong astonishment to the simple workman.

With some knowledge of mechanics and geometry he will arrive without difficulty at a true and exact calculation of forces. He will need only to acquire experimental knowledge to moderate the rigor of his mathematical hypotheses. This quality of moderation is one that especially distinguishes the great master craftsmen from the ordinary workman, particularly when it is a question of constructing delicate machines. The workman never seems able to acquire a just idea of this principle of moderation unless he has in fact learned to practice it, and once he has formed wrong notions about it there is almost no chance of putting him straight.

Armed with these scientific attainments, our author will begin by drawing up a plan of classification according to which the various branches of industry will be attached to the natural substances which they transform. This will always be a workable plan, for the history of the arts and crafts is nothing but the history of nature put to use.

Then he will sketch out for each workman a rough memorandum whose outlines are to be filled in. He will require each one to discuss the materials he uses, the places from which he procures these, the prices that he pays for them, the tools he uses, the products he makes, and the whole series of operations he performs.

He will compare the memoranda furnished by craftsmen with his own original sketch; he will confer with them; he will make them supply orally any details they may have omitted and explain whatever they may have left obscure.

However bad these memoranda may be, when written in good faith they will always be found to contain an infinite number of things which the most intelligent of men would never have perceived unaided, would never even have suspected, and hence could never have asked about. Indeed, he will wish to know still more, but these matters will be part of the trade secrets which workmen never reveal to anyone. I myself have found by experience that people who continually busy themselves with something are equally disposed to believe either that everyone knows these things which they are at no pains to hide, or that no one else knows anything about the things they are trying to keep secret. The result is that they are always ready to mistake any person who questions them either for a transcendent genius or for an idiot.

During the time when the workmen are filling out their questionnaires, the author may busy himself with correcting the articles which our *Encyclopedia* will have handed down to him. It will not take long to see that, despite all the pains we have been to, a few gross errors have slipped in, and that there are whole articles in which there is not a shadow of common sense; but he will learn from his own experience to be grateful to us for those parts that are well done and to forgive us for those that are poor. Above all, once he has made the rounds of the workshops over a certain period of time, money in hand, and once he has been made to pay dearly for the most ridiculous fabrications, he will know what sort of people these artisans are—especially here in Paris, where fear of the tax collector keeps them in a perpetual state of mistrust, and where they regard every man who questions them at all closely either as a spy for the farmers-general* or as a rival craftsman who wants to set up shop. It seems to me that one might avoid these annoyances by seeking in the provinces all the information about the industrial arts that can be found there—the inquirer would be known for what he is, he would be talking to people who would not be suspicious of his motives, money is more valuable there, and time is not so precious. All of which makes me think that one would obtain information more easily and at less

* Under the Old Regime many royal taxes were "farmed out" for collection to a syndicate of financiers known as the *Ferme Générale du Roi*. The syndicate leased, for an agreed lump sum, the privilege of collecting as much as possible from the taxpayer.

expense, and that the information itself would be more reliable.

One must indicate the origin of each art and follow its progress step by step whenever these steps are known; or, if they are not, then conjecture and hypothetical history must be substituted for the historical reality. One can be sure that in such cases the imagined story will often be more instructive than the truth could possibly be.

But it is not the same with the origin and progress of an art or trade as it is with the origin and progress of a science. Learned men discuss things with each other, they write, they call attention to their discoveries, they contradict one another and are contradicted. These disputes make the facts plain and establish dates. Craftsmen, by contrast, live isolated, obscure, unknown lives; everything they do is done to serve their own interests; they almost never do anything just for the sake of glory. There have been inventions that have stayed for whole centuries in the closely guarded custody of single families; they are handed down from father to son; they undergo improvement or they degenerate without anyone's knowing to whom or to what time their discovery is to be assigned. The imperceptible steps by which an art develops necessarily makes dates meaningless. One man harvests hemp, another thinks of soaking it in water, a third combs it; at first it is a clumsy rope, then a thread, finally a fabric, but a whole age goes by in the interval between each of these steps and the one to follow. A man who first carried out the production of something from its natural state to its most perfect finished form would with difficulty remain unknown. How could it happen that a nation would find itself all of a sudden clothed in some new fabric and would fail to ask who was responsible for its creation? But such events never happen or, if they do, it is only at rare intervals.

Generally chance prompts the first experiments; either these are unfruitful and remain unknown, or someone else takes them up and obtains some successful results, but not enough to attract much attention. A third follows in the footsteps of the second, a fourth in the footsteps of the third, and so on until at last someone gets excellent results—this final product is the first to create a sensation. Or again, it may happen that an idea has scarcely made its appearance in one man's workshop before it bursts forth and spreads far and wide. People work at the same thing in several places, each one performs the same manipulations on his own initiative; and the same invention results. It is claimed by several people at the same time; it really belongs to no one; and it is attributed to the man who first makes a fortune out of it. If the invention is taken over from a foreign country, national jealousy suppresses the name of the inventor and his name remains unknown. . . .

There are trades where the craftsmen are so secretive that the shortest way of gaining the necessary information would be to bind oneself out to some master as an apprentice or to have this done by some trustworthy person. There would be few secrets that one would fail to ferret out by this method; all would have to be divulged without any exception.

I know that this desire for an end to secrecy is not shared by everyone. There are narrow minds, ill-formed souls, who are indifferent to the fate of the human race, and who are so completely absorbed in their own little group that they can see nothing beyond the boundaries of its special interests. These men insist that they deserve the title of good citizens, and I will allow it to them provided they will permit me to call them *bad men.* To listen to them talk, one would say that a well-executed encyclopedia, a general history of the industrial arts, should only take the form of a huge manuscript that would be carefully locked up in the King's library, hidden away from all other eyes but his, a state document and not a popular book. What is the good of divulging the knowledge a nation possesses, its private affairs, its inventions, its industrial processes, its resources, its trade secrets, its enlightenment, its arts, and all its wisdom! Is it not to these things that it partly owes its superiority over the rival nations that surround it? This is what they say; but this is what one might add: would it not be a fine thing if, instead of enlightening the foreigner, we could spread darkness over him or even plunge all the rest of

the world into barbarism? People who argue thus do not
realize that they occupy only a single point on our globe and
that they will endure only an instant. To this point and to
this instant they would sacrifice the happiness of future ages
and that of the whole human race.

They know as well as anyone that the average duration of
empires is less than two thousand years, and that in a briefer
period of time, perhaps, the name *Frenchman*—a name that
will endure forever in history—will be sought after in vain on
the surface of the earth. Such considerations do not appreciably
broaden the views of such persons; it seems that the word
humanity is for them a word without meaning. Even so, they
should be consistent! Yet in the very next breath they deliver
tirades against the impenetrability of the Egyptian sanctu-
aries; they deplore the loss of the knowledge of the ancients;
they are full of blame for the silence or negligence of ancient
authors who have omitted something essential, or who speak so
cryptically of many important subjects; and these critics do not
see that they are demanding of the writers of earlier ages something they call a crime when a present-day writer does it, that
they are blaming others for doing what they think it honorable
to do. These "good citizens" are the most dangerous enemies
that we have had in our capacity as editors.

In general we have tried to profit from criticism without
ever replying in our own defense when the criticism was sound;
we have ignored all attacks that were without foundation.
It is not a sufficiently pleasant prospect for those who have
been zealously blackening paper with attacks on us that if ten
years hence the *Encyclopedia* has retained the reputation it
enjoys today, there will no longer be anyone to read their
scribblings—and that if the *Encyclopedia* is then forgotten,
their diatribes will be even more completely so! I have heard
it said that M. de Fontenelle's rooms were not large enough to
hold all the writings that were published against him. Who
today knows the title of a single one of them? Montesquieu's
Esprit des Lois and Buffon's *Histoire Naturelle* have only just
appeared, and the writings that attacked them are entirely
forgotten.

We have already remarked that among those who have set themselves up as self-appointed censors of the *Encyclopedia* there is hardly a single one who had enough talent to enrich it by even one good article. I do not think I would be exaggerating if I should add that it is a work the greater part of which is about matters that these people have yet to study. It is written in a philosophical spirit, and in this respect the majority of those who pass adverse judgment on it are far from being up to the level of their own century. I call their works in evidence. It is for this reason that they will not endure; and for this same reason we may expect that our *Encyclopedia* will be more widely read and more highly appreciated in a few years' time than it is today. It would not be difficult to cite other authors who have had, and will have, a similar fate. Some (as we have already said) were once praised to the skies because they wrote for the multitude, they submitted to the yoke of prevailing ideas, and they kept within the ordinary reader's capacity for understanding; but these authors have lost their reputations in proportion as the human mind has made advances, and they have finally been forgotten altogether. Others, by contrast, too daring for the time during which their books appeared, have been little read, have been understood by only a few, have been little appreciated, and have long remained in obscurity, up to the day when the age they had outstripped had run its course, and another century, whose true children they were before it had even dawned, finally caught up with them and gave them in the end the justice their merits deserved.

7

REGRETS ON PARTING WITH MY OLD DRESSING GOWN

Or, A Warning to Those Who Have More Taste than Money

(First published in 1772.)

Why on earth did I ever part with it? It was used to me and I was used to it. It draped itself so snugly, yet loosely, around all the curves and angles of my body—it made me look picturesque as well as handsome. This new one, stiff and rigid as it is, makes me look like a mannequin.

As for the old one, it used to lend itself complaisantly to any demand I chose to make on it, for the poor are almost always quick to be of service. If a book was covered with dust, one of the flaps of my old dressing gown was always ready to hand to wipe it clean. If the ink was too thick and refused to run out of my pen—presto, there was the skirt of my old dressing gown ready to serve as a penwiper. You could see how many times it had done me this service by the long, black stripes it bore. Those stripes were the badge of an author, part of the evidence that I am an honest workman. But now I look like a rich loafer, and nobody can tell by looking at me what my trade is.

Wrapped up in my old dressing gown I didn't need to worry about the servant's clumsiness or my own awkwardness. Neither did I have to watch out for flying sparks from the fire or for water leaking in through the roof. I was absolute master of my old dressing gown, but I have become a slave to my new one. The dragon that kept guard over the Golden Fleece was no more uneasy than I am—I go about under a cloud of anxiety.

An infatuated old man who has given himself up, tied hand and foot, to the mercy and whims of a foolish young mistress, repeats to himself from morning to night, "Where, oh where is my good old housekeeper? What devil put a spell on me the day I let her go to make a place for this minx?" Then he weeps and heaves a doleful sigh.

Well, I am not weeping; nor more am I sighing; but I continually think to myself: A pox on the rascal who discovered the art of making a piece of ordinary cloth seem precious by the simple expedient of dyeing it scarlet! And may the devil take an article of clothing so precious that I have to bow down to it! Give me back my ragged, humble, comfortable old wrapper!

My friends, see to it that you hold fast to your old friends. And, oh, my friends, beware of the contamination of sudden wealth. Let my example be a lesson to you. The poor man may take his ease without thinking of appearances, but the rich man is always under a strain.

Oh Diogenes! How you would laugh if you could see your disciple now, wearing the ornate cloak of Aristippus. Oh Aristippus, how much base flattery did your cloak cost you? How can one compare your soft, servile, effeminate mode of life with the free, steadfast existence of the ragged Cynic? I have deserted my barrel, where I was lord and master, only to enter the service of a tyrant.

Nor is that all, my friends. Listen, and I will tell you what ravages Luxury has made since I gave myself up to the systematic pursuit of it.

My old dressing gown was in perfect accord with the rest of the poor bric-a-brac that filled my room. A chair made out of woven straw, a rough wooden table, a cheap Bergamo tapestry, a pine board that served for a bookshelf, a few grimy engravings without frames, tacked by the corners to the tapestry, and three or four plaster casts that hung between the engravings—all these harmonized with my old dressing gown to make a perfect picture of honest poverty.

Now the harmony is destroyed. Now there is no more consistency, no more unity, and no more beauty.

One can expect trouble when an old maid comes to keep house for a widowed Protestant clergyman with many young children—indeed when any woman comes to live in a widower's house. Discomfort is also in store for a new cabinet minister when he takes over from a disgraced predecessor, or for a Molinist bishop who has secured the diocese of a Jansenist prelate*—but all that is nothing compared with the trouble this scarlet intruder has caused in my house.

I can look without distaste at a peasant woman. I take no offense at the piece of coarse cloth that covers her head, at the loose strands of hair that fall over her cheeks, at the tattered rags that only half cover her body, at the short, threadbare skirt that comes only to her knees, at her bare feet caked with mud. All these are signs of a calling that I respect; they are misfortunes that go with a necessary but poorly rewarded occupation, and I sympathize. But my gorge rises at the sight of an elegant courtesan, perfumed though she may be, and I look in the other direction while walking away from her as fast as I can. Her coiffure with little curls in the English mode, her slashed sleeves, her dirty silk stockings and worn-out shoes reveal to me the necessary transition from yesterday's high living to today's squalor.

My study would have presented just such an incongruous appearance if the imperious scarlet robe had not forced everything else to conform with its own elegant tone.

I have seen my Bergamo tapestry compelled to give up its place on the wall where it has hung for so many years to make room for a damask wall covering.

Two engravings that were not without merit—Poussin's "Shower of Manna in the Wilderness" and his "Esther before the Throne of King Ahasuerus"—were shamefully exiled, one (the melancholy Esther) to make room for a Rubens portrait

* Hostile parties within the French church in the seventeenth and eighteenth centuries. See note, page 251.

of an old man, and the other displaced by Vernet's "After the Storm."

My old straw chair has been relegated to the vestibule; its place has been usurped by an armchair covered with Morocco leather.

Homer, Virgil, Horace, and Cicero have relieved the thin pine board of the weight that used to make it bow down in the middle, and are now shut up in an inlaid cabinet—of which they are more worthy than I.

A huge mirror fills the space over the mantel of my fireplace.

The two handsome plaster medallions that my friend, the sculptor Falconnet, made me a present of after he had repaired them himself—these have been dispossessed by a little statue of Venus stooping. Modern clay has been shattered by antique bronze.

The wooden table still held its ground, protected as it was by a great heap of pamphlets and loose papers piled up helter-skelter. This encumbrance seemed likely to preserve it in safety for many a long day from the humiliation that threatened to descend upon it. But notwithstanding my natural laziness, Fate at last worked its will with my table: the papers and pamphlets are now neatly stacked in the drawers of an expensive new desk.

How futile is our instinct to behave exactly in accordance with accepted conventions! Fine manners have ruined many a man; the most sublime taste is not exempt from change; change means throwing things away, turning things upside down, building something new; in the end there is nothing left in the family strongbox, and daughters must be married off without dowries, sons must make their way in life without a good education. Thus our delicacy produces many fine things, and at the same time many evils. It has put this expensive and pretentious desk in the place of my old wooden table. The same fatal taste for luxury has ruined great nations, and maybe someday it will bring my last goods and chattels to the second-hand market on the Pont St. Michel, where the auctioneer will call out in his hoarse voice, "Who'll give twenty louis for a Stooping Venus?"

The remaining space between the top of my new desk and Vernet's seascape, which hangs directly above it, was displeasing to the eye on account of its blankness, so this void was filled by a pendulum clock—and what a clock! A clock chosen by the wealthy Mme. Geoffrin, made of bronze inlaid with gold!

Then there was an empty corner beside the window. There was just room for a secretary, and one was put there.

But there was still an unpleasant bit of bare wall between the writing shelf of the secretary and the bottom of Rubens' fine portrait, a space that was promptly filled by two small paintings, the work of La Grenée.

Over here is a "Mary Magdalene" by the same artist, and over there is a sketch that is either by Vien or by Machy—you see, I have even gone in for sketches!

Thus it was that the edifying retreat of a philosopher was transformed into the scandalous likeness of innkeeper's private sitting room. This is how I mock the nation's poverty.

. Of my former modest surroundings I have kept only one reminder: an old braided carpet. This pitiable object, I know very well, hardly goes with my other splendid furnishings. But I have taken an oath, which I shall never break, that this carpet shall remain where it is, because the feet of Denis the Philosopher shall never soil one of La Savonnerie's* masterpieces. I will keep my old rug, just as a peasant, taken from his cottage to be a servant in the king's palace, carries his wooden shoes along with him. Every morning when I come into my study, sumptuously robed in scarlet, I shall look down at the floor and I shall see my old braided rug. It will remind me of what I used to be, and Pride will have to come to a standstill at the threshold of my heart.

No, my friends, and again no; I am not yet corrupted. My door is still open to anyone in need who turns to me for help, and he will find me as generous as ever. I will listen to his tale of woe, give him advice if he wants it, help him if I can, and in any event show my sympathy for him in his misfortune. My heart hasn't grown any harder; my head hasn't swelled; and

* A designer of beautiful carpets and tapestries.

my nose isn't any higher in the air than it used to be. I still
walk with an amiable stoop, just as in times past. My speech
is still without affectation; I am still easily moved to laughter
or tears. My luxurious mode of life is still new to me and its
poison has not yet had time to take effect. But who can tell
what the passage of time may bring? What can one expect of
a fellow who has forgotten about his wife and daughter, who
has run himself into debt, who has ceased, in short, to be a
good husband and father, and who—instead of putting his
savings prudently away in the bottom of a good, solid
trunk——

Ah! Holy Prophet! Lift your arms up to Heaven and pray
for a soul in peril! Say to the Almighty: If Thou hast ordained
by one of Thine eternal decrees that the heart of Denis is to
be corrupted by wealth, spare not the artistic masterpieces
which he idolizes—rather destroy them and plunge him again
into his original poverty! For my own part I shall say: O Lord,
I resign myself to the words of Thy holy prophet and to Thy
will. I surrender all my treasures into Thy hands—take all of
them—yes, all except Vernet's painting! Oh, leave me nothing
but my Vernet! It was no human hand, but rather Thine Own
hand, that made it. Respect the gift of a friend and Thine
Own handiwork. See that lighthouse, see the tower beyond
it and to the right; see that ancient tree, twisted and torn by
the wind. How beautiful that arrangement of masses is!
Below that dark area, see the cliffs partly covered with greenery.
They are painted exactly as Thy mighty hand must have
shaped them, exactly as Thy benevolence must have clothed
them. See that rough terrace that falls away from the foot of
the cliff toward the sea's edge. It is the very image of the depredations which Thou has permitted Time to make against the
most solid things of earth. Would the scene be different in any
detail if Thy sun really shone upon it? O Lord! If Thou de-
stroyest this work of art, man will know that Thou art indeed
a jealous God!

Take pity on those unhappy people who are to be seen
here and there along the beach. Is it not enough that they have
had to look with terror into the sea's abyss? Hast Thou

saved them only to send them again to their destruction? Hear the prayer of this one over here who thanks Thee for Thy mercy. Second the efforts of that man over there who is busy gathering up the remnants of his fortune. Close Thine ears to the curses of yonder madman—poor devil, he had counted heavily on his profits from this voyage; his thoughts were fixed upon a comfortable old age; this was to have been his last venture upon the sea. Dozens of times, in the course of this voyage, he has counted up on his fingers to see whether his capital has grown large enough to retire on. He has planned to the last detail just how he would invest it—and see now how all his hopes have been dashed to pieces: he has scarcely enough left to buy the few rags he will need to cover his naked limbs! Let Thy compassion be moved by the tenderness of yonder husband and wife. See how the poor woman has been terrified. She gives thanks to Thee for the evil that Thou has been pleased not to inflict. Meanwhile her child, too young to comprehend what mortal danger Thou hast held before his eyes and those of his dear parents but a moment ago, has turned his attention to the faithful companion of his travels and is buckling on his dog's collar. Have mercy on this innocent little creature!

See this second mother, who has just reached dry land with her husband. Not for herself did she tremble; she feared only for her little one. See how she clasps her baby close to her breast; see how she kisses it.

O Lord! Acknowledge the waters Thou has created: concede that they are as Thou madest them, both when agitated by Thy breath and when calmed by Thy hand. Acknowledge those somber clouds which Thou didst gather together but a little while ago and which Thou art now pleased to disperse. Already they begin to break up and float away; already the light of the day-star is reborn upon the face of the waters.

Calm weather is foretold by the red glow that brightens along the far horizon. How remote, indeed, that horizon must be! The sky seems not to meet the surface of the water; instead one has the illusion that it continues downward beyond the edge of the sea and curves around the entire globe.

Sweep away the clouds that remain, and let the troubled waters subside into complete tranquillity. Allow those sailors to get their stranded vessel afloat once again; aid their exertions and give them strength—and do not take my picture away from me! Let it remain with me so that it may be as Thy scourge to punish my human vanity. Already I am aware that people come here to see my painting, not to visit me or hear my words of wisdom. They come to admire Vernet in my house. The artist has humbled the philosopher.

Ah, my friends—what a splendid Vernet I possess! The subject is the end of a storm that has caused no loss of life. The waves are still high; the sky is still covered by clouds; the sailors are busy trying to get their damaged ship off the rocks; on the nearby hillside one sees the natives of the place running toward the shore. What insight the artist has! He has used only a small number of central figures to show every aspect of the situation at the moment he chose for rendering it on canvas. How true to life the whole scene is! How lightly, yet surely, and at the same time vigorously, every touch is put on. I mean to keep this token of Vernet's friendship as long as I live, and I want my son-in-law to hand it down to his children, they to their children, and they to the children that will be born to them.

If you could see with your own eyes what a fine thing this picture is, viewed as a whole; how everything in it harmonizes; how one effect is bound up with all the rest; how all are obtained without ostentation and without any apparent effort; how the faraway mountains at the right seem to dissolve in mist; how beautiful are the cliffs and the lighthouses that cling to them; how picturesque the old tree is; how the sloping beach is divided between light and shadow; how the light grows dimmer by degrees; how the figures are distributed; how lifelike, natural, and full of vitality and motion they are; how they draw the spectator's attention; the forceful manner in which they are painted; the purity of line that reveals their contours; the way they seem to stand out from their surroundings; the vastness of the space represented; the faithful rendering of water in motion; the clouds, the bits of clear sky, the horizon! Here, using a technique opposite to the usual one, the artist has illuminated his background very brightly and has left the foreground in shadow. Come and see my Vernet, but don't try to carry it off with you!

In time I shall have paid off my creditors, and my sense of guilt will be less lively. Then I shall be able to take undiluted pleasure in all my new possessions. But you need not fear that I shall fall victim to the frenzy that makes men want to go on endlessly heaping up beautiful things. I still have the same friends I used to have, and I have made no new ones. Laïs is mine; I am not hers. Happy in her arms, I am yet ready to yield her up to someone I love, provided she would make him happier than she makes me.

And, if I may whisper a secret in your ear, my wench Laïs, whose favors others buy at such a dear price, didn't cost me a single sou.